D1282871

Marketing and Modernity

EXPLORATIONS IN ANTHROPOLOGY
A University College London Series

Series Editors: Barbara Bender, John Gledhill and Bruce Kapferer

Marketing and Modernity

Marianne Elisabeth Lien

Oxford • New York

First published in 1997 by
Berg
Editorial offices:
150 Cowley Road, Oxford, OX4 1JJ, UK
70 Washington Square South, New York, NY 10012, USA

Berg is an imprint of Oxford International Publishers Ltd.

Library of Congress Cataloging-in-Publication Data

A catalogue record for this book is available from the Library of
Congress.

British Library Cataloguing-in-Publication Data

A catalogue record for this book is available from the British Library.

Cover photograph: © Eirill Wilde Wük

ISBN 1 85973 991 1 (Cloth)
      1 85973 996 2 (Paper)

Typeset by JS Typesetting, Wellingborough, Northants.
Printed in the United Kingdom by WBC Book Manufacturers, Bridgend,
Mid Glamorgan.

Contents

Acknowledgments

This book is based upon fieldwork in the marketing department of a major Norwegian food manufacturing company, which is referred to as Viking Foods. Research for this book has been financed by a Norwegian Council for Applied Social Research (NORAS) and the National Institute for Consumer Research in Norway (SIFO). This version is a revised edition of a dissertation at the Institute and Museum of Anthropology, University of Oslo in 1995.

I wish to express my gratitude to Viking Foods' management for granting me permission to conduct fieldwork within their organization. In particular, I am grateful to key informants in the marketing department for accepting my presence, for willingly responding to my many questions, and for sharing some of their thoughts, joys and worries, even during periods of great pressure. A considerable part of the empirical material that was made available to me contains information that was confidential at the time. I am grateful for the openness with which I was granted access to confidential material, and I hope that the present publication does not in any way violate the trust that was extended to me.

I am deeply indebted to Eduardo Archetti for guidance and support during the entire research period. Fellow anthropologists at the Department and Museum of Anthropology, University of Oslo have also provided valuable support and inspiration. I also wish to acknowledge the encouragement of colleagues at the National Institute for Consumer Research, and especially of fellow members of the 'food research group' as it gradually took shape. An earlier version of the manuscript was read by Daniel Miller and by Marianne Gullestad, whose comments have been valuable in the process of revision.

I also wish to express my gratitude to Eivind Jacobsen for first introducing me to studies of technology and science and for valuable comments on various parts of the text; but even more for generosity and affectionate support throughout. Last, but not least, I am indebted to my children Vidar and Torbjørn for demanding care and attention and thus letting me experience some of the dilemmas inherent in modern lives.

Marianne Elisabeth Lien

List of Figures and Tables

Figures

Tables

Part I

Introductions

Chapter 1

Exploring Modernity: An Introduction

Modernity is a concept that has received considerable theoretical attention in the social sciences. Yet it is rarely a subject of ethnographic research. In spite of an increased interest in anthropological studies in what may be termed modern ethnographic settings, few critically explore current theories of modernity in relation to the analysis of modern lives. To some extent, this may be attributed to the fact that universalizing assumptions inherent in most theories of modernity are not easily juxtaposed with anthropological explorations of the particular. The relativizing imperative inherent in much ethnographic research of the last decade does not lend itself to broad generalizations (Miller 1994). As a consequence, modernity is assumed rather than explored as an empirical phenomenon.

This analysis starts with two premises. First, modernity, whatever the term entails, cannot be fully understood by theoretical endeavours; it must also be the subject of empirical research. Secondly, a concept of modernity necessarily implies an idea of that which is not modern. Often, this remains implicit in the debate, as if the nature of the dichotomy is somehow self-evident. The present analysis is an attempt to explore such dichotomies in a more explicit manner. This aim calls for a comparative approach.

One may argue that recent debates and assumptions about modernity frequently represent a continuation of the orientalist dichotomy of 'the West' and 'the rest'. According to Edward Said, Western assumptions about the Orient belong to what he calls the realm of *imaginative geography* (Said 1979). In a similar manner, assumptions about the nature of modernity seem to result from a notion of an imaginative past that serves to characterize the present. The problem is not so much the notion of a dichotomy in itself. The idea that there may be fundamental cultural differences due to recent and dramatic changes in the Western world can hardly be discarded, and serves at least as a basis for further inquiry. The difficulties associated with a modern–traditional dichotomy arise, however, when this dichotomy becomes self-evident and thus integral to our interpretation of the world we inhabit, rather than an analytical distinction that merits further inquiry.

This book is an argument neither in favour of, nor against a concept of modernity. Rather, it takes current theories of modernity as a starting-point for critical exploration. The aim of the analysis is to achieve a deeper understanding of modern, professional lives as they unfold in a particular ethnographic setting, and then to consider these experiences in relation to other life experiences that would generally be labelled 'traditional'. Through such comparison, the analysis seeks to challenge current theoretical assumptions of modernity.

A Modern Place

The analysis is based upon an ethnographic study of the struggles and concerns of young professional men and women situated in a marketing department of a major Norwegian food manufacturer called Viking Foods.[1] It draws attention to processes by which food products and advertising are gradually constructed, and focuses especially on the product managers' conceptualizations of both products and consumers and on the dilemmas involved in transforming raw material into culturally meaningful products.

Advertising has been analysed by social scientists primarily as a system of signs, or as mediators of cultural meaning (Williamson 1978; Leiss, Kline and Jhally 1990). Yet commercials and advertisements are not only 'webs of significance',[2] they are created for the purpose of selling certain products. Approaching advertising as a source of insight into cultural meanings, we must also ask who gets to define and express those meanings, and to what ends? As Scholte notes, we must keep in mind that *'few do the actual spinning, while the . . . majority is simply caught'* (Scholte 1984:140; Paul 1990). One aim of this analysis is to draw attention to the people 'who do the spinning'. This implies an inquiry into the marketing profession, and into the epistemological and material processes involved in the transformation of our daily food.

I approached the marketing department with an expectation of being able to study food production as culinary culture in the making, assuming that my informants shared an interest in food and cooking. As it turned out, this was hardly the case. Instead, I encountered a group of people whose professional interest was in the field of marketing rather than in the field of making meals. Food seemed to represent, not so much an element with which to experiment and create tasteful combinations, as rather a raw material that might or might not be transformed into a profitable product within the narrow confines of a market segment. Any evaluation of quality ultimately depended on whether or not consumers would accept and choose the final product. Consequently, consumers' attitudes were an issue of great concern. Uncertainty associated with what consumers want was also to some extent a source of discomfort.

As an attempt to reduce uncertainty in marketing decisions, a considerable effort was being made to acquire and produce *knowledge* that might help to predict these matters. Knowledge and interpretation are vital both to material processes of transformation generally conceived as technological processes, and to the combination of symbols, images and words involved in the construction of verbal and visual communication. Yet interpretation is fraught with uncertainty as well. What is a good advert? How can creativity be measured? What is the value of a brilliant idea? And what should poultry really taste like? As they strive to come to terms with such issues, product managers confront a broad range of dilemmas of a more general kind. This includes a struggle for order and a continuous effort to overcome ambivalence. These dilemmas bring us to the heart of several topics that are central to contemporary debates on modernity. In fact, the marketing department may serve as an excellent example of a place that features a range of salient characteristics associated with high modernity, such as modern reflexivity as described by Anthony Giddens (1991) and the modern struggle against ambivalence as described by Zygmunt Bauman (1990, 1991).

Nevertheless, when considered in light of ethnographic accounts of non-modern places, features that at first glance appear to be typically modern turn out to be not so modern after all. This analysis aims beyond the modern vs. traditional dichotomy, exploring instead the contextual premises of allegedly modern characteristics, and the relationships between them.

Western Modernity

Most authors agree that the term 'modernity' denotes characteristic features of a particular phase that is located in time and space. Giddens (1991) emphasizes especially the European Renaissance, exhibiting what he refers to as a historical shift from fatalism to modernity. According to Giddens, Machiavelli's book about the Prince, which is celebrated as an originator of modern political strategy, marks the transition to new modes of social activity from which fate is excluded (Giddens 1991:110). He cites Machiavelli, who formulates his understanding of fate and fortune as follows:

> *I believe that it is probably true that fortune is the arbiter of half the things we do, leaving the other half or so to be controlled by ourselves. Those princes who are utterly dependent on fortune come to grief when their fortune changes. I also believe that the one who adapts his policy to the times prospers, and likewise that the one whose policy clashes with the demands of the times does not* (Machiavelli 1961:130–1).[3]

Machiavelli foreshadows a situation in which a medieval notion of fate is replaced by an approach that opens up the possibility that man may influence his destiny. Furthermore, Machiavelli draws attention to the changeability of 'the times', emphasizing the need to adapt to the changes of the situation. As I shall demonstrate, this understanding is at the very core of marketing as well. According to Giddens, Machiavelli foreshadows a world in which the notion of risk and risk calculation has practically replaced notions of fate, and in which the universe of the future may be shaped by human intervention (Giddens 1991:109).

For Giddens, the territorial delineation of modernity becomes something roughly equivalent to the industrialized world. While industrialism represents one institutional axis of modernity, capitalism represents another, implying *'a system of commodity production involving both competitive product markets and the commodification of labour power'* (Giddens 1991:15). Bauman also makes a historical delineation when he refers to modernity as:

> *a historical period that began in Western Europe with a series of profound social-structural and intellectual transformations of the seventeenth century,*

and achieved its maturity: 1) as a cultural project – with the growth of Enlightenment; 2) as a socially accomplished form of life – with the growth of industrial (capitalist and later also communist) society (Bauman 1991:4).[4]

In spite of some disagreement in the literature as to when and where modernity may be identified,[5] the historical confinement of the term modernity seems to be of little concern to these authors. Instead, they seek to identify the *characterizing features of modernity*, including the institutional arrangements, modes of behaviour and underlying dichotomies that may be associated with the modern condition.

The characterizing features that are thus described, are, however, rarely based on empirical enquiry or comparison. Rather, the characterizing potential of the features described seem to derive primarily from *an assumed contradiction with that which is not modern: the traditional*. Like modernity, the traditional is often thought of as a historical phase, denoting remnants of a Western European 'past'. Alternatively, the traditional may be spatially located as contemporary, but culturally distant, enclaves that are assumed to represent a certain historical continuity. Yet the comparative potential inherent in such dichotomies is seldom explored.

According to Giddens, the modern world may be characterized by its dynamic character, a feature that according to Giddens is evident by the fact that the *'pace of social change [is] much faster than in any prior system'* (Giddens 1991:16). On the basis of these general observations, Giddens sets out to explain what he refers to as *'the peculiarly dynamic character of modern life'*. Three main elements are identified:

1. *The separation of time and space*, as expressed for example by the invention of the mechanical clock and the global map – tools that according to Giddens are constitutive of quite basic transformations of social relations (Giddens 1991:17).
2. *The disembedding of social institutions*, i.e. the 'lifting out' of social relations from local contexts. Disembedding mechanisms include symbolic tokens (such as money) and expert systems, the latter deploying modes of technical knowledge that have validity independent of the practitioners who make use of them (Giddens 1991:18–19).
3. *Institutional reflexivity*, i.e. the regularized use of knowledge about circumstances of social life as a constitutive element in

its organization and transformation. Modern reflexivity implies a susceptibility of most aspects of social activity to chronic revision in light of new information or knowledge. Thus, the reflexivity of modernity actually undermines the certainty of knowledge, and may be described in terms of an integral relation between modernity and radical doubt (Giddens 1991:20–1).[6]

The notion of doubt is further elaborated by Bauman (1991). According to Bauman, modernity may be thought of as: *'a time when order... is reflected upon; a matter of thought, of concern, or a practice that is aware of itself, conscious of being a conscious practice and wary of the void it would leave were it to halt or merely relent'* (Bauman 1991:5). However, the struggle for order is simultaneously *a fight of determination against ambiguity, of semantic precision against ambivalence* (Bauman 1991:7). As ambivalence is necessarily also a side-product of classification, any attempt at classification will call for an even greater classifying effort (Bauman 1991:3). Thus, the modern struggle against ambivalence becomes both self-destructive and self-propelling.

All these elements may be classified as 'acultural' in the sense that they could, *in principle*, be found anywhere. Yet, according to Giddens, they are intrinsic to the condition referred to as high modernity, a condition that originated in post-feudal Europe but is now increasingly global in its impact. Giddens's three elements can easily be recognized as empirical features that characterize transatlantic academic networks in the early 1990s. Moreover, as subsequent chapters will demonstrate, some of these elements are strikingly apt descriptions of certain empirical traits that characterize the marketing department. Thus, for anyone familiar with Giddens's and Bauman's descriptions of the modern condition, my present analysis may be read simply as an empirical exploration of modernity, and to some extent that is what it is.

Yet the aim of the analysis is slightly more ambitious. Even if empirical material supports Giddens's theses, the question still remains as to whether these alleged characterizing features of modernity are context-bound cultural features of the modern Western world – whether they characterize a cultural transformation that is, in principle, independent of a Western context – or whether they simply reflect universal traits of mankind that are neither context-bound nor particularly modern. In order to illuminate these issues, I will draw attention to the contextual aspects of these allegedly modern characteristics.

Two issues are relevant. One evokes the assumed dichotomy between the notion of the modern vs. the traditional, and may be phrased as follows: *What is it exactly that makes modernity 'modern'?* More precisely: in which ways do empirical findings that are assumed to characterize modernity resemble features found in societies generally described as traditional, and in which ways do these features differ in the modern context? This discussion requires a comparison by analogy, in which I rely on selected extracts from the vast multitude of anthropological representations of traditional societies (see Chapter 2). It should become clear in the course of the discussion that these analogies do not in any way do full justice to the rich nuances of the texts to hand. Even so, I contend that the exercise is useful, as it draws the attention to 'differences that make a difference', and thus helps us to identify phenomena for further analysis.

The second issue relates to the notion of Western modernity, and its relationship to the characterizing features of high modernity as described above. Charles Taylor brings attention to an important distinction between theories of modernity. On the one hand, there are what he refers to as 'cultural' theories of modernity, which characterize the transformations that have issued in the modern West, and in which: *'the contemporary Atlantic world is seen as a culture among others, with its own specific understandings, e.g. of person, nature, the good, to be contrasted to all others, including its own predecessor civilization'* (Taylor 1992:88).

'Acultural' theories of modernity, by contrast, describe these transformations in terms of some culture-neutral operation, such as for instance in terms of some specified social or intellectual changes that could, in principle, affect any society (such as: mobility, the rise of instrumental rationality, industrialization). According to this particular outlook the transformation would be defined *not in terms of its specific point of arrival* (i.e. modernity) but rather *as a general function that can take any specific culture as its input* (Taylor 1992:89). According to Taylor, the overwhelming majority of interpretations in our culture[7] tend to be 'acultural'. Miller makes a similar point in his discussion of what he calls *'the universalizing tendencies of theories of modernity . . . failing to account for the diverse contexts within which the dilemmas of modernity are manifested'* (Miller 1994:11). Except for some notable exceptions, such as for instance Weber's Protestant Ethic, the transformations are largely described *as if* they were due to some culture-independent operation. Although Taylor does not address his critique specifically to any particular author, his critique is highly relevant to readings of much of the current debate, including the analyses of modernity provided by Giddens (1991) and Bauman (1991).

In his discussion of Western modernity, Taylor draws attention to what he calls 'modern inwardness', i.e. an underlying opposition in our languages of self-understanding between the 'inside' and the 'outside' (Taylor 1992:93). He states: *'We think of our thoughts and feelings as "within" us. Or else, we think of our capacities and potentialities as "inner", awaiting the development which will manifest them or realize them in the public world . . . We are creatures with inner depths, with partly unexplored and dark interiors'* (Taylor 1992:94). This notion of an inner self is, according to Taylor, a characteristic feature of modernity *as it has developed within the historical and cultural context of the Western world.* Relying upon the history of ideas, he argues that the Cartesian notion of a disengaged subject articulates one of the most important developments of the modern era. This idea of disengagement has had a profound influence on a wide range of modern institutions, including government, military organizations and methods of administration, and has brought about a *'growing ideal of a human agent who is able to remake himself by methodical and disciplined action'* (Taylor 1992:99).

Contemporary theories of modernity tend to be acultural or universal in their scope. To the extent that contextually grounded analyses are thus avoided, this implies that the cultural configurations of Western modernity are largely left unexplored. The aim of the present analysis is to explore these configurations as they are expressed among young marketing professionals. I contend that it is precisely through analyses of the day-to-day practices of modern men and women that we are able to understand the configurations of modernity. This implies an account of mundane details of everyday life at a level of description that differs significantly from that of general theory. Yet by considering the struggles and thoughts of these men and women, we are in a better position to explore the characteristics of modernity. In particular, the present ethnography lends itself to a thorough discussion of the relationship between reflexivity and modern inwardness, as it is expressed through a search for authenticity (see Chapter 10).

Marketing: Global Structures and Local Practices

Marketing is both practice and discipline. As for the former, marketing is whatever people in the marketing department do that they refer to as marketing. I will refer to this as *marketing practice*. Marketing practice is necessarily localized, influenced by culturally informed interpretations of the ways in which things ought to be done. In addition, marketing represents a vocation, a profession, and an institutionalized discipline. As such, it offers a continuous source of information and validation to which one may turn for advice, and – at the same time – an institutionalized expert authority from which one's own status as a professional may be honoured or disqualified. As a discipline, marketing may thus be defined as an *expert system*, a disembedding mechanism that *'brackets time and space through deploying modes of technical knowledge which have validity independent of the practitioners and clients who make use of it'* (Giddens 1991:18). This expert system operates on a global level, and may be approached as what Appadurai refers to as a deterritorialized structural condition mediating flow of cultural idioms and commodities on a global scale (Appadurai 1990).[8] At the level of ethnography, however, this local–global distinction is far from clear-cut. In the marketing department, marketing is simply a way of knowing; a socially and culturally recognized skill that enables a marketing expert to interpret and make use of information in a manner that is recognized as proper and useful. Marketing is knowledge 'how to'.

While each single judgement is locally grounded, it is still informed by an expert system that reaches far beyond the local context. Marketing thus represents an empirical arena in which the local and the global interact. Because of this particular combination of local embeddedness and global connections, marketing represents an excellent empirical case for studying the interplay between the local and the global. This is further enhanced by the fact that marketing practice is, as we shall see, a field of activity in which a considerable effort is devoted to elaborating cultural differences within a continuum of familiarity on the one hand and foreignness on the other (see Chapter 9).

For some authors, globalization is primarily conceived of in terms of processes of cultural homogenization, or, as Hannerz (1990) argues, part of the emergence of a world culture. Modern consumerism is often attributed a key role in such homogenizing processes, frequently exemplified by transnational marketing efforts for uniform brand products such as Coca Cola. For scholars in the West, this understanding is often accompanied by a certain disenchantment and nostalgia, as when the 'homogenization' argument is transformed into an argument about 'Americanization' or 'commoditization' in a negative sense (Appadurai 1990; Turner 1987).

An alternative view, frequently sustained by ethnographic studies, emphasizes the wide variation in terms of local appropriation of consumer goods, of global 'narratives', or of modern conceptual terms (Friedman 1991; Miller 1992; Hviding 1994; Gewertz and Errington 1996; see also Miller 1995a). Elaborating the salience of what may be referred to as 'localizing processes', cultural 'heterogenization', or 'indigenization', such approaches serve to disprove common assumptions about the homogenizing effects of global interaction.

The following analysis may lend itself to each of these arguments. It provides an account of the way in which marketing, a deterritorialized expert system that is influenced by liberal ideologies originating in the US and Western Europe, disseminates into the Nordic context, in which values of equality, equity and social democracy are strongly held (Dahl 1986). The Norwegian marketing professionals may be approached as mediators who possess not only local knowledge, but also what Hannerz (1990:246) refers to as 'decontextualized cultural capital'. Thus, in Hannerz's terms they represent a kind of cosmopolitans with a key role in bringing about a degree of global coherence. As such, the study may emphasize the homogenizing effect of globalizing processes (Moeran 1993). At the same time, interpretations and applications of marketing knowledge in this particular context are also highly local, and in some ways very Scandinavian. The study is therefore also an example of the heterogeneity of globalizing processes. Rather than producing arguments in favour of a 'localizing' or a 'globalizing' perspective, I approach marketing as a double-edged process in which both processes occur simultaneously, and sometimes in a reciprocal manner. The focus of interest is therefore not so much the extent to which marketing contributes to global homogenization, but rather the consequences of this particular system of knowledge for the organization of cultural differences at a local level. In order to achieve this, it is necessary to distinguish between the conditions under which transcultural exchanges occur, and the distinct items that are exchanged. In other words, it is necessary to distinguish between marketing, as a decontextualized system of knowledge, and the cultural idioms and commodities that marketing mediates.

A particularly fruitful approach to marketing in relation to globalizing processes implies a recognition of the role of marketing in providing a framework within which cultural diversity may be organized. Theoretically, I am indebted to Richard Wilk (1995), who argues that to the extent that a global hegemony may be identified, it is a hegemony of form rather than of content. According to Wilk, global structures organize diversity rather than replicate uniformity. Rather than simply disseminating various sets of uniform messages all over the world, marketing may thus be analysed as a global structure for communicating difference, or a uniformly structured system of activities through which a wide array of culturally differentiated idioms may be transmitted. The question that needs to be addressed is thus not simply whether the cultural items that are mediated through marketing practice are 'local' or 'global', but rather how differences are constructed through the interplay between global structures and local interpretations in a specific empirical setting.

Towards a Better Understanding of Materiality

Theories of modernity and of globalizing processes constitute an important framework for the subsequent analysis, and are applied extensively in final discussions (see Chapters 9 and 10). Yet, at the level of detailed ethnographic analysis, they are hardly sufficient. During fieldwork it soon became clear that the construction of food products in the making is more than an elaboration of meaning. It involves a construction of materiality as well. In a sense, this fact appears so obvious and simple that it hardly needs further elaboration. Nevertheless, a review of anthropological contributions to the literature on consumption and consumer goods suggests that this may not be as simple as it seems.

As a broad generalization, one may reasonably claim that the anthropology of consumption is basically an anthropology of the meaning of consumer goods. This observation also applies to anthropological studies of food and eating,[9] in which the social and symbolic aspects of food are invariably emphasized, while the material aspects are taken for granted. This approach may be seen as part of a Durkheimian legacy that implies that practically all cultural domains, including consumer goods and food, are *'ultimately treated as symbolic of underlying social relations'* (Miller 1995b:415). While this approach is fruitful for understanding certain aspects of consumption, it hardly enhances an understanding of the complex interaction between processes of production and consumption. It is particularly inadequate for an analysis of how food products come to be as they are.

One aim of this book is to contribute to a better understanding of the interaction between the material and the social dimension of material artefacts. This implies that I am interested, not only in the material and symbolic dimensions of foods as such, but also in the way this interaction is ideologically and epistemologically informed.

Food products that reach the consumer are already fully equipped with textual and figurative communication, indicating what it is, its specific characteristics, name, possible modes of preparation, proper occasions for use, national origin, ingredients, nutrient contents, etc. As such, manufactured food products are both *functionally and symbolically encoded*[10] (Mackay and Gillespie 1992). Furthermore, as the present study will illustrate, social and symbolic aspects are also taken into account in the process of material production. Thus, when food products appear in the grocery store, their symbolic and social meaning is *'literally baked into them'* (Hennion and Méadel 1989).

A fruitful understanding of food production must therefore be sensitive to interactions between the social and material dimensions. This requires an attention to the processes of construction, rather than to the final result. These considerations brought my attention to a body of literature generally referred to as science and technology studies (for an overview, see Mackay and Gillespie 1992; Jasanoff *et al.* 1995). This theoretical approach serves as a supplement to more general theories of modernity, and is particularly relevant to the analysis of processes related to product development.

Studies of Technology and Science

Science and technology studies (often referred to as the STS-approach) comprise two broad research directions that differ primarily with regard to the empirical object of study. One focuses on the social construction of scientific facts, and is generally referred to as *laboratory studies*. The other focuses on the social construction of technological and material artefacts.[11] In spite of an obvious difference in empirical focus, these two research directions share a common theoretical basis, which I loosely refer to as constructionism.[12] As such, the STS-approach has much in common with the phenomenological tradition as it is brought into focus by Berger and Luckmann (1967), and is rooted in the Kantian idea that the world of experience is structured in terms of human categories and concepts (Knorr Cetina 1995). Both approaches represent attempts to formulate theoretical concepts that are suitable for grasping technology and knowledge in the making. In addition, they share a methodological strategy that implies a close study of the processes and actors involved.

Laboratory studies focus on natural science in the making (Latour 1988). Refusing to take a stand on whether or not a scientific statement is true, the researcher addresses instead the processes through which an idea *gradually comes to be accepted* as true. In order to unravel the social construction of scientific facts, ethnographic methods are applied. Laboratory studies imply literally following the researchers around in their day-to-day practice, and focus especially on scientific controversies and 'unfinished' knowledge (Knorr Cetina 1995). On the surface, laboratory studies may resemble ethnographic studies of organizations. The difference, however, is significant in that laboratory studies generally do not focus upon the organization as such, but rather upon the major mechanisms of knowledge production occurring within organizations (Knorr Cetina 1995). Thus, even though organizational variables are not excluded, the empirical emphasis and analytical purpose of laboratory studies differ significantly from most organizational studies.

Latour approaches technological and scientific projects as attempts at mobilizing various groups of actors to support a particular technical solution or a particular scientific 'truth'. By focusing on the ways in which researchers establish networks of alliances, Latour is able to identify some of the struggles and negotiations that occur in the processes of scientific or technological development.

In his description of the building and shifting of alliances, Latour also draws upon ideas from Machiavelli's account of 'The Prince' (Latour 1988). Just as the princes of fifteenth-century Florence had to face up to the harsh realities of power through the enlistment and continuous control of allies, so too must the technical engineers of today. While the Machiavellian world is essentially social, in the sense that alliances link living human beings, Latour insists that we must include a concept of non-human allies as well, in order to understand modern 'Princes'. By identifying anything from kerosene (in the development of the diesel engine) to the wind (as a prerequisite for the functioning of a windmill) as allies that are made to be relevant during various processes of technological development, Latour suggests that the project of the technical engineers has in fact much in common with that of Machiavelli's Princes. According to this approach, non-human entities such as microbes, scallops and automatic door-closers are relevant as negotiating parties at the level of analysis[13] (Knorr Cetina 1995). Emphasizing the social constructedness of technological facts and artefacts, Latour parts with those who approach technology in a more narrow sense, as something that may be defined separately from its social surroundings (Sørensen and Andersen 1988).

The fruitfulness of this approach for an understanding of material products in the making is closely connected to the concept of allies, which is broad enough to include both human and non-human elements. Most importantly, this perspective allows analytical treatment of a product manager's various human and non-human allies *on equal terms*. From the perspective of a product manager, the propensity of sausages to absorb water may prove to be just as crucial for a stable alliance as Norwegian consumers' propensity to buy sausages. Furthermore, both of these propensities are both resistant and subject to manipulation, the former by means of salt, the latter by means of advertising.

Applying this perspective, I do not suggest that sausages have agency in a common-sense meaning of the word. However, I *do* suggest that material entities may be analysed as central 'participants' (together with human actors) in the alliances that product managers strive to establish. Obviously, the resistance of material foodstuffs is not a conscious decision, while the resistance of consumers may well be. Yet as long as the focus is narrowly confined to the marketing department and the negotiation of knowledge that takes place there, this difference is not of great importance. Both kinds of resistance are potential challenges that need to be understood by product managers, and then prevented if possible.

What then, is implied by the notion of a stable alliance? Stable alliances may be scientific truths, successful technological solutions (a windmill, a PC), and in the present analysis, a successful brand product. According to Latour, a technological solution is successful when it has the ability to align different forces so that they come to act together as one, in the manner of a *machine*. A machine, according to Latour is *'a machination, a stratagem, a kind of cunning, where borrowed forces keep one another in check so that none can fly apart from the group'* (Latour 1987:129). A machine thus domesticates different kinds of forces, such as natural forces, as in Latour's example of a successful ship model designed by the Portuguese in the late fifteenth century:

> the wood of which they were built and the way they were careened made them stronger than waves and tides ... They acted as one element; they had become a clever machination to control the many forces that tried out their resistance. For instance, all sorts of wind directions, instead of slowing the ship down, were turned into allies by a unique combination of lateen and square rigs (Latour 1987:221).

In addition to non-human allies, a machine may consist of social actors as well. In the case of the Portuguese carrack, the technological innovation allowed a smaller crew to man a bigger ship, thus rendering the captain less vulnerable to mutiny. In addition, the bigger size of the carracks made it possible to embark bigger guns, which, in turn, rendered more predictable the outcome of military encounters with foreigners (Latour 1987: 221). In this way, technological (and scientific) developments may be viewed as the result of particular configurations bringing together both human and material (natural) forces, thus creating what is often referred to as a 'seamless web' of technology and society (Hughes 1987). During processes such as the above *'machination of forces'* unreliable allies are slowly turned into something that resembles an organized whole. When such a cohesion is obtained we have what Latour calls a *'black box'* (Latour 1987:129–31). In science, we may think of undisputed scientific facts or knowledge of a doxic nature as black boxes; in the field of technology, stable technological artefacts may serve in the same way.

Unlike laboratory studies, which are based primarily on contemporary ethnographies, the constructionist approach to technology is primarily concerned with technological developments from a historical angle (Pinch and Bijker 1987). One central concept within the constructionist approach is that of *interpretative flexibility*, referring not only to the flexibility involved in social interpretations of technology, but also to that inherent in processes of material design (Pinch and Bijker 1987). According to Pinch and Bijker, the first stage of analysis should include a demonstration that the technical solution finally chosen was not the only possible solution. The final technological artefact appears, in other words, as only *one out of several possible versions* that have been considered during the development process. Interpretative flexibility usually refers to the cultural constructedness of material products (Pinch and Bijker 1987). I will demonstrate, however, that the term applies equally well to 'imagined products', i.e. ideas about products that might be developed, but where actual materialization has not yet taken place. Interpretative flexibility thus occurs at all stages of the product development process, from the vague idea of 'making something', to the final incorporation of particular products into the eating patterns of each household.[14] Food advertising serves as a mediator in this process. Through advertising, producers have the chance to create a message that reflects *their* interpretation of the food product. Ideally, if the advertising is carefully designed, this interpretation will also be incorporated by consumers in a way that makes them not only try out the product, but try it out in such a way and with such expectations that the use of the product soon becomes a habit. Advertising may thus be seen as a key instrument in producing reliable, *stable alliances* between the producer and the consumer. Generally in the context of market economies, it may be assumed that strong alliances with the consumers serve as a crucial element in securing the future existence (and position) of the producer.

Within the constructionist approach, each stage in which interpretative flexibility may be identified represents a temporary *controversy*. When a particular interpretation aligns sufficiently strong actors and interests for making decisions on further action, controversies may be closed. *Closure of controversies* may imply the temporary stabilization of an artefact in a particular material form, the culmination of open conflicts among various social groups involved, or, with regard to science, the transformation of a scientific hypothesis into a scientific 'fact'.

The relevance of the STS-approach for the present analysis is most salient in the part of the analysis that deals explicitly with food products in the making. Drawing on key concepts of the constructionist approach, I am able to formulate more specific inquiries related to how commercial food products come to be as they are, the types of negotiations that take place, and the particular configurations of human and non-human allies that may be mobilized in closing controversies.

Metaphors, Knowledge and Truth

The social production of foods for sale is closely linked with the social production of knowledge. This is particularly apparent during stages of controversy, when considerations retrieved from a repertoire of knowledge of both material and social conditions become relevant to particular decisions. Such configurations of knowledge also have a significant impact on closing of controversies, and consequently on the final characteristics of food products and food advertising.

According to Latour, knowledge may be defined as whatever enables a person to handle whatever s/he encounters with the familiarity of previous experiences (Latour 1987:219). This implies that whatever happens represents only *one instance of other events already mastered*. Such familiarity may be obtained through personal experience, or indirectly, through experience of others. The crucial point in the latter case is that some relevant aspect of the experience is transformed and transmitted in a form that enables others to become familiar with things, people, and events that were previously distant. Travellers' accounts, journals of scientific laboratories, maps and language laboratories are all examples of experience thus transformed.

Transmitting experience through written text is a very common endeavour in modern societies, and our common-sense understanding of knowledge is often associated with that of written information. This is the case in the field of food production as well, a fact that became increasingly clear as I realized that a significant

part of my field material would never have been obtainable had I
not had easy access to a photocopier.

In his discussion of knowledge, Latour reminds us that ways
in which experience may be transmitted reach far beyond the realm
of written text. He illustrates his point by referring to all the
instruments that enable a ship to manoeuvre safely in unfamiliar
seas. Ocean maps provide an obvious example of experience
transferred, enabling a newcomer to navigate by means of someone
else's experience; but then, so too is the quadrant, if you know
how to use it. Just like the ocean map, the quadrant will help the
navigator localize in advance the rocks below the ocean surface
instead of, as Latour puts it: *'being localised by them without warning'*
(Latour 1987:221). How then, do we delimit a concept of knowledge? Does it end where technology starts, including only the
printed directions for how to use the quadrant? Or does it comprise
everything that enables us to navigate through life by means of
the experience of others, including anything from market statistics
to bread and electrical ovens?

Obviously, an approach to knowledge that includes practically
everything around us is not very fruitful as an analytical tool.
Latour makes this point as well, emphasizing that the term
'knowledge', just like 'technology', 'profit' and 'power', creates
more problems than it solves, because it tends to split the subject-
matter in a way that makes us lose track of the processes in which
these aspects are interwoven, or as he puts it: *'divide up a cloth that
we want seamless in order to study it as we choose'* (Latour 1987:223).
Following Latour, we then end up with an approach in which
neither knowledge nor technology are analytically distinct
concepts, but rather dimensions of a set of negotiations that, in
turn, is localized in a specific sociocultural context.

How, then, do we sort out the empirical material in a way that
enables us to analyse how both discursive and material artefacts
come to be as they are? In line with the ethnographic approach of
laboratory studies, Latour suggests that we draw attention to the
day-to-day activities and struggles of informants, asking (with
reference to these actors' positions): *How are they able to act at a
distance on unfamiliar events, places and people?* And: *How can these
events, places and people be made familiar, since they are distant?*

In the present analysis, the quest of the actors (product managers in the marketing department) may be approached as a
continuous effort towards ensuring and strengthening the various

patterns of alliances (mediated through food products) between Viking Foods and the fuzzy category of potential allies generally referred to as consumers. In large measure, this is part of a continuous preparation to deal successfully with future challenges and possibilities posed by the context generally referred to as 'the market'. It is by making aspects of this context familiar that the producer is able to come to terms with potential allies in spite of the separating gaps represented by space, time and scale.

How then, is this achieved? According to Latour (1987), in the accumulation of knowledge one must invent means that are *mobile* and *stable*, ensuring that the movement back and forth does not lead to distortion, corruption and decay. They must also be *combinable*, so that whatever insight these 'experiences' reflect can be cumulated.[15] In the marketing department, the efforts at 'making distant events, places and people familiar' is achieved largely within the framework of knowledge referred to as marketing and market research.

In day-to-day activities and negotiations in the marketing department, references to marketing knowledge are rarely explicit, but represent an integrated part of the argument itself. Marketing knowledge thus appears largely as propositional claims of 'truth', either on the basis of models inherent in the institutionalized expert system, or by tacit recognition of individual competence. The fate of such propositions depends, obviously, on whether or not the speaker succeeds in making this particular configuration of knowledge socially relevant, an achievement that, in turn, depends upon the social context, the socially recognized competence of the speaker, and the relationship that exists between him or her and members of the audience. The transformation of an individually expressed proposition to a socially recognized 'truth' is thus a complex social process in which competence, context and expert system all play a part.

In the light of this, knowledge is more than an instrumental resource; as Latour suggests, it is also a matter of local recognition, and thus contextually defined. For the purpose of subsequent analysis, knowledge may be defined as *a component of culture that is recognized as knowledge within a given social context*. Marketing knowledge thus includes any statement, model or source of information that professionals in the marketing department recognize as relevant as part of their knowledge. Methodologically, this implies that written sources, such as marketing textbooks and other relevant literature, constitute part of the analysis in so far as they have been referred to as relevant sources by informants.

This approach to knowledge implies that I generally refrain from evaluating marketing both epistemologically (against any objective notion of truth – whatever that might be) and instrumentally (whether it works). Instead, I seek to explore the *ways in which* the most common conceptualizations of the relevant context (such as 'market' and 'consumers') are taken for granted as naturally occurring entities, existing independently of their processes of construction. This implies that I will explore the local configurations of knowledge with regard to their particular content, their relationship to other configurations of knowledge, and the impact that these might have on the processes of food production and marketing practice.

Propositional claims are often metaphorically structured. An analysis of knowledge in the marketing department must therefore include an analysis of the metaphoric structures in which knowledge is embedded. Lakoff and Johnson (1980) suggest that we approach metaphors as concepts that enable us to understand and experience one thing in terms of another. As such, metaphors are neither true, nor false. Rather, they tend to emphasize some aspects of a phenomenon, while veiling others. Metaphors thus have an impact on the way we think about the world. As metaphors create social realities, they may also serve to guide future action.[16] This calls for analysis of the performative consequences of various metaphoric structures (Fernandez 1974).

Metaphors may also be approached as ways of organizing and transmitting knowledge, and of justifying certain strategies. The ethnography reveals the most central conceptual underpinnings in day-to-day marketing practice. Through an examination of such metaphors, and of the particular contexts in which they are applied, we may gain a better understanding of how experience is transformed to knowledge, and how this knowledge, in turn, serves as a guide to future action expressed in marketing practice.

This analytical exercise constitutes the empirical basis for a more general discussion of modernity. The premiss of this endeavour is that the struggles and actions of marketing executives may illustrate much wider concerns of modern life. Through a rather detailed account of 'everyday life' in a marketing department, we are in a better position to appreciate and to challenge theoretical assumptions about fundamental characteristics of modern society.

An Outline

This book is divided into three parts. Part I consists of three chapters, and is titled *Introductions*. While the present chapter is a theoretical introduction, Chapter 2 serves as an empirical introduction, focusing on the setting, and on selected aspects of fieldwork and analysis. Chapter 3 introduces the structural conditions of Norwegian food marketing at the time when fieldwork was carried out. This chapter is especially relevant for readers who wish to compare empirical findings to studies of marketing conducted elsewhere. The description is based primarily on secondary sources, and is not part of the ethnographic analysis.

Part II, titled *Empirical Context, Concepts and Cases* is basically an ethnographic account, consisting of five chapters. Chapter 4 provides a description of aspects of the social organization of the marketing department, and describes the roles and responsibilities of product manager, emphasizing various interpretations on issues such as career, success and gender. Chapter 5 brings attention to key concepts and metaphors that are applied in general discourse in the marketing department. It focuses especially on the terms 'market', 'product', 'brand' and 'consumer', and presents these terms by means of a metaphorical approach. Chapters 6 to 9 are empirical case studies. Each chapter provides a chronological outline of events for one particular product or product group in the making, usually referred to as 'ongoing projects'. Chapter 6 introduces the 'poultry project' as it developed over a period of one and a half years. The poultry project represents the most coherent case description, and is particularly thorough with regard to aspects of product development. Consequently, it represents a 'test case' for the constructionist approach to products in the making. Chapter 7 provides a description of the process of creating an advertising commercial. It focuses on the various attempts at creating a TV commercial for a particular pizza product, emphasizing the efforts at establishing a differentiated product range, and the application of consumer segmentation strategies in marketing and product development. Chapter 8 describes a product range of frozen convenience foods that were already on the market when fieldwork started. It focuses on attempts at improving the existing product range, and the development of a TV testimonial. Although Part II consists primarily of empirical presentations, preliminary analyses are presented throughout, and constitute a basis for the subsequent discussion in Part III.

Part III, titled *Discussions*, consists of two chapters in which empirical findings are discussed in the light of more general theories, and in the light of comparative material. Chapter 9 focuses on the notions of sameness and difference in marketing practice. These notions are discussed in the light of totemic classification, globalization theory, and the notion of authenticity, which is salient to Western modernity. Chapter 10 focuses especially on the separations between the private and the professional that characterize the social organization of marketing and advertising, and the difficulties in evaluating creativity. Ambivalence is a central concept, and strategies for dealing with ambivalence are discussed. Finally, feelings of uncertainty, which are frequently expressed in the marketing department, are analysed in relation to reflexivity, authenticity and the modern inwardness. This constitutes the basis of a discussion of marketing and modernity.

Notes

1. Viking Foods is a fictitious name, as are all other names of persons and products.
2. Geertz 1973.
3. This and all other citations from Machiavelli derive from the Penguin English edition, translated by George Bull, and first published in 1961. Slight differences between the citations here and those provided by Giddens's (1991) are probably due to the fact that Giddens cites a different edition.
4. This understanding of modernity differs from Giddens's in the sense that while Giddens includes only capitalism and industrialism as the institutional axes of modernity, Bauman includes communism as well.
5. Definitions of modernity range from those of French historians, who define the modern state as an institution that existed from the thirteenth to the seventeenth century, to that of literary critics, whose confinement of the term modernity lasts from the beginning of the twentieth century to the 1950s (Bauman 1991:3).

6. A thorough account of the various contemporary writings on modernity would go beyond the scope and purpose of the present discussion. For an account of theories of modernity, see e.g. Miller 1994.

7. Although Taylor is not entirely clear as to the circumscription of 'our culture', I assume he refers to Western academia, or Western intellectuals.

8. This claim refers both to the fact that marketing is a system of knowledge of (assumed) universal relevance, and to the fact that although models, theories and information tend to originate in the Western world (primarily the US), these conceptual devices seem to disseminate with remarkable ease across cultural boundaries, relatively undisturbed by the various local contexts in which marketing is practised (Moeran 1993).

9. Influential studies on food or consumption often delimit the analysis from the material dimension of the object in focus, 'transforming' it, as it were, to a symbol or a sign (Douglas and Nicod 1974; Douglas and Isherwood 1980), a signifier of class (Bourdieu 1984), or an instance of objectification of culture upon the material world (Miller 1987).

10. Advertising serves as an extension of this functional and symbolical encoding of the material product, providing space for elaborating various aspects of the messages indicated above even more.

11. Mackay and Gillespie (1992) define three separate schools within the micro approach to what they refer to as 'social shaping of technology'. These include the social constructionist approach as advocated most notably by Bijker, Hughes and Pinch (1987), the systems approach as advocated by Hughes (1987), and the actor network approach as advocated by Callon (1986), Latour and Woolgar (1986) and Latour (1987).

12. The term constructionism derives from Knorr Cetina (1995). Other authors refer to 'constructivism', which I take to cover broadly the same approach.

13. This approach has been accused of extending a notion of agency to things, a position that is clearly at odds with most current social theory (see for instance Collins and Yearly 1992). I suggest, however, that it need not be taken that literally.

14. For an excellent illustration of changes of interpretations of foods at the stage of consumption, see the account by Levenstein (1985) of the American response to Italian foods.

15. In modern societies, scientific laboratories represent a hallmark of this endeavour, making the notion of a 'laboratory' the conceptual metaphor of scientific accumulation of knowledge in its pure form (Knorr Cetina 1995).
16. Such action will, of course, fit the metaphor. This will, in turn, reinforce the power of the metaphor to make experience coherent (Lakoff and Johnson 1980:156).

Chapter 2

Setting the Scene

The ethnographic analysis is based upon fieldwork in the marketing department of a major Norwegian food manufacturer, which I refer to as Viking Foods. A major part of the ethnographic material was collected during nine months of fieldwork (October 1991–August 1992). Additional data on selected cases and issues were also gathered after the end of the fieldwork period, through occasional visits, correspondence and conversations on the phone. The present chapter provides an introduction to the setting, and describes selected aspects of methods and analysis.

The present study is both something more and something less than an ethnographic analysis of a modern organization. In order to illuminate how food products come to be as they are, there is a primary focus on *mechanisms* and *processes* as they unfold in a chosen ethnographic setting, rather than on the unique peculiarities of the organization itself.

With this in mind, I searched for an enterprise that, apart from being fairly large and influential in the Norwegian market, was also 'typical' enough that my findings might be assumed to have some general relevance. As it turned out, these criteria were more than fulfilled. From early 1989, when I made an initial inquiry about the possibility of conducting fieldwork in a Viking Foods marketing department, until 1992, when the bulk of fieldwork was carried out, the company experienced several mergers, making it one of the most influential and diversified private enterprises in food production in Norway.

Because of these recent mergers, I came to know individuals whose professional experience reached far beyond the marketing department of what was now referred to as Viking Foods. For some, their original employer had merged with the larger company, leaving them to cope as best they could with the codes and practices of a new work environment. Others had been part of Viking Foods even before the mergers. In addition, a significant portion of the people at the marketing department belonged to a category of marketing professionals who were young, ambitious and highly mobile (see Chapter 4). Many had been appointed to their present position after a period of initial training elsewhere. Because of this, many of my informants were well informed about practices elsewhere, and would often contribute their personal reflections and comparisons concerning what they felt to be peculiar to Viking Foods, and what would be likely to take place anywhere.

A Part-time Society

> Instead of being a full-time member of one 'total and whole' society, modern man is a part-time citizen in a variety of part-time societies. Instead of living within one meaningful world system to which he owes complete loyalty, he now lives in many differently structured 'worlds' to each of which he owes only partial allegiance (Luckmann 1978:282).

The marketing department of Viking Foods departs significantly from the stereotype version of a 'local village' of anthropological discourse. Perhaps most ethnographic field-sites do. Yet, as a trained anthropologist, I often felt an urge to treat my field as if it were a separate and coherent sociocultural unit. This urge may partly reflect my previous field experience in a remote and fairly isolated community in Northern Norway (Lien 1989), but it also reflects the tendency in anthropological studies in general, and in organizational studies in particular, to assume a simple coherence between culture and place. Such assumptions are now increasingly challenged, not only as a consequence of migration, but also as a result of an increased awareness of the non-geographical boundaries between one's 'own' and 'others'' culture, boundaries that are particularly strongly felt in connection with 'anthropology at home' (Okely 1996).

There are basically two ways in which the marketing department differs significantly from the notion of a local village as a close-knit and coherent social and cultural unit. One relates to the temporariness of its members' presence, and is aptly summarized by Luckmann above. The other relates to the significance of the various contexts in which the organization takes part.

Obviously, a social setting in which people interact only during certain hours during the day, and that is separated as much as possible from anything that has to do with reproduction (activities that in modern Western societies are firmly conceptualized as a part of 'private life' as opposed to 'work life') can hardly be seen as a total ethnographic context, or a local village in the traditional sense of the term. Nevertheless, there has been an increasing tendency in organizational studies to treat organizations precisely in this manner: as separate, coherent sociocultural organisms characterized by a particular set of codes and values, often encompassed in the popular term 'organizational culture'.[1] Emphasizing thus the informal aspects of the activities going on at somebody's workplace, this tendency represents a reaction to, and modification of, a more rational and mechanical understanding of the way organizations function. As such, the emphasis on the cultural dimension within these studies may be justified.

The present analysis is not an ethnography of the organization as such, nor a study of 'organizational culture'. I contend that to the extent that culture is relevant, it is primarily through a variety of connections between the marketing department and the external world. Thus culture provides a contextual dimension that is central to the interpretation of ethnographic findings. This applies to several levels of analysis, including marketing as a framework of knowledge, Norway and the Nordic region, and Western modernity. Most importantly, the book represents an ethnographic account of modernity in the Western world.

The construction of food products in Norway in the early 1990s cannot be separated from processes of global (cultural and economic) integration. As we shall see, these processes activate notions of 'Norwegianness' and of 'national cuisine' in a very explicative manner. While the existence of Norway as a distinct nation-state provides both a general framework for distributing products, and a constitutive element in creating them, one might still argue that Viking Foods is hardly Norwegian at all. Its global dimension is most striking when marketing is treated as an expert system. Knowledge in Viking Foods is of a transferable kind. Its application is neither restricted to the field of food, nor to the limits of Norway – on the contrary, its key models and insights are assumed to be of universal value, and its general statements are assumed to be valid anywhere.

For professionals working in the marketing department, 'the food business' and 'Norway' represent contexts within which they happen to work, in the sense that their personal competence is *not* restricted to these particular fields. Their professional training and their particular experiences at Viking Foods enable them to enter a professional position practically anywhere, and to market practically anything. Their competence and professional sense of identity is thus neither spatially nor materially defined; rather it extends the notion of localness: a marketing professional is inherently a global expert. At another level, however, Norwegian culture and lifestyle represent a frame of reference which they apply, implicitly or explicitly, in their constructions of particular food products. In this way, central themes that may characterize Norwegian (Nordic) culture may represent a proper context of interpretation.

With these aspects in mind, one might argue that the village metaphor should be discarded altogether. Although I recognize the limitations of the village metaphor empirically, as well as for analytic purposes, I still insist on making use of some method-ological advantages connected with a 'field-as-village' approach.[2] Consequently, my fieldwork strategies are partly aimed at 'mimicking', as far as the setting permitted me to do so, methods that would have been applied in more traditional anthropological settings as well. Yet there were significant limitations.

Fieldwork in the marketing department was fieldwork among people who conceived of themselves as being extremely busy most of the time. Most staff members were continuously on the move, often leaving their offices for several hours, and while present, they seemed to be busy working, or talking on the phone. Except for a regular monthly meeting, there were very few occasions at which I could interact with my informants as members of a group, let alone sit around and chat. It soon became clear to me that simply being there, waiting for events to occur, was not a very good idea.

Consequently, I had to select a methodological approach that would provide access to the flow of events from the inside, from the perspective of individual informants, and more coherently than through occasional fragments of information. As most activities in the marketing department were conceptualized as 'projects',[3] and as most projects implied activities to launch or improve a specific product (or range of products), I decided to organize fieldwork around such projects.[4] I will refer to these selected projects as *cases*.[5] Each project was implemented by a product manager who was responsible for that particular product. Because of these connections between persons, products and projects, the choice of project was simultaneously a choice of key informants.

Hence, to the extent that a certain holism is aimed at, it is not to be found at the level of organizational culture, nor with reference to individual lives. Rather, I have tried to describe and to understand *each single case* holistically, i.e. by analysing all the various issues and considerations that are brought up in a non-discriminatory manner.[6] This implies that I embark upon each case without a set of rigidly defined research questions in mind, but rather attempting to record and later describe the course of events giving as much attention to trivialities and 'dead-ends' as to dramatic moments and turning-points. In this way the present analysis differs from research on marketing practice carried out in the field of Marketing and Economics (see for instance Helgesen 1992). Furthermore, I contend that it is through such adherence to a holistic ideal (within the limitations that the complexities of the field represent) that the anthropological approach may provide a unique type of insight into modern practices, and therefore, to some extent, into modern lives.

My selection of cases had immediate consequences for the gradual establishment of close relationships to key informants. Generally, the tight schedule of most product managers implied that the only way that I could develop a fairly close relationship to any of them was by following them around. I also found that the most interesting and informative conversations often took place immediately before or after meetings, in the elevator, or during a coffee break, i.e. at moments when we were both on the verge of 'doing something else'. The fruitfulness of such brief conversations usually required that I should have already acquired a fairly good knowledge of the current issues. Because of the problems of establishing key informants among those product managers who were *not* informants on selected cases, my active selection of cases also turned out to be a selection of key informants.[7]

During fieldwork it became increasingly clear to me that the social setting I gradually got to know was precisely what Luckmann refers to as a 'part-time' kind of society (Luckmann

1978:282). My informants, like myself, were modern men and women, in the sense that the time we shared was indeed 'part-time'. For me, as well as for them, frequent and stable interaction in the marketing department did not automatically provide a free road of access into other spheres of life. Although friendships were not uncommon, especially among individuals of similar age and life-situation, the fact of working together did not *in itself* imply the development of other, personal relationships.

Because of these rather obvious social characteristics, and much to my regret, the ethnographic setting did not provide the opportunities for total personal involvement in the field. My experience of fieldwork therefore departs somewhat from the frequently stereotyped (and idealized) version of ethnographic fieldwork as a 'total experience, demanding all of the anthro-pologist's resources; intellectual, physical, emotional, political and intuitive' (Okely 1992:8). Especially, when it comes to personal and emotional involvement, the limitations were strongly felt. Having my home, family and personal social network safely within reach, I was never confronted with some of the hardships, psychological as well as practical, that fieldwork experience may entail. Most important, perhaps: I never really 'needed' my informants for anything other than information to complete my work, as other needs related to my physical and emotional well-being were fulfilled elsewhere.

Paradoxically, however, one might argue that precisely this disengagement of professional needs from other needs put me in a position to experience life in the marketing department in much the same way as it was experienced by my informants. In spite of the salience of work in the lives of these young professionals, life happened elsewhere as well. In spite of all the time spent in the offices after hours, there was always another place called 'home', providing (we may assume) a space for acting out very different roles, and often conveying an atmosphere of comfort and rest.

For them, as for me, the intrusion of this 'elsewhere' into the confines of the marketing department was generally limited to a telephone call negotiating something like 'Who goes shopping?' and 'What do we need?' Occasionally, a major life event occurring 'elsewhere', such as the birth of a child, or a fiftieth birthday, might also be celebrated and made publicly known by the announced sharing of cake and coffee. Other than this, however, the intrusion of private life into the professional sphere was carefully controlled, and largely avoided.[8]

In hindsight, I therefore regard this particular fieldwork experience not just as a second-best version of the 'total experience' type of fieldwork, but rather as an experience of the fragmentation of life-worlds and the part-time interaction that is typical of modernity. My wish to be more thoroughly absorbed in the fieldwork ritual may thus be re-interpreted as a kind of nostalgia, a condition sometimes said to characterize Western civilization generally and social theory in particular (Turner 1987).[9]

While this experience of modernity is an experience I share with my informants, I should hasten to add that it is precisely my awareness of these facts that sets us apart. The fact that my work both requires and allows a *sensitization* towards these and other peculiar traits that are otherwise taken for granted is, I suggest, the main reason why there is still a certain distance between 'me' and 'them'. Finally, I should add that this process of sensitization is brought about not so much by the fieldwork in itself, but by the continuous comparison of this experience to other fieldwork experiences made possible by anthropological accounts.

Time and the Notion of Change

While anthropological studies have often focused on empirical settings that are fairly well defined along a spatial dimension, they have tended to neglect or understate the limits of their field according to a *temporal* dimension. The temporal delimitations of the validity of the findings are seldom made explicit, rarely problematized, and sometimes avoided altogether, blurred in the mode of the ethnographic present. According to Fabian, it is precisely this setting apart in time that has enabled the anthropologist to create his Other as something different (Fabian 1983).

During fieldwork, I often found myself preoccupied with the limitations set by the *time period* in which the fieldwork took place. While the validity of my findings seemed to reach beyond the boundaries of the local region, the temporal validity of my findings seemed at first to be very narrow indeed. This preoccupation was spurred and nurtured by informants, who would often remind me that my experiences during fieldwork were the product of the

most recent events, and *'totally different'* from the experiences I
might have encountered last year, or even next year. Even a year
after I concluded the greater part of the fieldwork I was being
told, for instance, that the salience of a phenomenon that I had
found to be very important, such as brand-building, was practically *'negligible when I was there, compared to what was going on
now . . .'*. All in all, this notion of temporality and change pervaded
both my data-material and my recollections and thoughts about
the field-site.[10]

Partly, this preoccupation with time reflects a general awareness
of change in Norwegian public discourse, which has been particularly salient in the field of food-marketing and food-policy debate
in the late 1980s and early 1990s (Lien 1992, 1995a). This awareness
of change must be interpreted in light of processes of global
integration in general, and of an increasing internationalization
of the Norwegian food market in the early 1990s in particular (see
Chapter 3).

At the same time, my awareness of the importance of time may
also reflect a general preoccupation with time among anthropologists doing anthropology 'at home'. Hastrup notes that *'once
we move into our own culture areas, it would seem that a new kind of
awareness about the temporal discourse is required'* (Hastrup 1987:99).
On the basis of this observation she asks whether the ethnographer
working within her own civilization reads the 'sign of time'
differently from her colleagues working with remote, primitive
peoples. I will not pursue this discussion here, but briefly state
my belief, as Hastrup does, that 'this is possibly so'.

I share with my informants a preoccupation with time as a
common denominator for structuring the flow of events, for
separating them from each other and for making sense of them
all. Consequently, I feel obliged to draw attention to the temporal
delimitation of some of my findings. Apart from this, I will
demonstrate the various ways in which the notions of time, and
especially of change, inform the construction of reality and the
actions taking place in the marketing department; both as a space
in which each actor is moving forward (individual careers), and
as a collectively shared future coming up, which actors in the
marketing department must constantly try to interpret in order to
adapt to it.

A Note on Comparison

Ladislav Holy (1987) has drawn attention to the discrepancy between the current lack of methodological attention to comparison, and the fact that comparison is still widely practised within anthropology. Cross-cultural comparison, once a characterizing feature of anthropology, has gradually been replaced by a more interpretative approach. In this process, a focus on comparison has to some extent been replaced by a focus on epistemology, as problems have increasingly been identified at the level of description rather than at the level of generalization (Holy 1987). Consequently, the word 'comparison' literally disappeared from the vocabulary of methodological discourse; not because it was never practised, but rather as a reflection of the fact that, to the extent that it was carried out, its primary function was to highlight cultural specificity.

To the extent that I make use of cross-cultural comparison, my strategic approach is rooted within an interpretative paradigm, and aims primarily at facilitating description. Within the interpretative approach, the over-arching purpose of comparison is description, and as such the strategy has more in common with non-comparative description than with the cross-cultural testing of hypotheses that was practised earlier (Holy 1987). Thus the purpose of comparison in the present context is primarily to *evoke analogies*, which may serve to illuminate particular aspects and possible implications of the empirical findings. Thus it is comparison, as long as we understand comparison as an inherent aspect of the processes of translation, description, and explanation (Holy 1987; Overing 1987).

As an aspect of translation, one may argue that comparison has always been part of the ethnographic method – implicitly or explicitly. Earlier, when the anthropological gaze was primarily directed at distant and 'primitive' societies, the direction of translation was necessarily *from* the 'strange' *to* the 'familiar'. In the present account, the empirical focus is a context that is fairly familiar to most Westerners in academia, including myself. In this way, it is an instance of 'anthropology at home',[11] in which the encompassing context shared by informants, most readers and myself is the context of modernity, or even Western modernity.

This particular situation poses epistemological problems that are relevant to studies of modernity, as well as 'anthropology at home' in general: namely, the problem of identifying the characteristics of a cultural phenomenon which is simultaneously infusing our gaze. More precisely: How can we separate the characterizing features of modernity from our own ethnocentric preoccupations as modern individuals? Daniel Miller touches upon this problem when he summarizes the dilemmas inherent in studying modernity as *'how we can observe and understand the consequences of a framework for experience that is clearly and increasingly a significant part of all our lives?'* (Miller 1994:76).

A comparative approach represents one way of dealing with this problem. Through ethnographic accounts from societies that are distinctively non-modern, anthropological literature offers an opportunity to confront some of our highly ethnocentric assumptions about what modernity entails. Clearly, this requires a comparison between cultural contexts that, in many ways, are incommensurable. I contend, however, that such incommensurability should not inhibit us from making comparisons. Firstly, comparison has always been part of the anthropological endeavour, at least implicitly. For a large part, comparison in anthropology involves a high level of involvement with incommensurable systems (Evans-Pritchard 1962; Overing 1987). Any attempt to characterize modernity necessarily evokes an image of the opposite, and therefore, to some extent, the 'incommensurable'. Yet this does not imply that comparison must be avoided. Instead, I suggest that we should strive to make our comparisons explicit. Secondly, any attempt to define a 'commensurable' context is, in itself, highly problematic. As Judith Okely notes, 'the division between "known" or "other" culture can be defined neither by national nor geographical territory' (Okely 1996:1). The delineation of a 'commensurable' context is therefore fraught with difficulties in the first place, as similarity at one level does not necessarily imply commensurability at another. Commensurability is therefore not something that may be defined *a priori*, but is rather a matter of empirical inquiry (Overing 1987).

Notes

1. For a more thorough discussion of the term, see Czarniawska-Joerges (1992).
2. By this term, I refer to a certain persistence and continuity that is obtained through months of participant observation, and that often allows the establishment of relationships that are closer and more personal than what is required for a formal qualitative interview.
3. Projects vary considerably, both in length, investment of resources, purpose, and thrust of activities. While some imply the production of an advertising campaign, others imply material improvement of existing products, or even new product development. Sometimes, a project requires the full-time occupation of a several persons; at other times a project may be a part-time activity for everyone involved. Generally, however, most projects demand the full-time attention of the responsible product manager.
4. Three of the most interesting and extensive projects are presented as cases in Part II. During fieldwork, I also followed other projects that are not presented in this book (for further information and more case studies, see Lien 1995b).
5. In the process of selection, both practical issues and theoretical interest were taken into account. Especially, I was interested in projects that involved considerations relating both to the material and to the symbolic aspects of the product. I also preferred projects that seemed to imply considerable attention and a certain commitment on the part of the persons involved. Consequently, all cases are major endeavours in the marketing department. Furthermore, I was primarily interested in products that involve a close consideration of Norwegian eating patterns, such as for instance dinner products and convenience foods, rather than for example condiments and drinks.
6. While selected *cases* represented my main focus, the fieldwork process includes a wide range of activities, both related to the cases and of a more general kind. These activities include the general tool kit of anthropological fieldwork method, such as interviews and conversations, the gathering of written material, simple statistical inquiries and participant observation.

7. In hindsight, I realize that this passive selection of key informants also implied an unfortunate male gender bias during data-gathering. Accidentally, my selected empirical cases were all implemented by male product managers. To some extent, especially during the latter part of my fieldwork period, I tried to balance this by deliberately approaching female product managers for semi-structured interviews and informal discussions. In spite of these efforts, my data do not illuminate the situation of female product managers as well as they might if I had followed them throughout their day-to-day dealings with selected projects.

8. The presence of such control mechanisms may be illustrated by the instances in which unwritten limits are transgressed. Carrying responsibility for small children may for instance bring about such transgression. Too much of such intrusion of the private sphere into the professional sphere may, however hamper the parents' career. (For a more thorough discussion, see Chapter 4).

9. Turner describes four major dimensions of what he calls the nostalgic paradigm: the historical decline and loss, involving a departure from some golden age of 'homefulness'; the sense of absence and loss of personal wholeness and moral certainty; the disappearance of genuine social relationships; and finally, the idea of a loss of simplicity, personal authenticity and emotional spontaneity (Turner 1987:150–1). The celebration in anthropological discourse of the traditional fieldwork experience may be seen as an expression of such nostalgic yearning, pertaining to all four dimensions.

10. Note that the term 'field-site' itself indicates something that can be delimited in space. I could have translated this to 'field-period', in order to emphasize the arbitrariness of selecting spatial rather than temporal delimitations. For convenience, and considering the established conventions of ethnographic jargon, I have decided not to do so,

11. 'Anthropology at home' refers here not so much to a shared geographical region as to a shared familiarity with a certain textual style, interpretation and reflexivity that is inherent in the professions of marketing and social sciences alike.

Chapter 3

Structural Conditions

During the latter half of the twentieth century, the Norwegian food market has undergone a change from scarcity to affluence. In the early post-war period, food was in great demand, and the main challenge of food policy was simply to ensure a steady increase of production. Within a few years, scarcity was replaced by an adequate supply, and a steady increase in welfare in the population was paralleled by a proliferation of food products on the Norwegian market. Nevertheless, domestic producers still enjoyed a high level of state protection, mainly through agricultural protective measures.

Viking Foods is one of the major food manufacturing companies in Norway, and a major supplier of a variety of manufactured foods to Norwegian consumers. Although Viking Foods is a private enterprise, state agricultural protection represents both constraints and possibilities for Viking Foods. The purpose of the present chapter is to provide an understanding of the contextual background of food manufacture and food advertising in Norway, by means of which the relevance of the empirical findings may be evaluated. This chapter focuses especially on conditions that are specific to the particular period in which fieldwork took place. However, to the extent that they illuminate the current situation, broader descriptions of the development of modern food manufacture and advertising are included.

Modern Food Manufacture: Between Technology and Economics

The creation of the modern food industry is closely connected to the rapid pace of urbanization, both in North America and Europe, during the nineteenth century. Vast urban markets increasingly dislocated from the areas of agricultural production posed new problems of food preservation. In the early consolidation of the food industry, canning, refrigeration and technological break-through allowing the production of powdered milk represented major mass-industrial solutions to urban consumer demand (Sorj and Wilkinson 1985). Within the pre-industrial epoch, transformation had been the key to preservation, through the use of fermentation, smoking, drying, etc. With the establishment of refrigeration as an industrial method of preservation, large-scale production and distribution was made possible *without* any major alteration of the original agricultural product (Sorj and Wilkinson 1985). To some extent, the effort to preserve the perceived 'freshness' of agricultural products is still a basic aim of industrial production. In fact, many of the food science innovations during the post-war period involve such advanced preservation techniques (Fine and Leopold 1993).

Apart from this, there is also a tendency within processing industries by which the original agricultural product is no longer an end itself, but is reduced, as it were, to the status of input, or a means by which a final product may be realized.[1] In modern food manufacturing, as we shall see, both of these tendencies (preservation and transformation) are readily identified.

During the nineteenth and twentieth centuries, systems of food production and distribution have been subject to an ever-increasing *delocalization* (Pelto and Pelto 1983). This implies, among other things, that foodstuffs are transported over great distances. Delocalization affect foods in at least two ways. First, long-distance transport often takes time, which, owing to the organic nature of food, represents a constant threat of deterioration. Transport thus calls for ever-more advanced techniques of preservation, in order both to ensure safety and to prevent economic loss. Secondly, long-distance transport usually implies that the number of passage points and actors involved in handling the food are both numerous, complex and unfamiliar to consumers. Yet the intimacy of eating requires a certain sense of trust in food suppliers, which is far more absolute and pressing than the trust required for the purchase of many other consumer goods (Fine and Leopold 1993). Both of these aspects represent continuous challenges to modern food manufacture. Among other things, they provide the framework in which a current emphasis upon food safety, risk and trust in food advertising may be understood (Lien 1995).

Gradually, as the demand for food products in industrialised countries has turned more in the direction of convenience foods, the thrust of innovation in food manufacturing has shifted from that of preservation to preparation. From the perspective of food manufacturers, convenience foods also represent a strategy for countering the problems associated with saturation of the domestic food market. The rationale is very simple: when basic demand for food has been met (in terms of mere quantity), the only way of increasing profit is by increasing the 'value added', in order to make consumers spend more money on essentially the same quantities of food. Increased levels of processing represent one such strategy for adding value. Another strategy implies exploiting the borderline between food and 'mere pleasure' in terms of products practically devoid of any nutrients (coffee, spices, Coca Cola). Thus the high level of processing in the modern food industry may be seen as a result of a close interrelation of technological innovation and consistent efforts to increase profits characteristic of modern Western capitalist enterprise.

In Norway, the food manufacturing industries are generally referred to as a protected sector, in the sense that they are protected from foreign competition (Steen 1989). This does not imply that competition is non-existent. For many types of products, the domestic competition between various companies may still be fairly sharp.

A Protected Food Market

The Norwegian food market is characterized by a high level of regulation and protection aimed at ensuring the viability of Norwegian agriculture. This is partly due to a strong and well-established agricultural sector, whose interests are ensured by a wide variety of regulative measures, including import barriers[2] on foreign food products and state subsidies for domestic production. In practice, the prices on most domestic agricultural products are established by annual negotiations between the farmers' organizations and the state. The strength of the agricultural interest in Norwegian politics is due (in part) to historical conditions that have made agriculture a backbone of political culture. Until recently, these interests have been locked into a political system that in many ways imposes agricultural interests on other sectors and on other interests[3] (Jensen 1994).

One salient characteristic of the Norwegian agricultural sector is the institutionalization of agricultural wholesale and distribution systems through the farmers' cooperative corporations. Owned by the primary producers, these cooperative institutions are among the most important channels of food distribution in Norway, and as such they also have the power to control or regulate a significant part of the food market. The farmers' cooperatives function both as marketing and distributing organizations in their own right, *and* as main suppliers to other, privately owned food companies (including Viking Foods). Furthermore, they represent a significant purchaser of agricultural primary production, and are even obliged to purchase whatever their members may produce. Because of their dominant position, the farmers' cooperatives also represent an extension of state regulation in the sense that the agricultural authorities delegate some regulating measures to the producer cooperatives. Altogether, these different functions (member organization, sales and distribution channel, and regulatory body) give the farmers' cooperatives a strong and complicated position in the Norwegian food market and agricultural system.

As a result of regulative and protective measures, competition in the Norwegian food market has traditionally been limited, especially with regard to food product groups that are domestically produced. By the early 1990s, there was little or no competition in the markets of fresh meat, milk and dairy products, egg and poultry, grain mill products and certain vegetables.[4] The significant market shares of the farmers' cooperative bodies have been politically approved of, as a high market share ensures the role of the farmers' cooperatives as *market regulators*. When it comes to combined manufactured food products, bakery products and confectionery, however, the degree of competition in the Norwegian market is considerably higher (Dulsrud 1994).

For private manufacturers such as Viking Foods, these protective measures represent a mixed blessing. Most importantly, they serve to curb or prevent certain types of foreign competition. On the one hand, this implies that private manufacturers are more or less dependent on the farmers' cooperatives for stable supplies of various raw materials, and cannot benefit from lower prices on the world market. On the other hand, private manufacturers may also benefit from the protective measures, which efficiently serve to keep foreign food manufacturers out of the Norwegian market. For many product groups, the main competitors of private manufacturers are domestic, and large, multinational food manufacturers represent less of a competitive challenge than they might have done in a less regulated market. In this respect, private manufacturers are 'free-riders' on a system of regulation that is designed to protect the interests of domestic primary producers. Yet, for product groups such as meat and poultry, the main competitor for private manufacturers may be identical with the main supplier, i.e. the farmers' cooperative. *Vis-à-vis* this highly protected body, private manufacturers may hold a relatively weak position, while *vis-à-vis* foreign competitors, the position of private manufacturers may be correspondingly strong.

Finally, we should note that protective measures work both ways. Just as a high level of agricultural protective measures prevent foreign producers and manufacturers from entering the Norwegian market, tariff barriers within the European Union prevent Norwegian manufacturers from expanding towards the European continent.[5] Thus domestic and foreign protective measures set an upper limit in terms of market expansion, and thus limit the possibilities for benefiting from large-scale production, or what is generally referred to as 'economy of scale'. Partly as a result, the general prices of food in Norway have been relatively high compared to other European countries (Kjærnes 1994).

The high level of regulation and protection in the Norwegian food market differs significantly from the competitive, 'free' markets frequently described (and often assumed) in textbooks on marketing. Heavily influenced by US market ideology and practice, such textbooks tend to portray an image of a market that is far less regulated and far more open to competition than is the situation in the Norwegian food sector (see for instance Kotler and Armstrong 1987). In the early 1990s, however, many of these regulations were challenged as part of a general tendency towards greater efficiency and deregulation.

Norwegian Food Business in the Early 1990s: Major Challenges

In the late 1980s, a dramatic restructuring of the retail food trade took place, in terms of unprecedented price competition and a concentration of ownership at the retail level. At the same time, the prospect of increased international competition on the domestic food market gained much attention in the media and in politics. These challenges coincided with what was perceived in Viking Foods as a process of major restructuring – a process that was still going on during fieldwork. This restructuring was explained with reference to (1) concentration and integration in food retail, and (2) international integration and deregulation. These tendencies were generally described as *the* main challenges for Viking Foods in the early 1990s. Neither the process of retail concentration nor that of internationalization is unique to Norway.[6] Yet each challenge is interpreted from a local position, and acted upon in terms of the specific configurations of the national market.

One key impetus to processes of change in the Norwegian food market in the early 1990s was the prospect of international integration and harmonization of trade regulations (Steen 1991a). This includes several processes of integration that to some extent develop independently of each other. In what follows, I will draw attention to two separate processes that, from a Norwegian perspective, are among the most significant in this particular period: the GATT-negotiations (General Agreement on Tariffs and Trade)[7] and the expansion of the European Union (EU) and related European bodies such as the European Economic Area (EEA). These steps towards international integration were considered to be particularly dramatic for Norwegian food production and consumption, because of an exceptionally protective domestic food policy and relatively high and uncompetitive prices on many food products. In 1992, when fieldwork was carried out, Norway was not a member of the European Union, yet the Labour Government had ensured the prospects of a possible membership in the near future, and a public referendum was scheduled for November 1994. In the mean time, extensive harmonization with the EU food regulations was being implemented, as part of a Norwegian adjustment to the EEA.[8]

In the early 1990s, public debate on food and agricultural policy was strongly affected by the prospect of a possible Norwegian membership in the European Union. It was generally assumed that international deregulation would threaten the viability of the Norwegian agricultural sector and restrict the possibilities of maintaining an autonomous agricultural policy. On the other hand, competition from international food manufacturers and suppliers was assumed to be likely to benefit Norwegian consumers in terms of significant price reductions on a wide range of agricultural products owing to the relatively high domestic prices.

Similarly, the Norwegian participation in the GATT negotiations (the so-called Uruguay round) was assumed to pave the way for a more internationalized domestic food market. One aim of the Uruguay round was to liberalize the global food market. Once the treaty was signed in 1994, it implied that Norwegian import quotas were to be replaced by high import tariffs, which could be sustained temporarily, and then gradually reduced. In spite of the far-reaching implications of the GATT negotiations for Norway, its salience in public debate was rather limited compared to the attention given to the European Union.

The prospects of enhanced international integration provided a structural framework to which Viking Foods marketing professionals found it necessary to adapt.[9] In retrospect, and with the Norwegian voters' narrow majority against membership of the European Union in mind, one might conclude that the process of internationalization and deregulation was indeed slower than some foresighted marketing professionals might have assumed. However, when fieldwork was carried out, Norwegian integration into a European common market was a probable future prospect. As we shall see, the prospect of competing in a deregulated European market influenced and served to justify a wide variety of marketing decisions. For instance, the prospect of enhanced international competition on the Norwegian market brought about a discussion of Viking Foods' potential competitive advantages in a more competitive market. In this context, knowledge of Norwegian food, culture and preferences was considered to be one such key advantage (Chapter 8). This, in turn, fostered an enhanced and more explicit discussion in the marketing department on the notion of 'Norwegian food culture', and what a typically Norwegian product might be. Another example relates to the possibilities for market expansion, and to attempts to adapt both products and marketing strategies to a pan-Scandinavian or pan-European market.

Retail Concentration and Integration

Until the mid-1980s, the Norwegian food trade had been characterized by relatively high food prices. This was due in part to a relatively costly system of food distribution with little impetus for rationalization, and an almost total absence of price competition between actors in the distribution chain. This is aptly illustrated by the reply of a grocery wholesaler when asked why wholesalers made so few attempts to provide less expensive imported goods when they were still controlling the market (in the 1970s, see below): *'Why should we? We made good money and enjoyed stable alliances with the food industries, and a peaceful relationship to the retail business. In such a situation, why should we disturb the peace and quiet?'*[10] (Jacobsen and Dulsrud 1994:65, author's translation).

The 1980s brought an end to this harmonious alliance, when increasingly powerful retail distributors put pressure on suppliers to lower their prices. Four separate, but closely related tendencies may be identified: (1) retail concentration, (2) horizontal integration, (3) vertical integration, and (4) growth in the market share of discount outlets. All these tendencies are aspects of the general process that is referred to as retail concentration and integration. All these processes are also apparent on an international level.

Firstly, with regard to *retail concentration* in Norway, the number of retail outlets decreased from more than 8,000 outlets in 1982, to slightly less than 6,000 in 1992. During the same period, the relative proportion of large retail stores has slightly increased, at the expense of smaller stores (Jacobsen and Dulsrud 1994).

Secondly, the growth of centrally controlled retail groups (each consisting of one or more retail chains) implied a dramatic *horizontal integration* in the food retail sector, in terms of functional cooperation or common ownership. In 1981, less than half the turnover in the Norwegian food market occurred in retail chain stores. In 1992, five major retailing groups controlled more than 96 per cent of the total food turnover (Nielsen Norway 1993). Moreover, the three largest retailing groups (*Norgesdetalj, Hakongruppen, Forbrukersamvirket*) controlled more than 75 per cent of the total food turnover, reflecting a level of concentration that is exceptionally high compared to that of other European countries.

For producers and food manufacturers, this implies that distribution can no longer be taken for granted. Access now depends upon a contract with a few major decision-making units within each chain or retailing group, rather than with a large number of autonomous shopkeepers. On the one hand, this concentration represents a more simplified process of negotiation (if you get access to one, you get access to all). On the other hand, horizontal integration implies that each producer is far more vulnerable to decisions at the retail level, while the retailing groups have acquired a correspondingly strong countervailing power to confront large, more or less monopolistic food producers.

Thirdly, in the early 1990s, major retailing groups established exclusive delivery contracts with major wholesalers. This process of vertical integration has later been further emphasized through joint ownership, and has brought about a process of rationalization and enhanced cost-effectiveness. In general, better logistics and product strategies have contributed to lower prices (Jacobsen and Dulsrud 1994). However, to the extent that such vertical integration implies an even stronger concentration of power in a few hands, it contributes to the vulnerability of producers and manufacturers mentioned above.

As a result of vertical and horizontal integration, the countervailing power of the retailing groups has been dramatically strengthened. This is due partly to the sheer size of turnover in each retailing group, but also to their tendency to establish exclusive, long-term delivery contracts with chosen suppliers, tailored and increasingly efficient systems of distribution and, in some cases, shared ownership (Jacobsen and Dulsrud 1994).

Fourthly, as an aspect of this process, there has been a dramatic increase in discount grocery in Norway. In 1985, the discount outlets accounted for about 2 per cent of total sales in the grocery market in Norway. By 1993 discount outlets accounted for as much as 31 per cent of the total grocery sales (Nielsen, Norway 1993). Within the discount segment, three major chains (RIMI, REMA and PRIX) control about 91 per cent of total sales (Nielsen Norway 1993). Compared to other European countries, both the size of the so-called discount segment and its level of concentration in the early 1990s was exceptionally high (Jacobsen and Dulsrud 1994). Discount outlets are generally characterized by competitive and relatively low prices, and by a relatively narrow product range. For producers, this implies an enhanced pressure towards products that may be sold at a low price. In addition, it implies that marginal products are more difficult to sell. This is not because there is no consumer demand, but because the discount chains generally do not accept products that are designed for narrower consumer segments.

In the marketing department, the countervailing power of the retail sector was generally interpreted as a rather problematic challenge. The post-war period was often described by a gradual shift of power from the producers (in the early period of scarcity) to the wholesale sector (during the 1960s and 1970s) and finally to the retail sector in the 1980s. However, this third period differs from the earlier ones in that it put an end to what some actors would describe as a harmonious alliance between producers, manufacturers and the wholesale sector (see the citation above). Nevertheless, the dramatic restructuring of the retail sector is not entirely against the interests of the wholesale and manufacturing sectors. According to Jacobsen and Dulsrud (1994), several central actors within food industry production and wholesaling emphasized the growth of the retail chain as a useful lever to bring about a more rational and cost-efficient food production and distribution, a process that was considered to be extremely important in the light of the prospects of international integration and a more competitively oriented food market. For instance, the concentration in the retail sector also contributed to speeding up a process of international integration through cross-border retailing, as exemplified by Norwegian retailers' involvement in European retail alliances, the shared ownership of a Norwegian retail chain with the Swedish chain ICA, and an expansion of two of the major Norwegian retail chains into the other Nordic countries.

To summarize, retail concentration and integration in the early 1990s represents a major challenge for Norwegian manufacturers, primarily in terms of intensified pressure towards lower prices and an enhanced demand for high-market-share products at the expense of products that have lower turnover. In the marketing department these tendencies are particularly important to bear in mind in the sense that they provide a justification and structural framework for the ongoing effort at 'building brand products'.

The Social Organization of Advertising

From the perspective of consumers in almost any part of the industrialized world, advertising appears as a massive locus of information and attention, occupying both public spaces, and printed and electronic media. This impression reflects a continuous increase in advertising in many parts of the world.

From the viewpoint of economics, the growth of advertising is often explained by reference to stagnant or saturated markets. This is especially relevant to the food sector, where advertising growth is often described as a survival strategy for food manufacturers that operate within the relatively stagnant food markets of industrialized countries in the Western world. Another strategy, mentioned above, is that of product diversification, enhanced food processing and brand proliferation, which *also* requires that considerable resources are spent on advertising (Leopold 1985; Balasubramanyam and Nguyen 1991). However, the growth of advertising may also be understood as a self-reinforcing process in which one actor's investment causes other actors to invest even more. Alternatively, the reinforcement may be explained by reference to the marketing profession, who, like most other professions, are likely to work deliberately towards establishing the indispensability of their specialized services.

In the nineteenth century, advertising was practically synonymous with printed advertisements in newspapers, i.e. brief notices of information about the availability of the advertisers' services or products. In this period, the role of advertising agents was confined to that of brokers mediating contracts between the newspapers and the firms, for which they received a set provision. At first, advertising agents were agents of the newspapers, authorized by the publishers to make contracts with anyone who wished to advertise. For these services, they deducted a proportion of the money paid by the advertisers (Hower 1949).

However, the role of a newspaper agent was soon to be transformed into that of an independent middle-man. In the United States in the 1850s advertising agents became traders in advertising *space*, which they bought from the newspapers, at first piecemeal and then wholesale, and then offered to any advertiser who wanted to buy (Hower 1949). In Norway, the first commercial independent advertising agency was established in 1878, inspired by similar agency concepts in Germany and England (Dalseg 1983).

Although there is a considerable amount of literature on advertising as it appears in public, relatively few studies have been published on the everyday activities and organizations of advertising agencies. Among these, two detailed ethnographic accounts both place a great emphasis on the relationship between agency and client (Hower 1949; Moeran 1996).[11] The first description of a long-term relationship between agency and client dates back to the US in 1875, and the establishment of the so-called open contract. Up until this period, American advertising agents had primarily been traders of space, with their loyalty with the publishers rather than with the advertiser. According to Hower, this organizational set-up was challenged when an advertising agent named N. W. Ayer & Son managed to convince a major advertiser to embark upon a long-term contract in which the agent should place the company's advertisements for a year at the lowest price that could be obtained. In return, the advertiser would know exactly what Ayer paid for space, and would pay a commission to Ayer of 12.5 per cent of the actual cost of the space (Hower 1949). Thus the advertising agent shifted his source of income, and probably also his loyalty, to a specific advertiser. Through this experimental contract, Ayer was able to curb the price competition with other advertising agents, while the advertiser could rely more on the validity of Ayer's advice (Hower 1949). This contract represents one of the very first examples of the relationship of advertising agency and client as we know it today.

The historical shift that is described through the story of Ayer & Son includes elements that are still salient features of the agency–client relationship, such as the *long-term contract* (later referred to as an *account*), the salience of *loyalty and trust*,[12] and, finally, the gradual shift of the role of the advertising agent from that of a trader of newspaper space to that of an expert offering advice. The latter implies a shift of the role of the agency from a supplier of commodity to a supplier of knowledge. Increasingly, this has come to include not only insight into the most efficient placement of adverts, but also competence in visual and textual design. In Norway, the increased emphasis on visual design became apparent in the early 1920s (Dalseg 1983). The establishment of an account serves to ensure a long-term relationship of cooperation in which an advertising agency serves as the steady supplier of both strategic advice and advertising material for a long period of time.

While the advertising agencies compete for the most lucrative accounts, the situation of major Norwegian advertisers is one in which they can pick and choose. Generally, advertising agencies do not simultaneously serve clients that are also competitors of each other. However, when major advertisers are involved, the latter may establish so-called 'split accounts', in which their advertising budget is diverted to different agencies, each taking care of a different part of their product range. Split accounts may also imply letting one advertising agency handle strategic advice, while another takes care of the production of advertising material. Nevertheless, the presence of competing advertising agencies represents a constant threat to each advertising agency, as clients will normally not spread their accounts too thinly. Consequently, the saying 'one man's meat is another man's poison' (*den enes død er den andres brød*), is a fairly apt description of the relationship between agencies, giving the client the upper hand in the relationship.

An advertising agency is usually organized according to a basic internal division between the so-called creative (*'kreative'*) and the so-called consultants (*'konsulentene'*). While the exact organizational set up may differ slightly, this division serves as a main organizational principle in advertising world-wide (Myers 1983; Moeran 1996).

The creative staff often comprises several 'creative teams', consisting of an art director who designs the visual features, and a copy writer who formulates the text. Sometimes a creative director, or a senior art director is involved as well, holding a superior position and an overall responsibility for the creative aspect of the project. In addition, for certain assignments, advertising agencies make use of external creative professionals, such as for instance film producers.

Among the consultants, the most important figure is that of an agency middle-man,[13] whose main responsibility is to deal with clients and to ensure the continuation of long-term accounts. Sometimes referred to as senior consultant (*'senior konsulent'*), sometimes as assistant manager (*'assisterende direktør'*), the position of this agency middle-man is aptly described by Myers (1983) as the one who has the job of harmonizing the ideas of the creative team with the demands of the client. In the present analysis, this position will be referred to as the *account manager*. *Vis-à-vis* the client, the account manager serves to certify that the interests of the client have been taken into account. In this way, latent conflicts between the client and the creative team, or between aesthetics and commerce, are embedded in the social structure. The consultancy staff usually also includes persons who carry out practical and secretarial tasks that are necessary in order to make a project run smoothly. The most important feature, however, is the fundamental division of labour between the creative staff on the one hand and the internal agency consultants on the other.

Advertising in Norway

The most significant growth in Norwegian advertising has taken place during the post-war period, and especially since the mid-1950s. From 1949 to 1960, the volume of Norwegian advertising increased almost tenfold. From 1960 to 1980, a tenfold increase took place once again. During the same period, the number of advertising agencies in Norway grew from eleven in 1949, to 26 in 1960, to a total of 61 in 1980 (Helgesen 1983).

Until the mid-1960s, a legal restriction ensured that foreign capital would not exceed 33 per cent of the stockholders' capital of Norwegian advertising agencies. In 1965, as this restriction was abolished, Norwegian advertising agencies were rapidly internationalized, through extensive international cooperation and, gradually, also foreign ownership. Internationalization at this time implied primarily 'Americanization', as the foreign agencies were mostly affiliate companies of large multinational advertisers based in the United States. By the early 1970s Norwegian advertising agencies were therefore integrated in a wide international network of advertising agencies, both in Europe and in the US (Helgesen 1983).

In the late 1980s, a period of prosperity and growth in Norwegian advertising business came to an end. A general economic decline led to some bankruptcies and a large number of agency fusions and reductions of advertising personnel. Thus in the early 1990s, when fieldwork took place, the situation for individual agencies was perceived as extremely competitive.

At the same time, the prospect of commercial broadcasting in Norway represented a significant challenge, and also a much needed possibility for expansion for Norwegian advertising agencies. Until the late 1980s, the Norwegian Broadcasting Association had constituted the only Norwegian television station available to all. At the end of the 1980s, several commercial alternatives were available through satellite and cable-TV; but owing to the limited dissemination of cable-TV, their audience was limited. In 1992, however, a second national commercial TV channel (TV2) was introduced, independent of the cable system and available over almost all of the country. Anticipated since the early 1980s (Helgesen 1983), this development represented a very dramatic change in the channelling of Norwegian advertising resources, and a reorientation in terms of ways of communicating advertising messages. Thus in 1992 advertising by means of TV commercials represented for many advertisers a new kind of endeavour of which most had had fairly limited experience.

Since 1985, there has been a steady growth of food advertising expenditure in Norway, both in absolute numbers and as a percentage of total advertising. At the same time, there has been a dramatic increase in the proportion of food and drink advertising expenditure spent on TV commercials, primarily at the expense of printed adverts, as illustrated in Table 3.1:

Table 3.1. Total food and drink advertising expenditure in Norway 1985–1994

	1985	**1990**	**1992**	**1994**
Food and drink* (f&d) advertising expenditure (NOK† 1,000)	199.305	308.733	539.358	801.599
F&d advertising as % of total advertising expenditure	7%	11.2%	14.7%	16.8%
Percentage of f&d advertising expenditure spent on TV commercials**	–	–	42%	65%
Percentage of f&d advertising expenditure spent on printed food adverts (newspaper and magazines) ***	–	79%	40%	20%

* Food and drink advertising includes pet food as well, which in 1992 amounted to 2.3 % of the total food and drink advertising expenditure.
† Norwegian Kroner.
** In 1985 and 1990, food advertising as TV commercials was not separately recorded.
*** 1985 figures are unavailable.
(*Source*: Norwegian Advertising Statistics; cited with permission).

Notes

1. According to Sorj and Wilkinson, the full significance of this
   development emerged with the margarine industry, when the
   industry took as its starting-point not the preservation of the
   agricultural product, but cheaper alternatives to existing foods
   (1985:307).
2. Until the 1990s, import barriers were established by means of
   total import prohibition or seasonally variable import quotas.
   Since January 1995, as a consequence of the WTO agreement, a
   system of import tariffs has replaced the previous import
   quotas.
3. For a description of the relation between agricultural and
   nutritional interests in Norway, see also Kjærnes 1995a.
4. With regard to fresh milk, there was no import. With regard to
   dairy products, there was very little import in 1992. With regard
   to poultry, there was no import, and in 1991 the farmers'
   cooperative for eggs and poultry (PRIOR) held a market share
   of 83% on wholesale poultry (raw material), and close to a
   monopoly on manufactured products. With regard to meat,
   there was practically no import, and the farmers' cooperative
   for meat (NORSK KJØTT) held a fairly strong position, with a
   market share in 1992 of 51% of wholesale raw material, while
   its manufacturing counterpart (GILDE) held a market share of
   44% on manufactured meat products. With regard to vegetables,
   potatoes and berries, import was regulated by seasonal quotas
   designed to meet consumer demand that were not fulfilled by
   domestic production until 1994. In 1991, the farmers' cooperative for fruits and vegetables (GARTNERHALLEN), held
   a market share of 20–30% on fresh produce, and the level of
   competition was somewhat higher than for other agricultural
   products (Dulsrud 1994).
5. In 1990, the export of fish constituted 89% of the total food
   export. Of this, more than half was fresh or frozen. Production
   of agricultural or manufactured food products has traditionally
   been negligible (Steen 1991b). This low level of food export is
   due not only to foreign import barriers, but also to non-
   competitive prices on foods produced in Norway.
6. For a broader description of retail internationalization, see
   Hallsworth 1992.

7. In 1994, GATT negotiations were further institutionalized in what is now referred to as the WTO (World Trade Organization).

8. The most significant step towards European integration was taken in spring 1994, through an agreement between the European Union and the EFTA countries. This agreement implied full harmonization of food regulations with those of the EU, but largely excluded agricultural products from the intention of market integration. Thus, a certain level of European harmonization was realized even before the final referendum.

9. In 1992, the need to adapt to a more integrated European market had long been foreseen by managing directors in Viking Foods. According to one informant, the processes of preparing for a more open market had started as early as 1987.

10. Incidentally, in her analyses of central Norwegian cultural categories, Marianne Gullestad (1992:140) introduces the concept 'peace and quiet' as one example of cultural categories that *'are used to justify without themselves needing justification'*. According to Gullestad, *'peace and quiet epitomizes the preferred cultural solution to the multiple tensions within Norway'*, such as for instance between individual and society, between withdrawal and conflict, and between freedom and equality (Gullestad 1992:163).

11. Ralph Hower (1949) first published his remarkable account of the history of an American agency called N. W. Ayer & Son as early as 1939. Brian Moeran's book is an ethnographic study of a Japanese advertising agency (1996).

12. For a discussion of these aspects of the relationship, see also Moeran 1996.

13. Myers (1983) refers to this middle man as an 'account director', while Moeran (1993, 1996) refers to a similar position as an 'account executive'.

Part II

Empirical Context, Concepts and Cases

Chapter 4

The Marketing Department

Viking Foods is a well-established, major Norwegian food manu-facturing company. In the late 1980s and early 1990s, Viking Foods was going through a period of significant expansion. This was partly due to several mergers with minor companies, but also as a result of a corporate policy that emphasized the consolidation and expansion of Viking Foods' position on the Norwegian and Scandinavian market. These expansive strategies were part of an overall effort to be prepared for increased international competition on the Norwegian market as a result of anticipated import liberalization (see Chapter 3).

The administration unit of Viking Foods[1] consists of several organizational units, including the marketing department, the product development department, and the personnel management (staff). In addition, there are several production plants located elsewhere in Norway. The Viking Foods marketing department[2] serves a coordinating function between industrial production on the one hand and sales on the other. With first-hand knowledge of what is usually referred to as the 'market', the marketing department is also expected to foresee the possibilities for market growth and profitability of new products. This gives the marketing department a central function also in decisions related to product development. Altogether, the marketing department has by far the most significant function in major decisions related to both the creation of new products and the modification of existing products, and to the marketing activities for both.

The Offices

The physical location of the marketing department is in the administrative building of Viking Foods, which is situated in the outskirts of an urban area in central eastern Norway. A large neon representation of the Viking Foods logo is easily visible from the highway, and serves to differentiate this building from neighbouring buildings, housing companies with other logos.

The main entrance of the building is a large hall, in which two receptionists are always present, registering visitors and transferring telephone calls. Along the walls, tall glass cabinets serve as exhibition shelves for some of the Viking Foods products. The marketing department is located on the second floor. Other departments in the same building include the department of product development, a smaller marketing department and staff. The building is therefore usually referred to as the main centre of administration of Viking Foods.

In order to enter the marketing department, one has to pass through a locked door that is automatically unlocked only upon the insertion of certain card, combined with a four-digit code. All employees carry such cards, and need to remember the code in order to move around in the building. Visitors may receive temporary cards at the receptionists' desk.

The entrance door opens up into a large rectangular room, furnished with a round coffee table and some soft chairs. In addition, there is a secretary's desk on the left-hand side, situated next to the entrance. Along the walls there are individual offices, separated from the area in the middle by glass walls and doors that are usually open. Most of the offices are rather narrow and rectangularly shaped, and only have room for a desk, an office chair, a computer and a telephone, shelves along the wall, and a small, low table with a chair for visitors. These are the offices of product managers (*'produktsjefer'*) and product secretaries (*'produktsekretærer'*). A few of the offices are about twice as big as the others, squarely shaped and more open, and are furnished also with a large table and several chairs. Here we find the marketing director (*'markedsdirektør'*), the assistant marketing director (*'marketingdirektør'*), marketing managers (*'marketingsjefer'*) and sales managers (*'salgssjefer'*). At the far end of the central area, there is another room, fairly large, and closed in by walls that are partly glass, but fitted with curtains that may be drawn. This is the meeting room, seats about 20 persons, and contains a large table, chairs, an overhead projector, a white screen and a blackboard. In addition, the marketing department contains a smaller meeting room, a copy room with two copy machines, shelves with various kinds of office equipment, and a kitchen, with cupboards, kitchenware (primarily coffee cups), a microwave oven, a coffee maker and an electric stove.

Considering the centrality of the marketing department in major decisions, and in the organization as a whole, we might expect a very busy atmosphere, a buzzing activity of people working, talking, coming and going. Generally, however, this is not so. Entering the marketing department, a more typical impression is that of a large open space, few people, and limited interaction. Apart from a secretary (*'sekretær'*), who is practically always present, one never knows who is going to be there. Some of the offices will be empty and dark. In some offices the lights will be on, but the chairs will be empty. In other offices, a person will be present, working at his/her desk or on the computer, or talking on the telephone. Occasionally, someone will cross the central area to fetch something, or to have a conversation with someone at another office. Now and then people will enter or leave, usually exchanging some words with the secretary upon departure.

Generally, there is an atmosphere of quiet activity. Wall-to-wall carpets absorb the sounds of people walking, and when there is a meeting somewhere the doors are usually closed. The continuous low-frequency buzz from computers, and the clicking sounds as fingers press the keys, are disrupted by incoming telephone calls and the sound of voices answering. Everyone seems to be doing something; and informal idleness is seldom seen. The coffee table in the central area is rarely used. At lunch-time everyone goes to the large canteen downstairs, and for coffee-breaks most people simply fetch a cup of coffee to their office.

The offices are inhabited by people who, as a rule, consider themselves to be hard-working and fairly busy. Their time-schedules are generally filled ahead of time, allowing few possibilities for spontaneous meetings. As a result of this, trying to catch a product manager for an interview on the spot is difficult. Sometimes, the time pressure seems to preclude any conversation whatsoever. Other times, there is a flexibility that allows a few exchanges of ideas, right there and then. But as a general rule, an interview that exceeds 5–10 minutes in duration must be planned days, and sometimes weeks, ahead of time.

What do these people do all day? What is it that makes them so busy, and where do they go when they are not present? Before exploring these issues in more detail, let us take a look at the organizational hierarchy.

Organizational Structure

Organizations are socially constructed and reconstructed in everyday actions (Czarniawska-Joerges 1992:34). A wide range of metaphors have been used to describe an organization, each emphasizing a different aspect, including those of a machine, an organism, a brain, and *a* culture (!). The most important insight derived from such metaphors, however, is that organizations are complex, abstract entities that are hard to describe in their totality, simply because they can only be experienced as social encounters that are more limited in terms of time, space and personnel. Obviously, organizations do not exist only in our imaginations. Their central role in allocating and controlling vast resources (human, technical, financial) make modern organizations a massive source of influence upon the social and material landscape of modern societies, and as such they represent a framework that is more than imagery. Yet, their very abstractness also makes organizations into something more than a mere accumulation of resources. Because they are also imagined, organizations exist even when nobody is there. As Czarniawska-Joerges point out, organizations do not cease to exist on Sundays *'because their rules of construction currently entail not coming to work on Sundays'* (Czarniawska-Joerges 1992:34). Thus an organization is a socially constructed entity that structures the total organization of the everyday lives of its members, encompassing both the external private sphere and the professional sphere of the organization itself.

One way of imagining organizations is by means of organizational maps. As an anthropologist in the marketing department I was very quickly introduced to various drafts of such maps. As the beginning of my fieldwork happened to coincide with a period of reorganization, due to a recent fusion of Viking Foods with another industrial food company, the organizational map was still very much 'in the making', and no printed version existed. Encountering an institution during the process of a major reorganization implies that informants' descriptive models of the organization are, to an even greater extent than in more stable periods, provisional, preliminary, and also contested. This gives the researcher privileged insight into the dynamics of a formal organizational structure, both as an instrument of power and control, and as a medium for collective self-reflection. Most importantly, the recent fusion seemed to bring about a special attention among informants to the arbitrariness of organizational maps.[3]

As I began fieldwork in Viking Foods, my first introduction to the organizational structure was in the form of sketchy models composed of boxes and arrows, drawn by informants during our conversations. The boxes were filled in with names and titles, indicating various persons and positions, and the arrows linked them together in a way that was supposed to indicate their relationship as well as their respective locations in the organizational hierarchy. The hierarchical order was usually implicitly indicated in the map, by means of a vertical orientation in which being 'above' indicated a hierarchical superiority.

All maps were partial, indicating a particular branch (or function) of the organization only. Some maps were confidential, referred to as preliminary drafts, to be agreed upon in the near future. Some maps also had a built-in reference to the process of transition, indicating both the formal structure as it had been, and the structure as it was going to be after the D-day of reorganization.

Empirical analyses of modern organizations have repeatedly revealed a lack of consistency between the structure of an organization as visualized in organizational maps and the prevailing patterns of activity (see for instance Silverman 1970; Meyer and Rowan 1977). A formal organizational map should therefore not be interpreted *a priori* as a blueprint reflection of how the organization works. Still, the organizational map cannot be neglected in favour of day-to-day activities, especially not in a situation when these activities have to do directly with negotiating and establishing consensus around this map.

Following Meyer (1983), we may perceive the organizational structure as '*the collective social codification of what is going on in a given activity domain*' (Meyer 1983:263). The most formal and authoritative organizational map represents one visual expression of this, encompassing both a normative and pragmatic dimension. It represents an attempt at making sense of a set of relationships and procedures, by means of emphasizing and making explicit an underlying hierarchical structure. In addition, an organizational map is consensual, in the sense that, once decided upon by management, it represents the only legitimate version of the organizational structure, or what Latour (1987) would refer to as a 'black box'. Below is an organizational map of the marketing department during the period when fieldwork was carried out (Figure 4.1). The number of persons in each position is indicated in brackets.

A person's position in the organizational structure is a central piece of information that guides the allocation of tasks and responsibilities within the organization. Reference to one's position also constitutes an integral part of self-presentation, such as for instance when introducing oneself on the telephone, which is usually done by giving name, position and company. Most positions in the marketing department are defined in relation to other positions, and especially in relation to one's immediate superior. This is often referred to as 'reporting to someone' (*'rapportere til'*). A product manager may for instance define his/her position as follows: *'I am AA, product manager in the marketing department. I used to report to BB, but now I report to CC, who has become our marketing manager after the recent reorganization'.*

The term 'reporting to' is indicated on the organizational map as an arrow pointing upward (see Figure 4.1). This is complemented by a formally defined responsibility on the part of the person being reported to. A marketing director does, for instance, carry a superior responsibility for the group of persons who report directly to him or her.

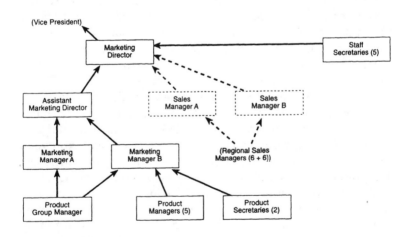

Figure 4.1. The Marketing Department

The main functions of the marketing department are marketing and sales, the latter primarily coordinating deliveries to wholesalers and retail chains. The marketing director is responsible for coordinating activities in both of these domains.[4] The responsibilities of the assistant marketing director[5] differ from those of the marketing director in that the assistant marketing director deals with marketing only. The assistant marketing director is responsible for marketing specific products, and for marketing activities that are not directly linked to specific products, such as seasonal sales, campaigns, in-store activities, strategic marketing and new business.

According to the organizational map, staff secretaries report directly to the marketing director. Their duties include various secretarial functions, such as transmitting telephone calls, writing, archive work and copying. Although they formally report to the marketing director, this does not give them a superior position in relation to the others in the structural hierarchy. Secretarial functions are generally understood as a set of functions serving *all* other positions to some extent. This means that a product manager may ask a secretary to carry out a task without having to formally get acceptance for this from the marketing director.

In Figure 4.1, two positions share the title 'marketing manager'. Their functions are, however, rather different, as a result of the recent merger. Marketing manager A carries the responsibility for merchandising, managing the company's corporate identity, and new product development. Marketing manager A also has a superior responsibility for some of the activities carried out by the product group manager. Marketing manager B carries superior responsibility for all product managers, product secretaries and product group managers. In addition, he is responsible for the marketing of so-called brand products (see Chapter 5).

Next to staff secretaries, product managers constitute the most numerous group of employees within the marketing department. Each product manager is responsible for a clearly defined range of products, for which he or she serves as a coordinating link between production, marketing and sales. In addition, the product manager is responsible for planning and implementing marketing activities for the products.

In more practical terms, this means that the product manager collects various types of relevant information, and follows up on various aspects of the processes from production to sales, such as product quality, content, production activities, legal regulations, sales statistics, storage, consumer profile, consumer complaints and much more. On the basis of this type of information, the product manager makes judgements and decisions about the products, for instance to carry out additional market research, to launch a new variety, to develop a new package, to launch an advertising campaign, or to get rid of the product.

The product group manager differs from the other product managers in that he is also involved in new product development, and functions as a coordinator for a broad category of products. Because of this triple function, he reports to both market managers (see Figure 4.1). In most other respects, the responsibilities and tasks of the product group manager are identical to those that have been described for the marketing manager.

A product secretary is a temporary position for persons with less experience than product managers, and their title is generally changed to 'product manager' within a couple of years. The responsibilities of product secretaries are generally the same as those of product managers. Because of the similarities between these three positions, I will refer to this entire group as product managers.

If we include the three product secretaries and the product group manager, the product managers in the marketing department include altogether eight people. In addition, there are five product managers in an adjacent marketing department, amounting to a total of thirteen product manager informants.

Having a Career: Age, Gender and the Notion of Success

The product manager's position is generally conceived of as a stepping-stone for a career in the field of marketing. A successful product manager will therefore only stay in this position for a few years, until he or she is promoted to a more prestigious position. Ambitions with regard to upward mobility are most explicitly stated among the younger and more educated product managers. Thus one of the more ambitious informants told me early on that if he were to remain in this position for more than, say, 2–3 years, he would be very disappointed. (As it turned out, he didn't: a couple of years later, he had already been promoted twice.) However, there is a marked difference between the younger and older generation, both in terms of educational background, and probably also in terms of realistic options for moving up, rendering the younger ones at an advantage.

Succeeding as a product manager is closely connected to success with projects for which one is held responsible. Succeeding with a project implies, first and foremost, the recognition of success by others, primarily those whose judgement is highly valued and/ or influential for one's promotion. The recognition of a successful project depends on various measurements such as sales statistics, market share, product profitability and sometimes also the measured 'effect' of marketing on sales volume and market share. However, the effect of marketing upon sales is hard to measure. Although increased demand may indicate that a marketing campaign has been successful, it does not usually indicate why this is so. Furthermore, if the demand remains stable, this may be due to other factors than the campaign itself, such as price reductions or promotions implemented by competitors, or simply a lack of distribution. Finally, as the retail outlets are increasingly incorporated into a few large retail chains, the chain management's decision about whether to offer, where to place, and how to promote the product is crucial. This makes the sales statistics less reliable as indicators of the success of a marketing campaign and of consumer preferences.

Furthermore, sales statistics must be considered in the light of external conditions that may have had an influence on the project, such as the presence of competitors in the market, the goals and expectations connected to the various phases of the project (for instance, high marketing costs and a low market share may be acceptable shortly after a new product is launched), and internal conditions within the organization that may have had an influence on the project (for example, sudden changes in the company's policy that are detrimental to the profitability of a particular product).

In addition to the success of specific projects, the success of a product manager is likely to be evaluated in terms of more subjective criteria related, for instance, to social performance on the job and dedication to the company and to specific tasks. Such criteria are hard to pinpoint, and less explicitly mentioned during interviews with marketing managers. Yet they constitute significant elements in the product manager's own interpretations of what it takes to be a good product manager (see below). On the basis of this, we may assume that they are also at work in promotion.

If we take a closer look at the gender distribution in the marketing department, we find that all leading positions are occupied by men. This includes all positions from that of marketing manager upwards to the marketing director (see Figure 4.1). In other words, all managers in the marketing department who have somebody else 'reporting to them' are men. At the other end of the organizational hierarchy, we find the five staff secretaries, who are all women. Product managers are the only group within the marketing department that comprises both men and women. Altogether, the proportion of women among product managers in the two marketing departments is a little less than 40 per cent, with five out of thirteen product managers being female (see below).

Most product managers have the equivalent of a Master's degree in Business Administration from a Norwegian school of business studies, or an equivalent degree from a university abroad. Two out of thirteen product managers have no such degree, but have followed courses in related subjects at an undergraduate level. These are slightly older than the others.

The product managers differ from other employees in the marketing department in that they tend to be younger than the person they 'report to'. Their working experience tends to be less than 10 years, and their age tend to be somewhere between the mid-twenties and the late thirties. Thus, a typical product manager is male, highly educated within marketing, and fairly young. However, there are exceptions to this general pattern.

The marketing managers and marketing directors are generally older; but again we find a certain variation. Their educational background is usually similar to that of the product managers. However, the type or amount of education does not seem to be a significant factor differentiating product managers from those further up in the organizational hierarchy. The difference that 'makes a difference' seems more related to working experience and reputation.

The age of staff secretaries ranges from the late twenties to the late fifties. Being a staff secretary is not as much a transitional position in the local hierarchy as is that of being a product manager. While a promotion to marketing manager is a likely prospect for a successful product manager, the secretaries' possibilities for advancing within the organizational hierarchy are far more limited.

What Do They Do All Day? Results from a Time Expenditure Survey

The tasks and activities of product managers are very varied. Variations occur both from day to day and from one time-period to another for each individual person, and also between individuals. According to some informants, there is no such thing as a typical day in their kind of job. In order to get a better overview of the activities of product managers, I conducted a time expenditure survey. This came as a result of a pressing need to find out what everybody was actually doing when not present in the office, and how they spent their day at work. All product managers (including product secretaries and the product group manager) were asked to record and categorize their activities for a period of five days. Out of 13 potential respondents, 10 managed to fill out the questionnaire.[6] In spite of a tendency for under-reporting among some product managers, the survey yielded considerable information about both activities and social interaction, and enabled me to describe, with far more accuracy, a 'day in the life of a product manager'.

The working day of a product manager is characterized by frequent shifts from one activity to another, a wide network of communications, and a considerable amount of time spent in meetings or talking on the telephone. The general impression is that of a busy day, in which more than half the working time is spent in meetings with other people. The product managers registered from six to more than twenty different activities per day, calculated as an average for each respondent over the five-day period. For the group as a whole, the mean number of different activities per day is sixteen. As the survey method tends towards under-registration, this number should be interpreted as a conservative estimate of a typical day; the actual number of activities is likely to be slightly higher.[7]

Meetings constitute the most time-consuming activity for the product managers, both individually and for the group as a whole. The average number of meetings is four per day, and this occupies more than 50 per cent of the total registered working time (see Figure 4.2). While there is some individual variation, *all* product managers participate in meetings on a regular basis.

About two-thirds of the registered meetings are face-to-face conversations between two persons only. This implies a total of

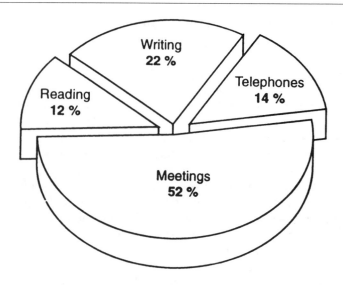

Figure 4.2. Time expenditure by product managers I (mean estimates over a five-day period)

2.6 such meetings per day on an average basis. Mostly, such meetings are informal encounters of relatively short duration. The remaining one-third of the meetings include at least three persons. These are mostly regular meetings that are planned some days ahead of time, and are generally of longer duration. In fact, meetings including three or more persons occupy almost two-thirds of the time allocated to meetings, while meetings including two persons only occupy only a little more than one-third of the total meeting time.

For many of the product managers, frequent telephone calls represent a steady source of interruption during the day. The mean number of telephone calls for the group as a whole is seven calls per day, although for some respondents the average number is considerably higher. Again, the mean should be interpreted as a low estimate. The amount of time spent on the phone is 50 minutes per day on an average for the group as a whole, indicating that phone calls tend to be frequent, but of relatively short duration. But again, there are considerable variations: one respondent spent as much as 38 per cent of his registered working time talking on the phone. The telephone links the product manager to a wide network of persons and institutions, including advertising agencies, media agencies, production plants, individual consumers, staff employees and colleagues located in other parts of the same building. Altogether, an average of two-thirds of the registered working time is spent on exchanging information orally, either over the telephone or at meetings (see Figure 4.2).

The rest of the time is spent either reading or writing, including computer work. On average, the product managers registered five different activities each day implying either reading (3) or writing (2). The amount of time spent on reading varies from day to day, and days when one does not read anything at all are not infrequent. Writing is reported as slightly more time-consuming than reading, constituting 22 per cent of the registered time, while the comparable figure for reading is 12 per cent. Altogether, an average of one-third of the registered working time is spent either reading or writing (see Figure 4.2).

Written documents include a wide range of material, from statistical information to written text. Examples of statistical information include for instance sales statistics, sales estimates, price lists, and invoicing and stock figures. Texts include external mail such as consumer complaints, magazines (specialized journals and popular magazines with food advertisements), market analyses, advertising campaign material, and internal notes such as meeting reports, press releases, drafts for briefings, letters and project plans.

Finally, the product managers were asked to categorize each registered activity according to whether it was related primarily to marketing, sales or production/product development. As indicated in Figure 4.3, marketing activities, as reported by the product managers, constitute more than half of the registered working time on an average basis (58 per cent).

For all product managers except one, the time spent on marketing activities exceeded that spent on any other activity. The average time spent on marketing activities varies from 39 per cent of the total registered time of one product manager, to 81 per cent of the total registered time for another. Activities related to sales and activities related to production each occupy about 17 per cent of the total registered time on an average basis (see Figure 4.3). For these activities, however, the variations between product managers are more dramatic, as time expenditure ranges from less than 2 per cent for some product managers to more than 30 per cent for others. Generally, the amount of time allocated to either production or sales rarely exceeds one-third of the total working time.

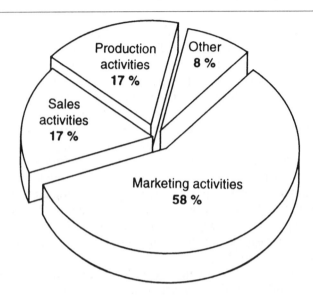

Figure 4.3. Time expenditure by product managers II (mean estimates over a five-day period)

Facing Up to the Tasks: Views from Within

When asked to describe what it implies to be a product manager, the informants emphasize two key functions: One is that of a *coordinating link* between production, sales, marketing, advertising agencies and consumers, the other is that of *having total market responsibility* for a defined range of products.

Being a coordinating link implies, according to informants, frequent contacts with a wide range of persons. One informant described his role as that of a spider: *'It is very difficult if you have to be away from work for several days, because you are kind of like a spider with very many points of contact, and you need to be in touch with them steadily . . .'.*

Having a total market responsibility implies responsibilities ranging from day-to-day trivialities, to more far-reaching strategic planning. One informant described it this way: *'A product manager is everything and nothing . . . You are the one who runs around and fixes all the little details, while at the same time you are the one who tries to think strategically about products and product groups.'*

One product manager described his role in fairly concrete terms, as being the one with the primary responsibility from the farm to the table. Another described his responsibilities in relation to a wider context of company goals, emphasizing his responsibility for ensuring that the short-term activities and goals are in line with the over-arching marketing strategy as it is defined in the strategic marketing plan of the department. Particularly, he emphasized the centrality of brand-building. The fact that the product manager usually received the flood of abuse when something went wrong, was often emphasized. As one product manager put it:

> *You are responsible for everything, even if you do not physically do it. For instance, if your product range includes sausages, then you are responsible for every aspect of those sausages. If something is wrong with the length of the sausages, then you carry the final responsibility, no matter if there was little you could actually do to prevent the mistake.*

The total responsibility often leads to a situation in which the product manager finds him/herself drawn between different interests, between the devil and the deep blue sea. The ability to handle this kind of pressure was emphasized, in addition to social skills such as that of making compromises, being flexible, and keeping a cool head in conflict situations. General social skills, such as being on good terms with all collaborating partners, and coaxing and speaking gently, were also emphasized as qualities important for being a good product manager. In addition, creativity, analytic abilities and structuredness were mentioned as important personal skills.

Holding a total responsibility is often conceptualized by product managers in terms of the local hierarchy. Thus, some informants describe themselves as a *president* (*'administrerende direktør'*) for their range of products. This particular analogy is clearly at odds with the actual organizational hierarchy, according to which product managers are located at the 'bottom', far from the level of president (see Figure 4.1). Product managers have no one in the marketing department formally 'reporting to them', and have few chances of delegating their tasks and responsibilities to others. This implies, for instance, that long-term strategic planning must be done in between all the other activities related to communication and coordination.

When, in spite of this inability to delegate, the term 'president' is frequently used by product managers, we may assume that the term serves as a metaphor that are especially suited to highlight certain aspects of the role of the product manager that are relevant to the actors. Alternatively, it may emphasize some aspects of the product manager's role that are frequently called upon by superiors, such as total responsibility and dedication to the task.[8]

In passing, we may compare the various functions of the product manager with the roles of the manager as described in the classical study of the nature of managerial work by Henry Mintzberg (1980). Mintzberg focuses on the multiple roles of a manager, and from his observations constructs a set of ten different managerial roles. These ten roles are grouped together as being either interpersonal, informational or decisional roles. If we compare these roles with the activities and role interpretations identified by product managers, we find that the product managers fulfil at least six out of the ten managerial roles. Product managers fulfil functions of what Mintzberg refers to as the roles of 'interpersonal liaison', 'informational monitor', 'informational disseminator', 'decisional entrepreneur', 'disturbance handler' and 'negotiator'. The roles that the product manager do *not* fulfil are those that are closely linked with the manager's function as the head of the company and its formal authority, i.e. the roles of a figurehead, leader, spokesman and resource allocator (Mintzberg 1980).

The product managers' role as coordinating links with total market responsibility for their range of products implies that each product manager is expected to engage in both short-term coordination, *and* long-term strategic planning. In practice, however, there seems to be a tendency that the day-to-day tasks are given first priority. As one product manager put it: *'You may be able to reserve three hours in the afternoon for strategic planning, but within those hours you might have to answer ten telephone-calls.'* Several product managers refer to the frequent shifts from one activity to another and frequent telephone calls as sources of interruption that tend to prevent activities that require time and concentration. Their working situation is often described as a constant running from one task to another, hardly ever finding time for working in depth on a problem, and always knowing that there is more you should have done. Incidentally, a similar set of expectations are described by Kanter, in her classic organizational study in a large American firm, in which business management is described as a very absorptive and time-consuming career (Kanter 1977:63; see also below).

In order to handle what is perceived as a heavy workload, many product managers report working overtime. The amount of hours spent on the job varies, both individually and over time. Still, a majority of the product managers report working 9–10 hours a day on average. Those who report working 'only' ordinary hours most of the time (8 hours), generally explain that this is not because they don't have a lot to do, but because of family obligations and small children.[9]

According to strategic documents, long-term planning and strategic analysis are to be given high priority by product managers. This is also emphasized by marketing managers, who maintain that product managers need to become better analysts, and to learn to think beyond the short-term sales results. Many product managers regret that they are not able to carry out these functions as well as they are supposed to. This concern is shared by marketing directors, who give great priority to long-term planning, especially in relation to what is referred to as 'brand-building'. At the time when fieldwork was carried out, this dilemma seemed to be unresolved, representing a source of frustration among the product managers.

My presentation of the time expenditure survey contributed to bringing this dilemma to the foreground, and several product managers took the opportunity to discuss these problems with their superiors. The marketing managers, however, seemed relatively undisturbed. One marketing manager responded that being disturbed by telephone calls from customers is a necessary part of having to deal with the outside world, and that having too many things to do is a normal state, not to be regarded as a problem. Neither was the need to work overtime. One marketing manager put it this way (addressed to me):

> You see, these are engaged people who are here because they are interested in what they are doing. If they feel the need to work after hours, there is nothing wrong with that. The job as a product manager is a kind of job that could be doubled or tripled any time, depending of how much you put into it. What distinguishes those with some years of experience from the beginners is perhaps that the more experienced are able to discriminate what absolutely needs attention from those tasks that they can forget about.

Through this statement, two central themes are illuminated. First, there is the recurrent dilemma of finding the right balance between work load and working hours, which relates to the individual dilemma involved in finding the right balance between private and professional activities in everyday life. Confronted with this dilemma, the marketing manager recognizes the heavy workload, but refuses to take responsibility for the consequences, maintaining that the ability to handle these issues is part of the product manager's own learning process. Refusing to see this as a problem, he refuses, in a sense, to deal with any intrusion of professional time upon the time that is generally conceived of in Norway as private or family time.

Second, and intrinsic to the argument above, is the notion of total dedication. According to the marketing manager, the product managers are engaged and interested people. As such, any attempt to withhold their engagement after hours would obviously be irrelevant, as it is the product managers' own decision.[10] This particular link between the notion of dedication and extra hours of work is hardly coincidental. In her study of a large American firm, Kanter argues convincingly that the organization's demands for diffuse commitment from managers (including working extra hours) represents one fairly concrete measure of *loyalty* in the face of organizational uncertainty (Kanter 1977:65). Although Viking Foods management keeps no records (as far as I know) of what goes on in the marketing department in the evenings, it seems reasonable to interpret the marketing manager's refusal to see overtime as a problem in the light of a more general understanding of working time as an aspect of dedication, and thus indirectly as a sign of loyalty.

Gender: The Invisible Difference

During most of my fieldwork period, gender was not a central issue. However, particularly towards the end of my fieldwork period, it seemed increasingly urgent to collect data that could illuminate gender differences. Partly, this came as a result of a growing awareness of the importance in the marketing department of separating private functions from the professional (see also Chapter 10). Just as important, however, was a growing awareness of a striking absence of the topic of gender differences in the marketing department.

Considering the issue of gender more carefully, two things appeared as particularly important: Firstly, in spite of a significant proportion of women among product managers in the marketing department (slightly less than 40 per cent), I was left with the impression of a masculine professional environment. This has less to do with the femininity of the individual women present, than with the invisibility of what I would personally conceptualize as a feminine discourse and style of interaction.[11] Secondly, I experienced what I will refer to as an absence and even a negation of gender differences, generally expressed in terms of a general consensus that – as far as professional matters are concerned – gender is not important. As I began to question these issues more explicitly, this general impression was further strengthened, as neither men nor women were particularly interested, and seemed to find my questions somewhat irrelevant. With regard to my queries regarding sex discrimination (systematic disfavouring of women), the issue was pushed aside or simply denied. As the issue of gender differences thus remained unelaborated, empirical data related to gender differences are limited. Nevertheless, the invisibility of the feminine dimension in the marketing department and the doxic status of gender-related issues call for some further elaboration.

One way of approaching gender in this particular context is through the interpretations and expectations associated with the role of the product manager and with the various possibilities of promotion. As we have seen, the job as a product manager is conceived as a stepping-stone for a marketing career. Consequently, it is important to be a *good* product manager, in order to be promoted later on. As indicated above, a good product manager is expected to be dedicated and engaged. This is also reflected in statements by product managers. One male product manager put it this way: *'You need some guts, you need to feel engaged, to burn a little bit, to be able to identify with ("leve seg inn i"[12]) the product. And then not to be reserved, to have the courage to speak in front of large audiences . . .'*

By this statement, the product manager indicates that engagement has to do with identification, thus pointing to the need to internalize the professional role to such an extent that engagement becomes authentic. A deep internalization of the professional role implies, in a sense, a blurring of the product managers' private and professional identities. More precisely, it implies a utilization of personal and private emotions ('guts', ardour, dedication) for professionally defined purposes. To the extent that such total dedication is achieved, it is likely to alleviate some of the discomfort that might otherwise be associated with a demanding job and long workdays. Obviously, if the product managers *are here because they are interested in what they are doing'* (see the citation above) they might as well spend the evening.[13] Furthermore, a product manager's presence in the office in the evenings may signify that he or she is a dedicated person.

In principle, these requirements have little to do with whether the product manager is a man or a woman. As most informants tend to maintain, there is no reason why women cannot be just as successful in these respects as men. And, as some women skilfully demonstrate, some women are. Nevertheless, I will argue that these interpretations of the role of the product manager are inherently masculine or male-oriented, both in the sense that they may in practice exclude women at certain phases of life, and in terms of the total dedication towards the professional role that this particular role interpretation implies. The latter contention is based upon a general understanding of gender as an underlying and constituting element of organizations and of occupational roles that may be present even when it is invisible in local discourse (Kanter 1977; Cockburn 1988:231; Kvande and Rasmussen 1990:31–2).

The first and most salient implication of gender is not related directly to biological sex, but to the different and culturally gendered roles of men and women in reproduction. Childbirth, an event that is culturally located firmly within the private realm, affects men's and women's professional lives differently. For men, the birth of a child is an occasion for celebration in the office and implies the right to take two weeks off at will, usually without economic compensation. For women, however, childbirth is only celebrated in their absence, if at all. In 1992, childbirth implied, for women, the right to 35 weeks maternity leave, with full wage compensation (or alternatively 44.2 weeks with 80 per cent wage compensation).[14] Adding four weeks of vacation, a woman having a child would therefore generally be absent from work for between 9 and 12 months afterwards.

In the light of this, the first year of motherhood is not easily compatible with the responsibilities of a product manager. Even though the tasks and responsibilities of women on maternity leave are temporarily handed over to someone else, the childbirth of a female product manager is likely to represent an undue inconvenience, rather than simply an occasion to celebrate. And even if maternity leave is certainly a socially acceptable cause of absence in the marketing department, it may still be at odds with the *dedication* that women have (or try to achieve) towards the job, and thus give rise to conflicting loyalties. These dilemmas are also discussed by Kanter, who writes: '. . . *pressures for total dedication . . . serve to exclude . . . women from employment as managers. Women have been assumed not to have the dedication of men to their work, or they have been seen to have conflicting loyalties, competing pulls from their other relationships'* (Kanter 1977:66).

Although gender differences are not necessarily a cause of unequal treatment *per se*, the consequences of motherhood definitely are. This was confirmed by product managers and marketing managers alike during a discussion of different product managers' likelihood of promotion, when it was agreed that women having two children could not expect to be promoted at the same pace as men with comparable working experience, simply because of their extended periods of absence. This difference is not argued in terms of gender differences *as such*. Rather, it is argued in terms of the implications of privileges in relation to giving birth (maternity leave) that 'happen to be' gender-specific. These privileges represent a significant external threat from the private sphere to professional continuity in the workplace.

In addition to the gender difference associated with childbirth, time expenditure surveys document significant gender inequalities in Norwegian homes with regard to the division of housework, even when both spouses work full-time (Norwegian Official Statistics 1992). Thus, as a result of gender inequalities in the private sphere imposing upon women what is referred to as a 'double burden', many women in the workplace are constantly under pressure in negotiating between hours spent at work and hours spent at home (Cockburn 1988). In this way, gender inequalities in the private sphere are likely to continue to affect the female product manager's professional career even *after* their first year of motherhood, and thus hamper (female) careers *beyond* the years of temporary absence due to maternity leave.

To summarize, gender is relevant in relation to promotion primarily in so far as it represents a threat to (and is re-conceptualized *in terms of*) an overarching separation of the private sphere from the professional.[15] The overlap, however, is far from incidental, as the separation between the private and the professional may be interpreted as an expression of a fundamental division between production and consumption in modern Western societies, a division that is also gendered in terms of a historical relegation of women to the private domain of consumption (Firat 1994).

Considering this relegation of women to the private sphere of consumption, the masculine orientation of the marketing department appears at first as rather paradoxical: if women are the primary consumer target group (and to a large extent, they are), why is their experience not utilized to a greater degree in the marketing department? Partly, the absence of women may be explained by a traditionally low proportion of women in the professional fields of marketing or economics. However, according to informants, this explanation is not satisfactory. Firstly, there has been a considerable increase in the proportion of women in such professions during the last decade. Secondly, according to informants, the proportion of women is actually higher in other fields of marketing, making food marketing a more male-dominated profession than the overall proportion of women in the fields of marketing and economics would dictate.[16] However, if we look at other areas of the public *food sector*, the masculine orientation is the rule rather than the exception, thus confirming the gendered private–public dichotomy (Kjærnes 1995b).

Another implication of gender, which is much less apparent in local discourse, relates to possible differences between men and women in professional identities and approaches to the job. As indicated above, the requirements for a good product manager relate not only to specific tasks to be carried out, but also to the *attitudes* associated with the various tasks. A male product manager described this attitude as engagement, the ability to 'burn', identification, guts and courage. As Cockburn (1988) notes, occupations are gendered, their specific gender resulting partly from the predominance of either men or women that is associated with the job. In the case of the product manager, the occupation is traditionally male. Thus, female product managers enter a world that has, until recently, been predominantly male. Consequently, they face up to role interpretations and expectations that have evolved in a masculine environment, and that are not necessarily identical to their own job experience and self-identity as professional women.

On the basis of research on men and women at various work-sites in England, Cockburn maintains that men appropriate not only technology, but work itself. According to Cockburn, there is no male equivalent for the term 'career woman', simply because it is assumed that if you are a man, your work will inevitably be your life project. Still, the project must be worked at with foresight and nerve (Cockburn 1988:180). Her male informants describe their role in terms of courage and commitment, and generally in a way that leaves women out, or renders their position in the male environment as somewhat unauthentic (Cockburn 1988:185). While the gender inequalities described by Cockburn are far more pronounced than those of the marketing department, the ways of conceptualizing a traditionally male occupation are rather similar. In the light of this, women's strategies for coping in this environment are particularly intriguing. Unfortunately, the data at hand do not allow a systematic gendered comparison of attitudes to work. Still, there are marked differences in terms of engagement between product managers. For some informants, engagement in marketing and sales seems to come easy. For others, and perhaps especially for those who have less experience, a feeling of total dedication towards making a profit appears to be more problematic. One female product manager was rather ambivalent towards this expectation. During an interview, she expressed her attitude as follows:

> Some say they can sell anything. For me, it's different. I find it hard to engage in products that go against my personal values. For instance, I would not be able to promote cigarettes. I find it difficult to think in economic terms all the time. Sometimes I think that working for an aid organization or something like that would be more satisfactory.

Obviously, these feelings of ambivalence are not shared by all female product managers. Nevertheless, the ambivalence and lack of total dedication expressed by this particular informant may be interpreted in terms of gender, and the fact that the informant is a newcomer in a male-dominated environment. According to Cockburn, a female newcomer into male-dominated territory is likely to feel out of place, as though *'on the outside looking in'*, as one of her informants put it (Cockburn 1988:203). The ethical considerations expressed by the female product manager may be interpreted as one way of trying to appropriate to herself a role that has previously been defined mostly by men. This interpretation is supported by a study of Norwegian women in the workplace, in which Sørensen (1982) argues that men tend to be characterized by what she calls a 'limited technical rationality', while women tend more towards what she calls a rationality of responsibility, in which consideration of individuals' needs and well-being play a key role. On the basis of this and other studies of women in the workplace, Kvande and Rasmussen (1990) identify what they call a 'critical potential' for women in the workplace. I must hasten to add that I consider such a critical potential neither to be exclusive to women, nor necessarily a dominating characteristic of female product managers. Still, the feelings of ambivalence with regard to her occupational role expressed by the female newcomer represent a kind of resistance that may be interpreted partly as one way of reconciling an orientation traditionally associated with femininity to a relatively male-dominated workplace.

To the extent that some women are still just as dedicated and skilfully instrumental as their male colleagues, this may be taken to indicate that the earlier collapsing together of sex and gender roles (relegating women to the private sphere) is increasingly contested. This does not mean that gender categories are no longer important, but rather that a current decoupling of sex and gender provides both women and men with more opportunities for representing both the masculine and the feminine in different situations. As Firat (1994) notes, referring to gender and consumption: 'increasingly we find both males and females representing the feminine and the masculine during different moments in their lives, . . . finding it possible to move from one (re)presentation of self to another in fragmented moments of everyday life' (Firat 1994:217).

In modern Norway, such fragmentation is perhaps most enhanced for professional women, who, in spite of their entry into a masculine environment, are still tied to the home in ways that tend to differ considerably from the ties experienced by male colleagues.[17] Yet, the practical management of home and family is not only a female affair. Although the unequal division of household labour still persists, we may increasingly expect men and women to take on different roles in relation to both the public *and* the private domain. To the extent that gender differences are invisible or doxic in the marketing department, it may be because gender is becoming less directly linked to biological sex, and more linked to the fundamental separation between the professional and the private domain.

Summary

The position of the product manager is located at the lowest level in the organizational hierarchy, and is generally conceived as a stepping-stone to a marketing career. A product manager serves as a coordinating link between a range of institutions (production, sales, marketing, advertising agencies, consumers), and carries a total market responsibility for her or his range of products. This implies frequent contact with a wide range of persons, primarily through face-to-face encounters and conversations on the phone, and some difficulties in giving priority to more time-consuming tasks related to long-term planning. It also implies a great deal of variation in the daily activities in terms of topics dealt with and persons talked to. Social and communicative skills are considered important, along with engagement and dedication to the job. A 'typical' product manager is a man of around thirty with higher education in the field of business or marketing. In spite of the smaller proportion of female product managers, and a total male dominance at higher levels, the issue of gender is rarely addressed in the marketing department, and women and men are considered to have equal opportunities for promotion. Gender becomes relevant for promotion to the extent that it implies absence of long duration, as in the case of the first year of motherhood. In such instances, the issue of gender is conceptualized and made relevant in terms of a more general separation of the private sphere from the professional sphere.

Notes

1. Viking Foods is a subsidiary of a much larger concern that was among the major industrial corporations in Norway in the early 1990s. This concern is also based in Norway, and owned primarily by Norwegian investors.
2. In the following analysis, Viking Foods' marketing department provides the primary location of empirical enquiry, while a minor part of the data material was gathered in an adjacent, but smaller marketing department. Data from other units of

the company are included in so far as they cast light on the processes and actors in the marketing department. Unless otherwise indicated, the present description refers to the marketing department in which most of the field research was carried out.

3. In the following description, I have chosen the time-period when fieldwork was most concentrated as a point of departure for my description of the organization, well aware that one year before, or perhaps two years ahead, the organizational map would have looked somewhat different. I have relied primarily on statements by key informants in the marketing department.

4. In the analysis that follows, I will focus primarily on the marketing branch of the marketing department as opposed to sales. (Sales managers are responsible for the activities of regional sales managers, who are located outside of the marketing department.)

5. The position of the assistant marketing director is partly a result of the reorganization that took place at the beginning of the fieldwork period. Before this, both marketing managers reported directly to the marketing director. Several informants (including the assistant marketing director) mentioned this as an odd position, created as a result of the problems of fitting what were previously two separate departments smoothly into one.

6. One of the remaining product managers was, after some negotiations, relieved of the assignment on the grounds that his tasks were very untypical, and in an area that had little relevance to my research interest. Two of the remaining product managers never felt they had the time to fill out the questionnaire, but agreed to provide the information orally instead, during an extensive interview focusing specifically on time expenditure.

7. Similarly, with regard to time expenditure, the estimates are generally low, as the average registered working time per day constitutes only six hours. As a regular working day lasts seven and a half hours (not including the lunch-break), and as many respondents work overtime, this indicates a tendency towards under-reporting.

8. One could for instance imagine a situation in which the managing directors appreciate the term 'president' because it entails association of total commitment and responsibility, i.e. personal qualities that they would like their subordinate product managers to possess; while the product managers, on

the other hand, appreciate the associations of power and status within the local hierarchy, i.e. characteristics that they would like the product manager's position to entail.

9. One interpretation may be that having small children is about the only legitimate reason for not working overtime. For a more elaborate discussion, see below.

10. The product manager's salary is set at a level that does not generally include extra payment for overtime.

11. The fact that my key informants were all men must be taken into account. This methodological male bias may especially have prevented me from establishing close relationships with individual women. However, with regard to the general impression of the marketing department as a semi-public place, the finding of the invisibility of a feminine dimension is still valid.

12. The Norwegian term *'leve seg inn i'* (literally 'live oneself into') is somewhat stronger than the English translation 'identify with', in the sense that it denotes a total absorption into something external. The term is frequently used about acts in theatre, who must *'leve seg inn i'* their roles in order to dramatize the characters in play.

13. Incidentally, this conceptualization of the role of product manager is very similar to current notions of the role of young social scientists within academia. As such, I could easily relate to the product managers' reflections on their job as a matter of engagement, guts and dedication.

14. Subsequently, the duration of maternity leave in Norway has been further extended and it has also become partly earmarked for the father.

15. This separation is also reflected in the circumscription of research, which often tends to analyse work and home-life separately, rarely making the one sphere of activities relevant to the other. According to Kvande and Rasmussen (1990), the tendency to separate 'family life' from 'work life' is extended through studies of women in the workplace as well, through an exclusive focus on women's socialization and family ties *at the expense of* conditions in the workplace as key factors for explaining female participation. This leads to what the authors call the mutual exclusivity of 'family life' and 'work life' (Kvande and Rasmussen 1990). I may add, somewhat reluctantly, that

the present field research only extends this tendency, as
the professional sphere is circumscribed as the locus of
inquiry.

16. This statement is merely based upon informants' impressions,
and is not substantiated by statistical data.

17. In their discussion of gender and modernity, Nielsen and
Rudberg (1994:48–9) argue slightly differently, however, as
they suggest that because of their attachments to the 'little
world' women tend to experience modernity in a different
way, which may possibly make women better equipped to
endure the hardships of modernity.

Chapter 5

Conceptualizing the Market

Viking Foods is a limited company, whose activities are founded upon the explicit purpose of maximizing profit. As a major Norwegian producer of manufactured foods, Viking Foods derives its profit from transactions with customers in retail or wholesale whose demand reflects (to some extent) the demand of Norwegian consumers. On an aggregate level, these transactions are generally conceptualized as 'the market' (*markedet*). The marketing department of Viking Foods may be regarded as an organizational unit whose primary purpose and field of activity is monitoring and strengthening the various alliances between Viking Foods and the market. This is achieved through development, design and marketing of Viking Foods products, and implies that the marketing department is given a key role in the joint effort of reproducing the organization as a whole.

The market is a key point of reference in the marketing department. Considerable effort is spent in describing, analysing and trying to interpret the various shifts and changes of the market, and in evaluating alternative strategies in relation to these. The concept of the market thus serves both as an all-encompassing *model of* the world as it is, and as a *model for* appropriate action (Geertz 1966).

The word market derives from the Latin term *mercatus*, meaning 'trade' or 'a market'. In early use, it referred primarily to a social gathering at a particular place, an image that is still relevant when thinking of the market as a physical arena where buyers and sellers meet to exchange goods. Historically, such market-places have often been the centres around which towns gradually emerged, and we often find market squares centrally located in what are now modern cities. Gradually, the concept of market-as-place has been substituted by an understanding of the market as *processes* of buying and selling, until finally, in the seventeenth and eighteenth centuries, the definite article that precedes the noun denotes *an abstract aggregate geographical form* (Dilley 1992). Referring to 'the Norwegian market', we imply both an aggregate of individual transactions and a certain spatial extension, although the meaning of the latter goes far beyond the original concept of a market square. Firstly, transactions of goods and services are no longer physically confined to a specific location or square, and the physical delineations of these locations do not always coincide with the organizational structures of which they are a part. Secondly, the market as a physical locale has become the subject of metaphorical elaboration.

Definitions of the market are always positioned. Marketing theory defines the market as *'the set of all actual and potential buyers of a product'* (Kotler and Armstrong 1987:204), a definition that clearly reflects the sellers' perspective. This is quite different from the perspective of, for instance, a consumer wanting to buy a car, for whom the market may be conceived as the totality of all firms and private persons who offer cars for sale within the vicinity of his or her home town. The meaning of the term market thus varies according to one's position in the buyer–seller relationship.

In general economic theory the market is often defined as all the buyers and all the sellers who transact some good or service. Although this description usually presupposes some kind of adherence to the ideal market principle of economic theory, this is not a requirement. Perhaps for the lack of more precise concepts, the term 'market' is frequently applied cross-culturally to transactions that to only a limited degree resemble the ideal free market of economic theory (Dilley 1992).

In the following, we will examine the various ways in which alliances between Viking Foods and the market are conceptualized in the marketing department. We will focus especially on four key concepts that are particularly salient in local discourse: 'market', 'product', 'brand' and 'consumers'. These terms are chosen because of their central roles in structuring events and for legitimizing action in the marketing department. Furthermore they are, as we shall see, also subject to rich metaphoric elaboration.

All four concepts are also analytical tools within the discipline of economics. One may argue that a market idiom pervades a significant part of Western public discourse, structuring and legitimizing events far beyond the confines of commercial transactions. Even in the marketing department, activities that are basically social are often structured in terms of market idioms.[1]

While these extensions indicate the extent to which economic theory has influenced Western discourse in general (Dilley 1992) and the subdiscipline of marketing in particular, they are not the topic of the present chapter. Yet the hegemonic influence of such market-oriented paradigms warrants a thorough analysis of these concepts, and the way they are conceptualized, both *beyond* and *within* spheres of transactional (market) exchange.

In the present chapter, I will explore the range of meanings and metaphoric connotations associated to each term, as they are applied empirically in local discourse and in practice in the marketing department. I will demonstrate that the ways informants in the marketing department talk about the market indicate meanings and connotations that reach far beyond the definition of a marketing textbook. Depending on the way it is metaphorically structured, the meaning of the concept may thus be extended in different ways. Four central metaphoric structures are identified. These are based on local discourse gathered through either interviews or empirical case material or at seminars or lectures with informants from Viking Foods. In order to achieve a coherent presentation of each term, quotations are necessarily disconnected from their empirical context. Subsequent empirical chapters will, however, provide sufficient detailed description to allow the reader to evaluate each term in the light of various contexts in which it is applied.

'The Market': Metaphoric Connotations

Market as Territorial Space

One of the most common ways of conceptualizing the market is in terms of a space. In its most basic form, this conceptualization of the market as territorial space is indicated by means of prepositions, as for instance in the following statements:

- *We are reaching a saturation in the pizza market* (Product Manager, Chapter 7).
- *We need to develop products with growth potential in the market* (Interview: Product Development Director).
- *Product x is taken out of the market ('ut av markedet')* (Interview: Product Manager).

- *When the prices you can obtain are really low, it is no longer interesting (for Viking foods) to be* **in** *the market* (Interview: Marketing Manager).
- *Pizza is the only market which is large enough to* **enter** *('gå inn i') with segmentation strategies* (Marketing Manager, Chapter 7).
- *Product y had been* **on** *the market ('på markedet') for forty years* (Interview: Product Secretary).

We see here a combination of spatial metaphors, one indicating the market as an entity that products may be entered into and taken out of, and that may be saturated at a certain point, the other indicating a territorial field that a product may be on or off. Thus, when trying to grasp the characteristics of a rather abstract entity like the market, informants turn to metaphors of something concrete. This use of metaphors is not uncommon. Salmond has suggested that *'nearly always, when we talk about abstract concepts, we choose language drawn from one or another concrete domain'* (Salmond 1982:81 referring to Ortony 1979:89). Even the company itself may be *in* or *out of* the market. By imposing spatial metaphors on some real or potential buyers, one may treat the market as a coherent entity, with an existence separate from and independent of Viking Foods. There is a market 'out there', which is, in a sense, living its own life, beyond the direct control of anyone at Viking Foods. This may seem a paradox, considering the fact that Viking Foods is among the most central actors who take part. Metaphorically, however, this interdependency is not recognized, neither is the impact of Viking Foods' decisions on the particular configurations of this territorial field. The most important issue is rather whether or not Viking Foods is present in this particular arena.

The notion of a market as a concrete space gives rise to several types of metaphoric elaborations, all sharing a preoccupation with the spatial delineations of the market. Sometimes the spatial extension of the market is identical with the geographic borders of the nation-state, as in the term 'the Norwegian market'. Sometimes the concept is narrowed down according to product category, as in the term 'the (Norwegian) poultry market'. When approached as an object of analysis, the spatial extension of the market is often conceptualized in terms of geometric figures, usually as a circular shape, as in the case of a pie chart.

In Figure 5.1. the pie represents the total market for a certain

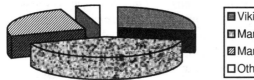

▣ Viking Foods 27%
▨ Manufacturer A 42%
▨ Manufacturer B 25%
☐ Others 5%

Figure 5.1. A model of the market for a particular product category

product category. The size of each slice represents the *relative market share* of the different companies offering this product. The market share is usually also indicated by a percentage. The brand with the largest slice is referred to as the *market leader*. This particular conceptualization of the market is often used in market analysis, as a description of the present situation or of the past. By means of a pie chart the abstract concept of a market may be reduced to a stable and finite entity, visualized as a pie to be shared. The market appears as something given, that may be split among a group of actors – an entity that no one can acquire more of, except at the expense of someone else. The circle leaves no 'other' category, no open space that remains to be filled. In this way, the pie metaphor draws attention to the presence of other actors in the market arena; actors whose presence and growth represents a more or less continuous threat. This takes us to the next metaphoric structure, which I will refer to as:

Market as Battlefield

Metaphors of war are frequently applied in descriptions of the market. This tendency is particularly salient among certain market research institutes, and in parts of the marketing literature. An example of this is an American video by an multinational market research company called Nielsen,[2] which is known in Norway by the name Nielsen, Norway. The video has been presented at several meetings arranged by Nielsen for their customers, including informants from Viking Foods' marketing department. The film opens by zooming in on a map of Europe. Dramatic music and heavy rhythms accompany the quick shifts of images as the camera zooms in on red national borders. Then the term *'Marketing Warfare'* lights up on the screen, while a male American voice says: *'The competition has escalated to new levels of **speed and precision**, critical* *decisions must be the right decisions . . . Only those who act now will prevail in the future . . . We are prepared for victory.'* (The rest of the video focuses on the services offered by Nielsen International.) Metaphors of war are also used in general discourse in the marketing department, as in the following quotations:

- *Keep on going, there are still vacant market shares to fight for! ('Stå på, det er fortsatt ledige markedsandeler å sloss om')* (Product Manager, Chapter 8).
- *We have to act today in a way that arms us ('ruster oss') for the competition of tomorrow* (Interview: Staff Director).
- *Company Q has lost market shares ('tapt markedsandeler') lately* (Interview: Marketing Manager).
- *We need to fortify ('befeste') our market position by establishing Viking Foods as a brand* (Interview: Marketing Director).
- *Tactical manoeuvres must be undertaken* (Product Manager, Chapter 6).
- *It is important that we hit with great precision ('treffer med stor presisjon')* (Marketing Manager).
- *[We need to be] creating products that are spearheads ('spydspisser') in the market* (Interview: Product Manager).
- *Product x is a miss ('skivebom'[3])* (Interview: Marketing Manager).

Here we see how conceptualizations of the market as territorial space are extended into something that, like territory in times of war, one must fight for, and that may be lost or won. Furthermore, the quotations demonstrate the use of vocabulary drawn from military technology, depicting the market as a battlefield and the products as weapons. Conceptualizing marketing activities as tactical manoeuvres, marketing and products as spearheads, referred a kind of warfare in which the product manager is like a warrior or a general at war. The metaphors may thus ignite a competitive and courageous spirit, emphasizing the need for both offensive action and strategic planning in a battle where a failure to fortify one's position inevitably implies loss.

As indicated above, products serve the role of weapons. Sometimes, however, the products may be more directly involved in the battle, as indicated in the following quotations:

- *We are now going to make three pizza brand products without cannibalizing ('uten å kannibalisere')* (Marketing Manager, Chapter 7).

- *If we eat each other, that's not a problem. I think a certain **competition** between our own products is healthy, as long as they don't **fight for the same space on the shelves*** (Interview: Marketing Manager).

Like companies fighting for market shares, products may also, in a sense, fight one another in order to acquire 'space on the shelves' – a scarce resource that is crucial for the products' survival (see also below). Ironically, the battle between food products is often described by metaphors of cannibalism, indicating that a product's success implies, figuratively, 'consuming' other products that are less successful. This brings us on to the next metaphoric structure, which I will refer to as:

Market as an Environment of Natural Selection (Evolutionary Approach)

Often when products are discussed, the market is referred to as a place where products 'live' or 'die'. Sometimes, the life cycle of a product is also depicted visually (see also Figure 5.5). Consider the following quotations:

- *Today, products' **life cycles are getting shorter and shorter** ... Somebody told me that out of 100 products launched in Germany a few years ago, only seven are still on the market* (Interview: Marketing Manager).
- *For most products, I think the **life cycle model** ('livssyklusmodellen') is correct* (Interview: Marketing Manager).
- *We follow up on trends and update the product in order to **keep it alive** ('holde det i live')* (Interview: Marketing Manager).
- *The reason that products are taken off the market is that they **do not have the right to live** ('årsaken til saneringer er at produktene ikke har livets rett')* (Interview: Marketing Manager).

We see here how the concept of the market is structured in terms that relate to life and death. The products are metaphorically conceived in a manner that resembles living species, and concepts from biology are applied (life cycle). Once they enter the market, however, the products are on their own, survival of the fittest is the governing principle, and those that are not fit enough will eventually disappear. The market thus provides the ultimate judgement, a final test in which failure is not coincidental. At the same time, the metaphor emphasizes the importance of adapting to the environment: i.e. of knowing the rules of the market. This brings us over to the final metaphoric structure, which I will refer to as:

Market as a Flux of Transformation

A wide range of expressions bring attention to the changeable nature of the market. These are particularly common when the market is the object of analysis. Consider, for instance, the following extract from a presentation for customers by a vice-president of Nielsen International, upon his visit to Norway in February 1994: *'According to a Chinese proverb, change is both danger and opportunity. We're prepared to take advantage of the new opportunities. In the following I will refer to some key trends changing the marketplace'* (Todd Bradley, Vice-President of Nielsen International, Feb. 1994). But the changeability of the market, and the company's need to adapt, is also a frequent topic of discussion in the marketing department, especially within the context of long-term strategic planning, knowledge and market analysis:

- *Keeping an eye on **consumer trends**, you can make the product **stay alive** much longer* (Interview: Marketing Manager).
- *Pizza z is not good enough, because the **market has become more sophisticated, the taste ('smaken') has changed**, it is the kind of product that **time has run away from*** (Product Manager, Chapter 7).
- *We need to develop in the direction of retail, and in the direction that the consumer **market changes**. On food fairs abroad, I observe what happens in these areas in other markets. **That will come to us as well*** (Interview: Marketing Director).
- *We are definitely getting better at **picking up signals** ('å plukke opp signaler') from consumers. One of the **signals from the market** is that E-numbers are no good'* (Interview: Assistant Marketing Director).
- *The advertising agencies **feel the pulse of the market** ('føler markedet på pulsen')* (Interview: Marketing Director).

We see here how the market is practically given a life of its own. Like a child, it is always changing. It grows more sophisticated as it no longer accepts what it accepted before, and because of this it is somewhat unpredictable. Like a fastidious child, it must be offered products carefully adapted to its changing taste preferences. The challenge is therefore to develop procedures to pick up signals fast enough, and to respond quickly. Adaptation is crucial, and must be achieved through careful interpretation and analysis of market and consumer information.

A considerable part of the discourse in the marketing department is based upon an understanding of the market as indicated in the metaphoric structures above. Alone, and in combination, these metaphors offer a rich source of connotations that help to structure experiences and serve as a guide for further action. When the metaphoric structures are applied in general discourse, speakers may evoke first one, then another, seemingly without any difficulties. This lack of any strict criterion for use is quite consistent with similar findings on the use of metaphors within scientific discourse (Salmond 1982). Rather than being interpreted as indicating a lack of logical structuring on the part of the informants, it should be seen as a feature of the use of metaphoric structures themselves, being at the same time open-ended and creative (Salmond 1982).

The market serves as a key concept in the reproduction of Viking Foods as a particular locality in time and space. By focusing on the market metaphors, we are able to grasp ways in which actors in the marketing department (through a collectively shared discourse) conceive of the locality's immediate context. And because this particular context happens to provide a crucial source of justification for the company as a whole, the discursive elaboration of an imagined 'market' serves, simultaneously, as a key factor in the reproduction of the locality itself.

This simultaneous production both of the locality and its context occurs not only at the discursive level. In the process of ensuring profit through producing and distributing foods for sale, Viking Foods also contributes to producing the market of which it is a part. However, in strictly metaphoric terms, the latter aspect is largely underscored, as the market is conceptualized as 'living a life of its own' (see above).

The relevance of this set of metaphoric structures, for the purpose of the present analysis, lies primarily in the way they serve to guide, structure or legitimize action. The linkages between metaphors and action may be perceived both directly, as in the cases when conceptualizations of the market inspire a certain attitude (for example, market as battlefield, product manager as warrior) or more indirectly, as in the cases when conceptualizations of the market simply serve as descriptive tools that help the marketing professionals sort information about the context to which they must adapt.

With this in mind, we may ask: what do these metaphoric structures tell informants about the proper way of being? Which aspects of their own roles, and of the roles of their products are highlighted through these metaphors? And what types of principles are legitimized by the different metaphoric structures?

First of all, we may note the *unpredictability* inherent in some of the market metaphors. Whether conceptualized in terms of processes of natural selection or battles of war, the metaphors seem to indicate that 'it is a jungle out there', where life is fragile and failures are frequent. The image of abrupt changes in likes and dislikes further emphasizes the unpredictability of the outcome.

However, one is not totally at the mercy of the unpredictable nature of the market. The metaphoric structures indicate at least two ways of ensuring a favourable outcome. Firstly, as in the case of natural selection, extinction is assumed to be due to maladaptation. Consequently, it is important to create products that are adapted to the environment. One must, in other words, *know* the market, a task which is not easy, considering its constant shifts and changes. Secondly, as in the case of war, strength is important in order to endure the fight and come out as a winner. But strength alone is not enough. Qualities like cunning, courage and cautiousness are just as important, and, last but not least: the ability to act *strategically*.

Metaphors are 'good to think', and as such they are also good for people who think out loud, together. More precisely, metaphors may enhance the process by which a person's understanding is adopted by another person. But in providing a set of images in terms of which we think about reality, they also contribute to shaping that reality. Metaphors may thus be self-fulfilling (Lakoff and Johnson 1980).

As indicated above, each metaphoric assertion about the market highlights a distinct aspect of marketing practice. Following Fernandez (1974), we may thus argue that each metaphoric assertion evokes a dominant state of mind, which implies a set of *performative consequences*, including giving priority to certain role interpretations and certain definitions of the medium (in this case the product) and to a general principle governing action. Based on the metaphoric assertions described above, various aspects of marketing practice may be tentatively summarized as follows (see Table 5.1):

Table 5.1 is based on an understanding of metaphoric assertions as *'a strategic predication upon a ... pronoun ... which makes a movement and leads to performance'* (Fernandez 1974:43). As such it summarizes potential performative consequences of the various metaphoric assertions. This does not imply that these metaphors and their performative consequences are necessarily suitable descriptions of actual marketing practice. Rather, the purpose of Table 5.1 is simply to suggest the flexibility inherent in the metaphoric assertions. The extent to which these performative consequences are also realized in practice is an empirical question to which we will return in subsequent chapters. While highlighting the unpredictability, changeability and risk associated with the market, the metaphoric structures simultaneously serve to underscore other aspects. One such aspect is the stability of demand. Comprising four million relatively affluent consumers, the Norwegian population may be said to represent a fairly stable and predictable source of demand. Furthermore, as was indicated in Chapter 3, domestic manufacturers benefit from protective

Table 5.1. Metaphors – performative consequences

Metaphoric assertion:	Performative Consequences:		
	Ideal-type actor	Role of product	Governing principle
Market is territorial space	Coordinator	Marking off boundaries	Entitlement and defence
Market is a battlefield	Warrior	Weapon	Courageous, strategic action, aggressivity
Market is an environment of natural selection	Fatalist	Living species	Survival of the fittest *Post hoc* explanations of failure and success
Market is a flux of transformation	Analyst and Interpreter	Mediator, seducing consumers	Reflexivity Adaptation through interpretation

measures intended to maintain domestic agricultural production. As a major and well-established Norwegian food manufacturer in a country with a high level of domestic protection, informants at Viking Foods *might* have emphasized the stability of the situation, rather than the unpredictability. In spite of this, however, unpredictability and risk are highlighted, while other aspects, such as stability and mutual dependency, remain veiled.

Products as Weapons – Products as Living Species

Entering the marketing department, one immediately notices a huge glass cabinet which is filled with all the *products* of the marketing department. Neatly organized according to their respective product categories, the products in the cabinets serve as a visual display of what the activities in the marketing department are all about.

The key linkage between the marketing department and Viking Foods is defined through the marketing department's responsibility for a specified range of food products. These products also serve as the linkage between Viking Foods and the consumer, thus representing its basis for maximizing profit. According to the vice-president:,

> the marketing department is supposed to make sure ('passe på') that we have products that will be profitable for us ('tjene oss') in the years to come, and that we manage to consolidate these products strongly enough both in the retail link and with the consumers ('å befeste våre produkter ... på en tung nok måte').

Not surprisingly, we find that the notion of products also serves as the most central organizing principle within the marketing department.

What is a product? Food products may be described as a totality that includes both physical properties, package design, the label and the accompanying advertising. This approach is in accordance with the way informants in the marketing department describe products. Several informants described products by evoking an image of various layers, in which the material properties constitute the core, while symbolic properties and advertising constitute its periphery. In order to explain this, one informant drew the illustration in Figure 5.2:

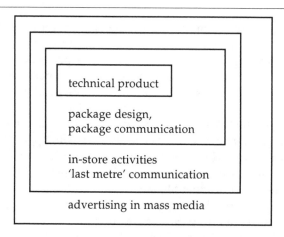

Figure 5.2. The Product

This understanding of the product was clearly inspired by a book on marketing called 'the metaproduct' (Linn 1985), a book which was frequently recommended to me. According to its author, a 'metaproduct' is far more than its technical and physical components: *'the metaproduct is the total invisible world of conceptualizations that we associate with a product'*. According to the author, a metaproduct may be created and developed in exactly the same way as the physical product, and this is what modern marketing is all about (Linn 1985). This understanding of products is dominant among the persons working in the marketing department, and is rarely contested. Interestingly, this image of the product is also referred to by persons working in product development. In fact, only one informant in the marketing department held a different opinion with regard to at least certain types of products, maintaining that: *'A sausage is a sausage, that is nothing to create an image around.'*[4]

Products may be categorized according to whether they are uniform (*'ensartede'*) or differentiated (*'differensierte'*). Uniform products are those that are similar from one manufacturer to another (e.g. frozen peas), while differentiated products differ more (e.g. frozen pizza). The same feature is also referred to by the terms generic (*'generiske'*) or unique (*'unike'*). Products that are differentiated are generally considered to be at an advantage, as a certain degree of uniqueness is a requirement for 'building brands', an activity which is highly estimated (see below).

Another way of comparing products is by ranking them by means of quality and price. The term quality is rarely defined, and its meaning may well differ from one product to another. Often, the meaning of the term remains implicit throughout discussions. When pushed to clarify the term, product managers often refer to the consumer as a point of reference, as in the following reply: *'What is quality? That's a good question. Taking pizza as an example, I'd say that it has to do with what the topping looks like. How is the sauce? How does the consumer perceive ("oppfatte") it? Quality is to satisfy consumer needs. The bottom should be crisp and tasty'* (Interview: Product Manager).

High-quality products may also be sold at a high price, but not always. Consequently, products may be compared by reference to both quality and price, as illustrated in Figure 5.3:

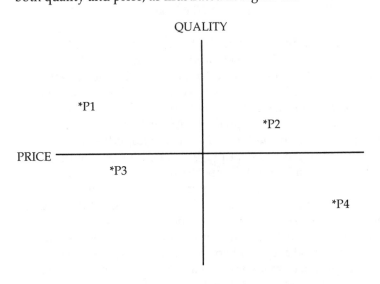

Figure 5.3. Products differentiated according to quality and price

Figure 5.3. represents one way of comparing different products according to quality and price. This particular figure was sometimes reproduced by informants during interviews.

While the products' degree of uniformity, quality and price serve primarily as analytical tools, products are also frequently described in more metaphorical terms. One may for instance develop *strategic products,* i.e. products that are not necessarily profitable, but serve to give a certain image to the company, or to a product range. Certain products may also serve as a spearhead in the market in order to keep a competitor at a distance, or to stop a competitor from an anticipated launch. These terms clearly correspond with the metaphors of the market as battlefield (see earlier in this chapter).

Another set of product metaphors relate to the image of the market as an environment of natural selection. We have already described how products are referred as 'having the right to live' on the market. Within a similar metaphoric structure, products are also considered as having potential for growth (*'vekstpotensiale'*); they stay alive (*'holder seg i live'*) as long as they are produced and sold on the market; and all products have a specific life cycle. Generally, this life cycle is depicted as an inverted U-curve in which the vertical axis represents the volume sold (alternatively:profit), and the horizontal axe represents time:

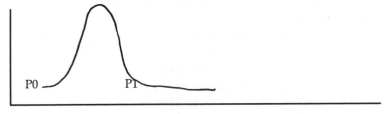

Figure 5.4. Products' anticipated life cycle

This image of a product's life cycle is sometimes used by informants to illustrate how the life cycle of products is becoming shorter and shorter (the slope is gradually turning sharper), and also to legitimize marketing expenditures. One marketing manager puts it this way:

> *The idea [in marketing theory] is that in order to prolong the life of a particular product or product group, you must enter right here [points to where the line starts to drop] with some kind of marketing activity. It might be a new package design, a slight change of content, or it may be an advertising campaign. What is important is that you do revitalize ['fornyer'] the product in a way that creates some activity around it. By keeping an eye on consumer trends and updating your product accordingly, you can make it stay alive much longer.*

A similar curve figures in marketing textbooks. In Kotler and Armstrong (1987), the idea of products as having a life of their own is emphasized by statements such as: *'management wants the product to enjoy a long and happy life'* (Kotler and Armstrong 1987:274).

The image of the product as a living species is closely related to the image of the market as an environment of natural selection. Just as with prehistoric species, no product can be expected to 'live' for ever. Still, survival may be prolonged, and this is achieved by altering the product in a way that makes it more adapted to the changing environment. The idea of *adaptation* is crucial: by adapting to consumer trends, the final moment of extinction may be postponed.

Although the idea that all products are bound to 'die' is frequently referred to in the marketing department, the image is not entirely uncontested. Several informants emphasize, while referring to the model above, that this principle does not apply equally to all products. Bread, butter and milk are often mentioned as examples of products for which the life cycle model does not necessarily apply. The importance of considering each product separately is thus emphasized. One informant maintains the manufacturer's own responsibility in making this model come true: *'I think we make it this way, simply because so damned many of the new product launches are a fiasco'* (Marketing Manager). Yet the basic principle of the product life cycle model (i.e. as a typical description, relevant to most products on the market) remains largely uncontested.

The life cycle model is subject to various types of elaboration. Different stages of products' life cycles may be referred to as stages of introduction, growth, maturity and decline, or they may be described by more elaborated models, such as the so-called BCG approach (see Figure 5.5 below). This model is developed by the Boston Consulting Group (BCG), a leading North American management consulting firm, and is frequently referred to in marketing literature (Kotler and Armstrong 1987:33).[5] In the marketing department, the origin of the model is rarely explicitly stated, neither is the term BCG used. Yet the model circulates as a piece of common knowledge that is rarely contested:

	Market share: HIGH	LOW
Level of Investment: HIGH	'STAR'	'BABY'
LOW	'CASH-COW'	'DOG'

Figure 5.5. Products' life cycle according to the BCG model (Reproductions provided during interviews by informants in the marketing department)

The main virtue of the BCG model is that it offers a tool for considering the product's viability, or whether or not it is worth spending money on. A marketing director puts it this way:

> *Let's imagine a model for the products' life cycle like this* [quickly draws Figure 5.4]. *If you look at the first upward slope, you can imagine that in the future this curve must be steeper. Products that don't quickly acquire a significant market share must be taken off the market sooner. This can also be illustrated in a different way* [quickly draws Figure 5.5]. *Imagine a line drawn from the upper right corner* ['baby'] *through star and cash cow and ending up in the lower right* ['dog']. *This is really the same model. Through marketing activity* [high investment] *we can turn the 'dog' into a 'baby', and hopefully make the product go through all the phases once more. But for each turn, we will be at a lower market share . . .*

This statement illustrates the way such models may serve as a guide for action. While the first life cycle model (Figure 5.4) serves to justify marketing expenditure in order to make the product stay alive, the BCG model (Figure 5.5) is more sophisticated in the sense that it legitimizes *either* increased marketing expenditure, *or*, alternatively, the elimination of a product from the market. As such, it is a very flexible tool, justifying whichever decision seems most appropriate.

The metaphoric image of products as living beings is further nurtured through frequent efforts at finding the right *name* for a product, and with trying to define such features as the product's *personality*. According to one informant, a product manager must have the ability to get into the spirit of the product, or identify with the product (*'leve seg inn i produktet'*, see also Chapter 4). These metaphoric structures all serve to personalize the product beyond the level of mere survival; the product becomes analogous to a person. The processes of *personalizing products* are particularly salient in discourse related to brands or brand products.

The Art of Building Brands

Brands are insubstantial things, mere symbols, names, associations. Sometimes they signal real differences between products. Sometimes they are mere illusion (The Economist, 7 September 1991).

Among the products displayed in the glass cabinet near the entrance of the marketing department, only some are *brand products* (*'merkevarer'*). Nobody knows exactly how many, as the criteria for classifying a brand product are highly variable, and frequently challenged. Everybody agrees, however, that not all products are brand products, that many products have the potential of *becoming* brand products, and that the establishment of brand products, or so-called brand-building (*'merkevarebygging'*) is part of the current long-term strategy of Viking Foods.[6] A senior marketing director puts it this way: *'Brand-building is "the thing". It is a signal from managing directors, from product managers, from advertising agencies, from everywhere. It is really nothing new. In a certain sense, it has always been there, but the consciousness around this activity is much greater now.'*

During my period of fieldwork, the importance of building brands was increasingly recognized, and strongly emphasized. Terms like 'brands' and 'brand-building' are thus frequently referred to, and serve as a major source of justification for allocating resources to marketing activities. According to the senior marketing director:

In order to establish a brand product, we must increase consumer awareness of the product, and thus bring it to the 'top of the ladder' . . .. There must be concentrated advertising over a certain period. The advertising must be noticed for at least 3–4 days in order to have an effect. Our budgets [for marketing activities] are really much too small. This has to do with increased competition for consumers' attention in the media, and implies that we must spend more resources on marketing [than before].

Some informants eagerly embrace the opportunity to work with brands: *'Brand-building? That's what I'm here for!'* (Product Manager). Others are somewhat less enthusiastic: *'Brands? Well, of course it is important. [Jokingly:] If I don't say that I'll be fired. But I'm not among the most eager brand-building advocates . . .'* (Marketing Manager).

This enhanced effort towards brand-building was partly due to an intensive education effort, launched by top management and directed at medium-level managers. In spite of a demanding workload, many of the product managers spent an entire week at a hotel in order to learn more about brand-building (the seminar was referred to as 'The Brand Days' ['*Merkedagene*']). The increased awareness of the importance of building brands is also reflected in social organization. During my fieldwork period, the marketing department consisted primarily of product managers and product secretaries. The following year, however, four of the former product managers were given the new title *'brand manager'*, a promotion that placed them slightly 'above' other product managers. The establishment of this new position implied the introduction of yet another level of hierarchic differentiation.

While practically everyone in the marketing department agrees that brands are important, there is no final definition as to what the term really entails. Definitions range from those that emphasize consumers' willingness to pay a bit more (so-called 'premium price'), to those that emphasize symbolic properties of the brand product and the positive associations that a particular brand evokes. A marketing manager puts it this way:

The physical characteristics of products are usually quite similar, right? So when I speak about a brand product, I refer to both physical characteristics, personality and price. By personality I refer to those associations that the product has, or gives. You may have a relationship to Blenda [washing detergent] which says 'Hi, Blenda!'. Blenda is a woman in her mid-twenties with long blond hair, white, natural . . . The brand is a person.

Consumer loyalty is another feature that is frequently mentioned: *'The challenge is to establish brand loyalty on a long-term basis. To build preferences, establish what we call "properties"'* [7] (Product Manager). When asked to clarify what he means by the term 'properties', the product manager explains: *'What I mean is that a product has a kind of monopoly on a particular association, such as for instance the way Evergood (coffee brand) "owns" the golden cup. No one else can use that golden cup that way. The golden cup is Evergood!'*

While most informants would agree that premium price, personality and brand product loyalty are all central features of brand products, there is some disagreement regarding the relative importance of each. Furthermore, other economic aspects are also mentioned as distinctive criteria. According to one marketing director, a brand product is defined by means of three variables:

1. Consumers' knowledge of the product;
2. Market share; and
3. Profit per item sold (*'dekningsbidrag'*).

Another marketing manager points to the centrality of brand products when negotiating shelf space with retail chains. He defines brand products by means of two criteria:

1. Products that the retail chains cannot go without; and
2. Products that consumers are willing to pay a little more for.

In most of these definitions there is a blurring of classification, cause and consequences. More precisely, the criteria that are used to classify brand products are often not separated from the various advantages that brand products bring about. A premium price may be considered a *result* of a particular set of positive associations among consumers, rather than an independent characteristic of the product itself. Nevertheless, it is frequently mentioned as a classificatory feature, thus making the definition somewhat tautological: 'Product x is a brand product because consumers are willing to pay more for it – Consumers are willing to pay more for product x because it is a brand product.' One informant explains the difference as follows: *'It is the so-called premium price that enables us to call it a brand product. But we must make sure to note the difference between brand products and commodities. There are certain commodities that are sold at a higher price simply because of lack of competition. That does not make them into brand products'* (Special Consultant, Staff).

The fact that brands are both desirable and hard to define provides fertile ground for internal disagreement regarding the classification of Viking Foods products. Some informants argue that, according to external brand-building experts, Viking Foods does not have a single brand product! Others are more pragmatic, and maintain that classification is more a matter of degree. Rather than transforming all products into brand products in a strict sense of the term, the main challenge is to establish products with a *brand profile*. Most informants would agree, however, that certain products in the Viking Foods product range are typical brand products. From the perspective of each product manager, the authority to classify products as brand products is a crucial asset, and one that renders each product manager somewhat vulnerable. One authoritative statement regarding Viking Foods brand products is a confidential document in which the entire product range is classified according to what is referred to as brand product strength (*'merkevarestyrke'*). The purpose of this document, prepared by staff, was to give an overview of the competitive strength of Viking Foods products, particularly with regard to anticipated foreign competition. The final assessment of Viking Foods' products was neither available to the researcher, nor to most product managers – a fact that indicates the sensitivity of the issue of brand assessment. Selected parts of the report were, however, made available to me upon request. In this part, brand products are defined as follows:

> *A brand product is a product with a dominant position, i.e. high market share, high degree of distribution, high knowledge (among consumers) and something 'unique'. For food products in particular: The customer is willing to pay an 'extra price' for the brand product, and a majority will choose the product in a situation with several competing alternatives* (Confidential report 1992).

Another example of an authoritative definitions of brand products is the one that was taught during the one-week seminar ('The Brand Days'). In the initial document, featuring a draft of the course design, a brand product was defined as: *'A product which is considered ("oppfattet") as special ("særpreget") in the market, with regard to: symbols, designs, characteristics, and to which consumer groups feel an attachment.'*[8] The document emphasizes the importance of focusing on perceptions in the market, rather than on the hopes and expectations of the manufacturer. At the seminar, however, a brand was defined slightly differently. According to participants' notes: *'A brand is a promise ("a bundle of advantages") with a distinct personality, identified and guaranteed by a name.'*

This definition emphasizes the notion of the brand as a potential contract between manufacturer and consumer, a feature that has also been emphasized in the current marketing debate in Norway.[9] Another aspect of the notion of brands is that of *product differentiation*, a feature that until recently has not been emphasized to the same degree. At the Brand Days seminar, this was emphasized as follows: *'[The concept of brands] rests on the idea that it is possible within a given product category to create a differentiation that is relevant to the consumer, and sufficiently significant to establish a preference against competitors.'*

With regard to metaphoric structures, much of what has been said about products also applies to brand products. Both may be conceived as potential 'spearheads' in the competition for consumers, and both are separate entities whose position must be defended. However, while products may also be thought to have 'personality', in the case of brand products this personality is subject to even more elaboration, carefully defined, nurtured through advertising, and carefully adapted to the notion of the consumer target group. An important tool in this process is the so-called Brand Strategy (BS), a document with a definite set of headings that serves as a kind of 'identity card' describing the product according to product characteristics, brand name, product advantages, target group, etc. In a way then, transforming a product to a brand product implies a profound *personalization of the product*, in which the division between product and consumer tends to blur. (See also Chapters 7 to 9.)

Still, there are important differences between products and brand products. While products' life cycles may be described by means of life cycle models, brand products are rarely described in those terms. Rather, they are 'precious jewels' that must be carefully tended. While products that 'don't have the right to live' are simply taken off the market, brand products can hardly be subject to such swift elimination. To the extent that former brand products might be judged so harshly, they would simply cease to be defined as brand products. Consequently, brand products never die!

This distinction is quite meaningful if we consider both the careful adaptation of a fully developed brand product to its so-called consumer target group, and the symbolic (metonymic) association between brand product and manufacturer.[10] Firstly, by being carefully adapted to the notion of psycho-demographic characteristics of a defined target group, not only is the brand product differentiated from other competing products, it also (ideally) 'resembles' or 'mimics' an imagined consumer category, to the extent that it may be described as its symbolic representation (see Chapter 7). Applying the terminology of an actor–network approach, the difference between a brand product and a non-brand product (commodity) may thus be analysed as a difference of translation, locating the brand product one step closer to the consumer, thus contributing to what Latour refers to as *machination of forces* (Latour 1987). If, or when, such translations do *not* succeed in aligning consumer interests, the product is by definition no longer a brand product. One might argue that the concept of brand products serves as mere illusion – representing the 'gold medal', which is only rarely achieved, but that still motivates and shows the way. Consequently, actual products may fail, and they may be replaced by other food products *without* altering the long-term ideology (strategy) of brand-building.

Secondly, a brand product is an asset of the company that, to some extent, exists in a symbiotic relationship with the company's trademark: successful brand products are supposed to 'rub off' on the general image of the company, while a favourable company name ideally lends credibility to its distinct brand products. For a food manufacturer whose trademark is considered an asset (such as Viking Foods), it is therefore important that the various products sold under the company name do not in any way degrade the company's image. For instance, in situations when strong pressure to cut prices forces manufacturers to lower quality standards beyond a certain point, they might choose to market the product under a different trademark. In this way, the company prevents the cheap, low-quality product 'contaminating' the trademark of the manufacturer.

From the perspective of investors and stockholders, strong trademarks or brand products are an important asset of any company. This has led some to argue that the value of brands should be reflected in the companies' balance accounts, just like the value of property and industrial equipment. In spite of the considerable effort that has been put into developing procedures for determining the exact monetary value of brand assets (for example by consultants such as Interbrand), some accountants warn against such attempts, pointing to the insecurity involved. By 1993, there are still no commonly shared procedures for estimating the value of brands in exact figurers, and practices vary widely.

In the light of the close association between the brand name and the manufacturer, the fact that brand products rarely 'die' is less surprising. Brand products represent the company in an almost metonymic manner. Symbolically therefore, the 'death' of a brand product would represent a serious threat to the image of the company as a whole.

Conceptualizing Consumers

A consumer is a human being who doesn't work in advertising.[11]

Most of the above descriptions of the market, of products and of brand products rest upon an idea of consumers: consumers constitute the market in the sense that without them there would be no transactions. Consumers are the final recipients of products, and an image of consumer target groups serves as the point of reference in construction of brand products. From the perspective of a product manager, consumers are the 'ultimate other' with whom food manufacturers interact, and on whom the future reproduction of the company depends.

On a more general level, the term 'consumer' refers less to a subcategory of human beings than to a social role that is situation-specific and closely linked to the act of consuming. According to Williams (1983), the English term 'customer' was gradually replaced by 'consumer' around 1950, a change that also reflects a changing relationship between the vendor and the buyer. He writes: *'customer had always implied some degree of regular and continuing relationship to a supplier, whereas consumer indicates the more abstract figure in a more abstract market'* (Williams 1983:79).[12] With reference to industrialized societies, everybody is a consumer part of the time (including marketing professionals), while nobody is a consumer all the time.

Unlike products, which are physically displayed by the entrance, consumers hardly ever appear in the marketing department, that is: *practically nobody ever enters the marketing department as consumers.* Yet the department is filled with people who are all part-time consumers in their various private capacities. When they enter the marketing department, however, they enter in the capacity of marketing professionals. This very paradox (ironically hinted at in the quotation on the product manager's notice-board) is a key feature of the notion of consumers in the marketing department to which we will return in subsequent discussions (see Chapter 12).

Except for occasional complaints over the telephone or in the mail, the only evidence of consumers' existence is indirect, through text, statistics and figures. Such information basically comprises two different ways in which consumers (more or less consciously) become visible to marketing professionals: either through their purchasing activities, recorded in the marketing department as *sales results,* or through their verbal responses to questions posed in market research surveys and recorded in the marketing department as *consumer-oriented marketing research.* Each of these constitute very important sources of information in the marketing department. Both are carefully recorded, frequently consulted, and readily available to product managers. Moreover, such types of information are frequently appealed to substantiate major decisions.

From the perspective of an outsider, the amount of such information is rather impressive. Several shelves in the central area of the marketing department are filled with market research reports, and each product manager has a considerable collection of ring leaf files in his or her office documenting various aspects of consumers' opinions or purchasing behaviour. From the perspective of informants, however, consumers are still considered to be highly unpredictable. Some claim that the information is insufficient, arguing that much more time and money ought to be spent on gathering data about consumers. Others emphasize that the data available are not utilized systematically enough. Most informants agree, however, that *too little is known about consumers,* and that an effort should be made to improve competence in this field. Such statements are consistent with the current literature of marketing research, which frequently emphasizes the lack of formality in decision-making processes, which is partly due to a low utilization of information input (see Helgesen 1992; Greenley and Bayus 1994). In other words, information about consumers is always *incomplete*. From the perspective of informants and authors of marketing literature alike, this is a major source of uncertainty in marketing decisions. The consumers are, by and large, an unpredictable element, and consequently one that needs to be better understood.

Despite the potentially relevant experience that product managers may have as consumers in the private sphere, this private experience is rarely integrated in marketing decisions, or at least not explicitly referred to. Instead, such experience is often discarded as subjective or non-representative. It thus seems reasonable to claim that knowledge acquired outside the realm of professional practice and training is *generally not made relevant* within the context of day-to-day marketing practice. A similar observation has been made by Robert Prus, with regard to what he claims to be minimal attention to social interactions and actual lived experience in marketing literature. He writes: *'One would expect to see more evidence of their [authors'] own lived experiences in their depictions of the market place. Instead, it is as though they operate with two largely non-integrated sets of knowledge – their own lived experience and what may be termed academic positivism'* (Prus 1989:29).

Once again, we are faced with what we may call a 'bounded-ness' of the professional context against the private sphere. In terms of the construction of local knowledge about consumers, this implies that there are implicit criteria by which 'knowledge', as it is contextually defined in the marketing department, does not comprise certain realms of personal experience. While both private experience and professional training may enable a product manager to encounter something with the familiarity of previous encounters (Latour 1987:219), only the latter is locally recognized as knowledge in the marketing department (see Chapter 12).

This implies that in their struggle to know more about con-sumers, informants rely heavily on external sources of information, most notably on consumer-oriented marketing research.

Conceptualizing Consumers through Market Research

An essential feature of the way information about consumers appears in the marketing department is that it is nearly always *commercially transmitted*. In other words, whenever needs for

information about consumer preferences or consumer characteristics arise, commercial marketing research institutes are consulted.
Unlike, for example, information about brand products, which is
generally the property of Viking Foods, information about
consumers is nearly always purchased.

Consumer-oriented marketing research may be conceived as a
subcategory of marketing research. Kotler and Armstrong define
marketing research as: *'The systematic design, collection, analysis and
reporting of data and findings relevant to a specific marketing situation
facing the company'* (Kotler and Armstrong 1987:95).

The term 'marketing' research includes a wide range of documents, which may vary considerably with regard to the degree of
analysis involved (from crude sales figures to sophisticated market
analysis), and also with the extent to which consumers are a central
focus of inquiry. While some types of marketing research may be
carried out on the basis of internal documents readily available,
consumer-oriented marketing research usually involves external
interpreters.

Consumer-oriented marketing research draws upon several
social science disciplines for methods and theory. Data-collection
methods range from statistically advanced analyses of quantitative
survey data to purely qualitative descriptions of consumers'
attitudes as they are expressed during so-called 'group discussions'. In Viking Foods, both of these methods are frequently
used. In what follows, I will give a brief description of both.

Qualitative group discussions are usually staged in order to
throw light on specific issues such as: 'What are the consumers'
perceptions of a particular product?', 'How is it usually prepared?',
'What culinary characteristics are considered important?' and
'How important is price?', etc. Generally, such questions are formulated by the product manager, and then handed over to the people
at the market research institute, who select an appropriate sample,
reformulate the questions if needed, stage the group discussion
and write the final report. Usually, the composition of the group
reflects certain predefined criteria related primarily to age and sex.
Other than this, informants in the marketing department rarely
know exactly how respondents are selected. Some suspect that
the people at the market research institute pick their own friends
and acquaintances, and worry that the sample is atypical of the
population at large. Others assume that they simply go out into
the streets of Oslo and pick among the people passing by.

Most informants in the marketing department are well aware that group discussions can never reflect the Norwegian population as a whole. Yet many product managers choose this market research strategy because it may yield different kinds of insight, especially with regard to the variety of associations, thoughts and preferences that products may evoke. A combination of qualitative group discussions and statistically representative surveys is often sought.

Quantitative consumer surveys differ from qualitative group discussions in their emphasis on representativity in the sample. Some surveys are specifically designed to describe current and potential target groups for certain products; these are often referred to as target group analyses. Others are more general, seeking to describe basic values and life-style characteristics of various segments of the population; these are often referred to as *consumer segmentation strategies*. While the target group analyses are usually ordered and paid for by a particular company, and are thus considered the exclusive property of that company (they cannot be sold twice), consumer segmentation surveys are commercially available to a wide range of subscribers.

Consumer segmentation strategies are of interest, not only to the marketing profession, but also to media institutions and political parties (Lien 1993). In Norway, several different consumer segmentation surveys exist. Some are conducted by market research institutes; others are the property of advertising agencies, and are offered exclusively to the agency's clients. In spite of certain methodological differences, the final results of these surveys are often remarkably similar, dividing the national population into various segments according to value orientation and/or life-style characteristics. Each segment is labelled by terms that differentiate categories of consumers in remarkably similar ways (Lien 1993).

Most consumer segmentation strategies that are available in Norway are linked up with international segmentation surveys with which the Norwegian company cooperates, and from which specific survey questions, analytical concepts and research designs are often derived. Consequently, by hooking up to a consumer segmentation strategy, one is able to compare, for instance, the exact percentages of various subcategories of the population in various countries.

The most successful and influential consumer segmentation

survey in Norway in the early 1990s is *Norwegian Monitor* (Lien 1993). *Norwegian Monitor* is based upon biannual interviews of a representative sample of approximately 3,000 Norwegian adults, carried out by a Norwegian market research institute called 'Markeds og Mediainstituttet' (MMI). MMI also offers other market research services, such as target group analyses and group discussions. The stated aim of *Norwegian Monitor* is 'to understand individual behaviour choices'. On the basis of a theoretical assumption that values are causally related to behaviour, a central part of the survey is a range of operationalizations of 60–70 predefined values (altogether approximately 180 questions). *Norwegian Monitor* is an exploratory survey is an exploratory based upon correspondence analysis, a method that *'seeks to provide a visual image of the relations between the variables, so that each variable is placed close to those which it is positively correlated, and far from those with which it is negatively correlated'* (Hellevik 1991:277). The analysis provides a visual image in which the vertical and horizontal axes reflect underlying dimensions. In *Norwegian Monitor*, the vertical axis is labelled 'modern-traditional', while the horizontal axis is labelled 'materialism–idealism'. In the language of statisticians, the axes represent the dimensions that are most suitable for distinguishing differences in the variables (see Figure 5.6).

Once established, this visual image serves as a conceptual tool that helps to describe not only the relationship between the values, but also that between individual consumers. Each individual respondent may, for instance, be visually located at a point somewhere on the chart, according to his or her average 'score' on each of the two dimensions. The idea that not only values, but also individuals 'belong' somewhere on the map offers a wide range of possibilities regarding target group analysis. Mapping the exact location of all persons who report not eating breakfast in the morning, one may, for instance, find that they tend to concentrate in the upper left corner of the sociograph. By means of further calculations using the arithmetic mean, this cluster may be reduced to a single mean point that shows the value orientation of the typical non-breakfast-eater (see Figure 5.6). If we substitute for non-breakfast-eaters, users of a certain brand of fish products, for example (and list their average scores on each single value, as shown in Figure 5.6), we have an example of a fairly detailed target group analysis.

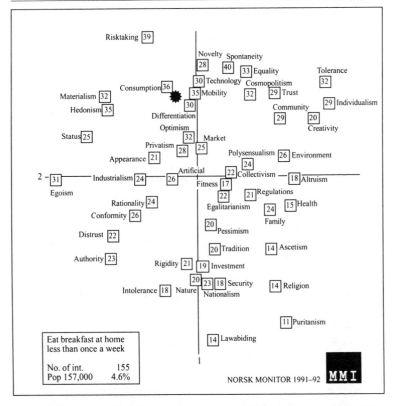

Figure 5.6. An example of a Norwegian Monitor target group analysis. Reproduced with permission from the publisher (Hellevik 1991)

Three characteristic features of *Norwegian Monitor* should be mentioned. First, *Norwegian Monitor* is (like most other consumer segmentation strategies), a presentation of the correlations between selected variables. It describes how certain values tend to appear together, but it does not tell us anything about causal relationships between each value and the behaviour of the target group. Secondly, in spite of its focus upon differentiation (between consumer segments and between values), the arithmetic mean serves as a central underlying tool of the statistical analyses. In *Norwegian Monitor*, the locations of both individual respondents and specific target groups are achieved by means of extensive use of the concept of the mean.[13] Thirdly, while the use of the arithmetic mean implies a consistent translation of qualitative information (value statements) into quantitative measurements, in the final presentation of consumer segmentation strategies these quantitative measurements have once more been translated into 'catchy' phrases. Thus, in all consumer segmentation surveys, categories of consumers that have something in common are systematically referred to as 'consumer segments', and each such group is often described using labels such as, for instance, 'frustrated', 'hedonist', 'mainstream', 'traditional', 'experimental', etc. Needless to say, these labels serve to facilitate presentation of a fairly complicated set of relationships to clients, including product managers in the marketing department. In order to further facilitate presentation, each segment is sometimes illustrated by means of a series of slides and verbal characteristics showing a person who typically represents that particular segment. Thus, 'catchy' labels and slides represent a rich set of stereotyped idioms that dramatically simplify complex statistical information, thus providing the marketing profession with a wide range of images that are 'good to think' (for a critical discussion, see Lien 1993).

In the marketing department, *Norwegian Monitor* is readily available to anyone who needs it. Like most other major manufacturers of consumer goods, Viking Foods is among its subscribers, and pays approximately Norwegian Kroner (NOK) 100,000 annually for regular updates. In spite of its availability, *Norwegian Monitor* is not as widely used as one might expect. Many informants express a certain regret that they do not use it more often:

> *I've read* Norwegian Monitor, *but very superficially, so I don't know it very well. Generally, I think we use it much too seldom. That's too bad. We could have got a lot of 'input' from* Norwegian Monitor, *I'm sure . . . This business is so imprecise ('er så lite eksakt') that wherever we **may** seek information, we **ought to**. Not the least for the sake of our own sense of reflection ('vår egen bevissthet'); reading such things forces you to have an attitude regarding which target group you want to address. Of course, it doesn't always fit, you need common sense as well . . .'* (Marketing Manager).

This statement reflects a general attitude among informants in the marketing department: *Norwegian Monitor* is potentially useful, but not fully utilized. The reasons for this may be several, but some informants emphasize its complexity as a problematic feature. Clearly, the volume of data is massive, and optimal utilization requires that one spends some time studying it. In the light of the experience of a heavy workload among product managers, this time may not be easy to find.

While the usefulness of *Norwegian Monitor* is generally recognized by most informants, many also emphasize its limitations. One of the marketing directors claims that too little time and money is spent on marketing research. He does not apply consumer segmentation strategies very frequently himself, but strongly encourages product managers to do so. When I asked whether he believes in this kind of information he smilingly replies, somewhat hesitantly: *'Well . . . I guess you could say I do. Anyhow, we don't have anything that's better. It's as close to heaven as you can get . . .'.*

Summary

The various metaphors and models of the market, of products and of consumers, are part of a shared set of interrelated categories and concepts that we may loosely refer to as a common pool of knowledge within the marketing department. As such, they serve both as statements about the world 'as it is', and as conceptual tools for incorporating new phenomena into a common classification scheme.

At the same time, the models and metaphors serve as guides for action. As many of the examples clearly illustrate, the division between a description and a guideline is not very sharp. As such, the metaphors and models serve also as tools that help product managers choose (or legitimize the choice) between alternative courses of action.

Metaphors are particularly powerful in mediating between the level of semantic classification and the preverbal experience of a moral domain. Beck (1978) argues that *'metaphors allow us to introduce non-verbal material into logically structured, semantic contexts'* and thus help to *'carry our understanding across the boundaries of verbal thought'* (Beck 1978:87–8). Metaphors such as 'market as battlefield' and 'product as living species' may be perceived as precisely such mediators, drawing upon a preverbal sphere of symbols, and introducing them into a level of strategic discourse and semantic classification.

The common pool of knowledge in the marketing department thus includes not only a set of models and concepts that help to structure and classify vast amounts of information, but also a set of meanings and metaphors that help distinguish between right and wrong, good and bad, in day-to-day choices of actions.

Notes

1. This is illustrated for instance when trying to convince someone else about a certain idea is referred to as 'selling the idea' (Chapter 6), or in the case of competitive presentations (Chapter 10).
2. Nielsen is an international market research company with branches in several countries. Nielsen Norway is a central market research institute in Norway, particularly known for its surveys on sales and market shares.
3. The Norwegian term *skivebom* refers to the field of shooting, depicting the situation when the bullet not only misses the bull's eye, but misses the entire target.
4. In his daily activities, this particular product manager spends more time on production-related activities and less time on marketing activities than the rest.
5. The BCG model referred to in the Marketing Theory textbook differs slightly from the model reproduced in Table 5.2 with regard to the dimension represented by the vertical axis. While informants in the marketing department refer to 'level of investment', Kotler and Armstrong label the vertical axis 'market growth rate' (Kotler and Armstrong 1987:34). Kotler and Armstrong's model corresponds, however, to certain written documents circulating in the marketing department.
6. It is often assumed that the use of brand names is an aspect of capitalist development. This is sometimes substantiated by the absence of brand names in medieval Europe, and by a description of the interrelations between mass consumer markets, the growth of large corporations, and marketing based on brand names as distinctive features of later periods of Western capitalism. According to Hamilton and Lai (1989), historical research from late imperial China has revealed that the notion of brand names is not unique to European capitalism.

The authors argue that brand names (product labels identifying seller, producer, or some claimed advantage of the product) were extensively used in China in the 1800s (and before) as aids in the marketing of products, in a manner that in many ways resembles the use of brand names today (Hamilton and Lai 1989).

7. English term is used.

8. This document was handed to me by the vice-president during an interview. According to him, '*it explains how we think with regard to brand products and brand-building competence*'.

9. During a seminar for the employees and clients of a major Norwegian advertising agency, Tom Blackett, British deputy chairman of Interbrand (consultants on international brand-building) put it this way: '*The entire philosophy around brand products is that the brand is a contract between customer and vendor. The brand guarantees the quality that the customer is looking for*' (*Kampanje*, 11, 1993:40).

10. Brian Moeran emphasizes the dual aspects of brands as well, as he states that '*branding . . . takes place at two different levels simultaneously: one in the sphere of institutional relations, the other in that of material objects*' (Moeran 1996:279).

11. Cited from the notice-board in a product manager's office.

12. In Norwegian, a similar linguistic transition seems to have occurred with regard to a substitution of *kunde* (customer) for the more abstract *forbruker* (consumer) (see also Lien 1994). In the marketing department, the term *kunde* generally refers to the major retail chains, with whom the manufacturer has in fact a regular and continuing relationship, while the term *forbruker* refers to individuals finally purchasing the product in the retail store.

13. Representations using the arithmetic mean are not unproblematic. According to some critics, the arithmetic mean may be a good measurement for phenomena that may be characterized along one quantifiable dimension, such as for example the height of military recruits. If, however, the phenomena in question are heterogeneous, and not easily quantified along one single dimension, the arithmetic mean makes little sense (Feldman *et al.* 1991). As both values and individuals are highly heterogeneous and complex phenomena, this critique applies to consumer segmentation systems as well.

Chapter 6

Materializing Good Ideas: The Poultry Project

The present chapter is an empirical outline and analysis of a series of events referred to as the poultry project (*'fjørfeprosjektet'*). It is a case study that exemplifies how a rather vague idea of 'making something with poultry' gradually materialized into a range of products offered on the market. The poultry project was started shortly before the start of my fieldwork period, and I was able to follow it throughout a period of almost two years. The poultry project provides an empirical example of a material product that is still very much in the making, thus offering an opportunity to explore the fruitfulness of analytical concepts derived from the constructionist approach.

Although the ultimate evaluation of a product takes place after the product has been launched on the market, there are many products 'in the making' that never get that far. When they don't, it is generally because of a lack of internal support necessary to carry it through the preliminary phases. During the first stages of product development, internal support is crucial. Product development projects are both costly and time-consuming, and the decision to allocate resources to the project requires a considerable confidence in the specific concept, or product idea.

Support for a particular project is ensured both through extensive documentation suggesting that the particular product will align key interests involved, and through the less tangible element of confidence inherent in personal relations, and particularly in the persons who are most heavily involved in project implementation. In the following cases, I will refer to such persons as the *prime movers* of the projects.[1]

The product development process implies phases of uncertainty, in which criteria for evaluation are actively searched for. I refer to these moments as stages of interpretative flexibility, representing temporary controversies concerning the characteristics of the product. Presenting the case, I will focus especially on such moments, when decisive criteria are being sought, and when major decisions are being legitimized. This allows a chronological outline, and opens up the ground for a comparison with other cases as well.

Norwegian Poultry Consumption: Conspicuous by its Absence

Compared to that in other countries, the consumption of poultry in Norway is exceptionally low. This was particularly salient around 1990, when Norway had the lowest per capita poultry consumption in the industrialized world. According to statistical material assembled in the marketing department, an average Norwegian consumed approximately 4.5 kg. of poultry in 1989. This was considerably lower than comparable figures from other countries at the time, including Sweden and Finland (6 kg./person/year), Denmark (12.5 kg./person/year), England and France (approx. 20 kg./person/year) and the USA (38 kg./person/year).

In the early 1990s, poultry products in Norway were primarily chicken. Turkey was only available frozen and whole, and other varieties of turkey products were practically non-existent. Chicken was also primarily available whole, either frozen, or freshly barbecued in the grocery store. In addition, barbecued chicken wings were a relatively popular and inexpensive snack. Furthermore, a frozen product range of various types of marinated chicken, ready to heat in the oven, had recently been introduced on the market, and was acquiring a significant market share. This product was launched by PRIOR, a farmers' cooperative organization with an overall market share in poultry raw material of almost 90 per cent. Fresh chicken, and selected parts of chicken (thighs, breast) were practically unavailable.

Case 1: The Poultry Project

A written document dated July 1991 marks the beginning of the poultry project. Referred to as the *'poultry project plan'*, the

document states the main content, purpose and resources involved
in what is later to be referred to as 'The Poultry Project'. The
document is written by Erik and Erling,[2] a product manager and
a former product development director who will be actively
engaged in implementing the project. The poultry project plan
opens as follows:

> *It has been decided that Viking Foods will carry out a serious total evaluation
> ('seriøs totalvurdering') of the poultry market, and of how we may utilize
> poultry as raw material in our production systems. We believe in the potential
> of the raw material ('råstoffet'), and it is therefore important for us to establish
> products with our trade mark ('varemerke') in the market before the expected
> import liberalization takes place.*

This opening statement refers a major decision, with significant
consequences for the allocation of resources, in terms of both
financial and personal engagement. By the time poultry products
were launched on the market a few years later, several million
NOK had been spent on the project, not including the salaries of
the personnel involved. However, upon writing the poultry project
plan, the product manager had no guarantee that the project would
ever be carried this far. All he knew was that the group of
managing directors had agreed to *start* the project. As I will soon
demonstrate, the *continuation* of the project would have to be
ensured many times yet. But first, let us take a closer look at the
introductory statement in order to elicit what this major decision
entails.

According to the introductory statement, *'we'* (i.e. Viking Foods)
will do something with an object, i.e. *'poultry raw material'*, in order
to achieve what is important to us, namely to *'establish products
with our trade mark in the market'*. What starts out as *'raw material'*
will, through some kind of transformation process that includes
'utilization in our production systems', be turned into *'products with
our trade mark'*. The market serves as the context within which this
goal is to be achieved. In a sense, the entire introductory statement
may be read as a presentation of a strategy for creating a new
linkage between 'us' and 'the market' by means of a certain
material transformation of 'poultry raw material' into 'products
with our trade mark'.

The advisability of establishing *'products with our trade mark in
the market'* is partly grounded in *'our belief in the potential of the raw*

material'. However, this belief is not sufficient to carry the entire project through, as it needs to be confirmed through a *'serious total evaluation of the poultry market'*. Continuation of the project thus depends on whether or not further investigations confirm the initial 'belief'. In the present context 'the market' represents both an *object of study*, and *an arena* in which it is important that Viking Foods' products are present (see Chapter 5).

According to the project plan, the activities should be timed in such a way that they precede the occurrence of another anticipated event, namely the import liberalization that is expected to take place. As was indicated in Chapter 3, this anticipated event serves as a key legitimator for several other activities as well. Note, however, that nobody knows yet *when* it will take place, *how* it will alter the present state of affairs, or even *whether* it will take place at all.

In the project plan, *'we'* refers rather loosely to Viking Foods. Later on we are introduced to three persons who will *'work with the project in the present phase'*, including Erik, Erling and a third person called Terje, a vice-president of the firm, whose involvement in project implementation will, as we shall see, be rather marginal.

In addition to these prime movers, an advisory group (*'styringsgruppe'*) has also been established. This group consists mostly of persons who hold central positions in management, and includes Terje, a staff director and two marketing directors from two different marketing departments. As it turns out, this advisory group will have a central function internally in supervising the proceedings, supporting (or opposing) major decisions and ensuring the allocation of resources to the project.

Why Poultry?

In the poultry project plan, poultry raw material (*'råstoffet'*) refers to chicken and turkey; two categories of slaughtered birds that are used as main ingredients in cooking in many parts of the world. Why does a group of marketing professionals suddenly state that they *'believe in the potential of'* this particular raw material? What is it about poultry that makes it interesting just now?

Studying the subsequent paragraphs of the project plan, we learn that the belief in poultry is substantiated by reference to three significant features of the Norwegian 'poultry market'. Firstly, PRIOR dominates the Norwegian poultry market, with a market share of 88 per cent. However, according to the document, PRIOR *does not seem to be interested in products with a higher degree of processing ("høyere foredlinggrad") than "Lørdagskylling"*.[3] Secondly, per capita poultry consumption is significantly lower in Norway than in other countries, such as Sweden, Denmark, England and the US. Thirdly, the present sale of poultry products on the Norwegian market is claimed to exhibit a *'significant growth'* (5–6 per cent per year).

Looking more closely at the three statements, we find that two of them depict a kind of absence. First of all, PRIOR, which holds a dominant position, seems to have no interest in poultry products that are processed beyond a certain degree. Secondly, a brief comparison with other nations quickly indicates a relative lack of demand for poultry in Norway.

In order to explain how this apparent absence of both consumers' and producers' interest in poultry products may serve to substantiate an alleged potential of poultry, we must turn once again to conceptualizations of the market. According to the introductory statement, the overarching purpose of the present endeavour is to *'establish products with our trade mark in the market'*. In the present context, the *'market'* serves as a spatial metaphor, a territorial context, in which *'products with our trade mark'* are to be located. The proposed timing, apparently reflecting a strategic consideration, further indicates that the presence of others is a potential threat, thus evoking metaphors of limited space (see Chapter 5). In the light of these metaphoric structures, the idea of absence may be understood as an *empty space waiting to be filled*.

However, the profitability of filling empty spaces would not be very promising without a concurrent anticipation of change. Obviously, one might argue that a relatively low level of demand for poultry products among Norwegian consumers might as well serve as an argument *not* to invest in poultry production. In the present case, however, this negative discrepancy is interpreted as an indication of future growth, rather than as indifference towards poultry as such! This is further substantiated by an annual growth (5–6 per cent) in the sales of poultry products. In other words, there is an implicit expectation that what goes up will continue to go up. Secondly, by basing the argument on a comparison of average per capita consumption in Norway and other countries, we may note an implicit assumption that differences in consumption between nations will eventually level out. While the former assumption rests on an extrapolation of current changes into the future, the latter rests on an anticipation of global homogenization of food consumption patterns. When applied together, these principles indicate that average Norwegian poultry consumption will continue to increase until it reaches a level of consumption that is closer to that of other nations.

Written by the product manager, the poultry project plan serves both as a temporal outline of tasks to be done, and as a piece of background information providing the rationale for the project at an early stage. Thus, it serves both as a guide for future action, a contract-like statement of tasks and responsibilities, and a statement ensuring legitimacy *vis-à-vis* resource allocators. As we have seen, the conceptualization of the market as a spatial territory, a territory in which the presence of Viking Foods products must be ensured, serves as a basic understanding on which the subsequent decisions and activities are founded. Basically, the role of the prime movers may be interpreted as that of ensuring Viking Foods' presence in this market (provided that it is profitable to 'be there'). This is ensured through a transformation of raw material into *'products with our trade mark'*.

As Machiavellian princes engage in fights to defend their territory, and to acquire territories that are new, so too must the product manager constantly be prepared to fight for a product's presence in the market. While the territory of the Machiavellian princes may be easily delineated geographically, the 'territory' of the product managers is defined by market metaphors.

Phase 1: Carcasses and Calculations: Acquiring Technological Know-how

The less a man has relied on fortune, the stronger he has made his position (Machiavelli 1961:50).

Once the introductory project plan is signed and approved of as a contractual document, an intensive effort at gathering information begins. According to the project plan, the key to profitability in poultry lies in 'optimal utilization of the carcass' (*'optimal utnyttelse av slaktet'*). The problem, however, is that Viking Foods' department of product development has no previous experience or competence with poultry products. Consequently, they will have to acquire competence and knowledge in a field with which they are as yet unfamiliar.

Many issues need to be clarified, such as: Which suppliers deliver the most suitable raw material? What is the optimal weight of the slaughtered birds with regard to further processing and profitability? How should the birds be cut in order to utilize the various parts most efficiently? What are the costs of various phases of the production process? What are the various possibilities of final products to be made from the different poultry parts? And what are the advantages and disadvantages of turkey vs. chicken? All these questions pertain directly to an overarching goal of profitability, and may be subsumed under the overarching question: *How do we utilize the poultry carcass most efficiently?*

In order to learn more about this, Erik and Erling basically do two things:

1. They communicate intensively in order to gather information about the general structure of poultry production both in Norway and abroad, and thus learn to know the poultry raw material indirectly, through the experience of others. Talking implies travelling, and this takes them to major poultry production plants in Europe and in the US, to annual international food conferences (see also Chapter 8). In the mean time, relationships to other actors in the field are established, both domestically and abroad. International specialized journals serve as another key source of information, in addition to written correspondence with other actors in the field. On the national level, suppliers of poultry raw material are particularly important sources of information.
2. They launch a six-week test production in a nearby laboratory in order to explore the nature and technological potential of poultry raw material. Through direct experiments with the raw material they accumulate what they consider to be indispensable experience and competence in poultry.

Test production starts on a Tuesday morning with the delivery of 53 slaughtered turkeys in two different sizes. In a fully equipped product development laboratory, eight turkeys of each variety are immediately cut and sorted into piles of meat, skin, bones and fat. An external consultant, Mr Biehl, known for his experience with poultry, does most of the cutting. Once the carcass is divided according to these categories, each type of material is handed over to two female laboratory assistants, who carefully weigh each pile of turkey raw material, and record the results in a laboratory journal. This information will later be used to calculate the profitability of various types of poultry carcass (*'utbyttekalkyle'*).

The meat is further divided into categories of breast filet, thighs and so-called MUK,[4] each of which serves as a basis for further processing. During the next few days, some parts of meat are marinated, cut, dipped in so-called 'Pandora' batter, flash-fried, frozen and vacuum wrapped individually. Other parts are prepared as so-called 'American boneless turkey breast' which implies that the part is roasted with the skin left on. Other parts are simply marinated and frozen for later use. Each procedure is carefully recorded, and each part which is wrapped and frozen is marked by type and date.

Test production continues during the next weeks, and is only interrupted by regular deliveries of slaughtered birds. Throughout the subsequent weeks, more than 70 turkeys and more than 500 chicken carcasses from four different suppliers are processed according to a tight and detailed schedule. At the end of the six weeks, raw material has been transformed into a variety of possible products, most of which are retrievable from the freezer, varying slightly in terms of ingredients and modes of preparation. Furthermore, selected parts of the labour process have also been subject to investigation, so that it is now possible to compare the time involved in for example, cutting turkey vs. cutting chicken. In addition, all possible products are recorded on a list, prepared by Erling, which includes no less than 110 varieties of turkey and chicken, featuring tenderloin steaks, batter-fried fillets, Chinese marinated chicken wings, Cajun marinated thighs, turkey wieners, turkey meat balls, chicken steaklet, chicken pâté, cold cuts, ham and much more.

Most of these products exemplify levels of processing that far exceed what is available in Norwegian food stores at the time. How do they come up with the new varieties? Erling explains that he tries out practically everything he can think of. Some of the products are varieties that he has previously made with pork. Others are varieties that he has picked up by studying poultry magazines, or seen in foreign supermarkets. Another important source of ideas is people in the trade:

Erling: *When I meet people who sell, for instance, breading-machines, or a particular range of marinades, I ask them about their experiences in the market. Such as, for instance, what other manufacturers are up to. And I make contacts with food manufacturers abroad, and learn from their experiences.*

Much of what he creates may thus be described as constructing copies of poultry products sold elsewhere.[5] In addition, through his experience with other meats (pork, beef), Erling has acquired a considerable repertoire of meat dishes. On the basis of this repertoire, he is able to construct copies of other meat products, the only difference being that this time they are made with poultry. As we shall see, this difference is sometimes not even detectable.

During this initial phase of the poultry project, the prime movers have gained some knowledge about how poultry products may be utilized. This implies that they have learned more about the nature and interests of a potential ally. In accordance with Latour (1988) allies may be defined as human or non-human actors whose interests or characteristics must be explored in order to ensure future alignment. Furthermore, it is fruitful to distinguish between primary and secondary allies. Primary allies are human or non-human actors whose final cooperation and alignment is crucial in order for the project to succeed. By secondary allies we refer to human or non-human actors whose cooperation or alignment is subsidiary to the continuation of the project.

The question of how to utilize poultry carcasses most efficiently (profitably) could not have been answered without consulting the turkeys and chickens themselves. The first phase thus introduces poultry raw material as a primary ally. At this point the specific nature of this ally is merely explored, through careful scrutiny of its content of fat, skins, bones, its physical and texture reactions to various treatments with heat, its ability to absorb various types of marinades, its physical appearance after various transformations and so on. These explorations will later be evaluated in order to decide whether and how the distinctive features of these non-human allies can be aligned with the broader interests of Viking Foods. At the moment, however, their distinctive features must simply be explored, or, as Latour puts it: 'localised in advance' (see Chapter 1).

In addition, we may introduce the concept of intermediary translators, defined as actors who are central to processes of translation between prime movers and their primary allies. The process of getting to know the characteristics of chicken and turkey carcasses involves a group of external product development consultants who serve as an intermediary link between the carcasses and the prime movers. Possessing specific competence in the field of food technology, they are able to explore and evaluate the raw material more professionally than the product development staff at Viking Foods. In this process, however, it is crucial that they describe their findings in a manner that the prime movers can make use of. In this way, the external product development consultants may be described as *intermediary translators* between the poultry raw material and the prime movers.

Phase 2: What Should Poultry Taste Like?

Test production has revealed some general features of turkey vs. chicken meat that enable Erling to predict more accurately how various types of raw material will respond to various kinds of treatment. He now knows exactly the amount of marinade that may be injected, and he also knows the extent to which various amounts alter the flavour. Furthermore, on the basis of his recently acquired knowledge about the differences between chicken and turkey, he now tends to favour chicken.

When test production is over, Erik and Erling get together in a meeting room in the marketing department, along with an assistant from the department of product development. Erling and the assistant have brought sheets of notes, which specify each variety by number, raw material and a brief description of the type of dish and the mode of preparation.

This marks the beginning of what I will refer to as the second phase, a process of narrowing down an almost infinite range of possible culinary varieties to a limited range of products with which they may proceed. In the present description, this phase lasts more than seven months, and includes a series of product presentation meetings taking place both during and after events described in subsequent sections. However, we should bear in mind that this phase is never quite finished, as products on the market are subject to continuous modification (see also Chapter 8).

The purpose of the present meeting is to select a limited range of varieties that may be presented to the advisory group, and a range of varieties that may be presented to consumers as part of a so-called qualitative survey (*'kvalitativ undersøkelse'*). In addition, they need to 'outline a strategy for selling the ideas further within the system'[6] (*'legge opp en strategi for å selge idéene videre i systemet'*).

The meeting starts with a detailed reading of the list of poultry varieties. Erling briefly presents each case and his assistant occasionally adds some information, while Erik alternatively nods, takes notes, and asks questions. The friendly and informal atmosphere of the meeting gives the impression of close companions working together towards a common goal. Someone else within the organization needs to be convinced about something, and this requires close cooperation. We may note, however, a certain sobriety on the part of Erik that stands in contrast to the enthusiasm of the other two.

Going through the list of 110 poultry product varieties, Erling informs the audience that some of the varieties have already been crossed off. They are what he calls *'fiasko'* (flops, failures) that either taste bad, look bad, or have other obvious disadvantages. This leaves them with a list of 72 products, out of which some are described as a success, while others are in the 'twilight zone', i.e. *'we have got to do something with it'*. As they go through the list, they categorize the 72 products, first according to whether they are made from turkey or chicken, and then according to subcategories such as whole chicken, chicken breast, tenderloin, chicken wings, chicken thighs, mixed ground meat products (turkey and chicken combined), turkey breast, turkey thighs and turkey wings, each category consisting of 3–15 products. In the end, they have a list of 21 different turkey products, 37 chicken products, and 15 products that are combinations of the two. Now the discussion focuses on the relative advantage of using chicken compared to turkey.

Erling: *Chicken gives us a greater range of products to choose from; as you can see, there is a greater number of chicken products on the list. Furthermore, I think it is easier to make people eat chicken than turkey. American turkey breast[7] could only be sold in some specialty stores in Oslo now. But chicken wings[8] can be sold anywhere, I promise you . . . When it comes to turkey, there is always turkey pastrami. When we can replace something else it is easier . . .*

Erik: *I agree that it is probably better to go via chicken, turkey is too foreign ('fremmed') for the Norwegian consumer, it would be going too far . . .*

Erling: (Looking at some notes) *Look, with the prices we can obtain for the residual chicken meat ('avskjær'), we will be able to sell the breast fillets at a very nice price. Especially if we can inject a marinade. And then we can sell chicken wings via fast-food[9] . . . According to my calculations one piece of marinated breast fillet will be about 150 grams, that means exactly one serving!* [Smiling . . .] *That is a great advantage!* [pause] *As for the sausages, poultry meat has a greater capacity for absorbing liquid than pork. This means that we can use less meat! But there is another problem. We are no longer allowed to call it 'wiener'. Not 'hamburger'[10] either.[11] We have to solve this somehow, otherwise we can just forget about the whole thing . . .* [pause] *Then there is PRIOR. Up until now we have accepted the price of 33 NOK/kg. But we know it is less expensive to make big chickens . . . We should be able to document this, however, before we enter into negotiations with PRIOR.*

Erik: *Well, about the qualitative market research. We should decide upon the varieties that we can pass on to group discussions. And I think it is important that we go out and gather some of the attitudes that we expect might be there. On turkey as well. And on the mixed products.*

Erling: *When I say I think we should go for chicken it is because I think it is much more difficult to make people eat something new, than to give them something that substitutes for something else . . .*

Shortly afterwards, they go through the list of products once more, in order to pick out the varieties for the presentation in the qualitative survey. As a general rule, a few varieties within each subcategory are included. When in doubt, they pick what someone says they prefer, unless someone else objects. For instance, having to choose between two kinds of meatballs, 104a and 104b, in which the former is more spicy, Erling suggests:

Erling: *104b is more like a 'Hokksund' variety,[12] so let's go for 104a.*
Erik: *I don't think we should do that in the present phase.*
Erling: *OK, let's take 104b.*
Erik: *Which of the turkey breast varieties are better? Smoked or not smoked?*
Erling: [Pointing to a smoked variety] *105a.* [Pause]
Erik: *Now, how many products do we have altogether?*
Erling: *13 chicken varieties and 8 turkey varieties.*

Erik:	*That's too many, but all right, we'll leave it at that.*
Erling:	*Make sure you try out the whole range though . . .*
Erik:	*Yes, except for chicken wings, because they are sold anyway.*
Erling:	*OK, what you say sounds convincing . . . When we meet the advisory group, shouldn't our aim be to present what we have done, and what we are planning to do?*
Assistant:	*Are we going to have an internal presentation?*
Erling:	*I'm allergic to internal presentations . . .*
Erik:	*I think there are so few people who really are involved, so we'll just get too many opinions in all directions . . . But when it comes to the advisory group, we have to prepare these products and let them taste. And that goes for the other marketing managers as well . . .*

While test production was directed at exploring and getting to know the raw material, the present challenge consists in summarizing and translating this experience in a way that makes it presentable both to the advisory group and to consumers who will participate in qualitative group discussions at a later stage. This implies a transformation of poultry raw material into a specified range of culinary concepts. The process of reducing the list of varieties from 110 to 72 potential products, and then selecting 21 presentable prototypes, may be described as a *tentative closing of controversies*. It is tentative in the sense that it is not considered as a final or irreversible decision: rejected prototypes may still be re-included. Yet it is necessary in order for the project to proceed.

During the process of selecting products for presentation, a range of different considerations have been taken into account. As the above quotations indicate, the arguments touch upon widely different dimensions, such as consumer preferences, taste varieties, possible points of sale, the absorption capacity of poultry vs. pork, culinary classification, legal regulations, production costs, price of raw materials, supplies of raw materials, and ways of presenting results to the advisory group. During test production, *material issues had systematically been treated separately from social and cultural issues* (i.e. material features of the raw material were explored *without* simultaneous considerations of consumer preference). Now, as the prime movers strive to make a coherent presentation, these different issues are brought together, thus exposing (to us and to them) some of the complexities involved.

The fact that poultry raw material has now been 'translated' into a preliminary range of culinary concepts does not imply that a final decision can be reached. As the discussion reveals, there are still many unresolved controversies with regard to the potential of the various culinary varieties, and to the relative advantages of chicken vs. turkey. In order to be able to proceed from here, two things need to be done. First of all, the advisory group must be convinced that the project idea still has potential in order to extend their support. Secondly, the interests and preferences of potential consumers must be explored. As the support of both of these actors is crucial for the project to succeed, we may refer to these as primary allies as well. I shall return to these in the phases three and four. But first, we need to conclude the second phase.

Exploring and evaluating different culinary concepts is a long process, including, among other things, four internal product presentation meetings in which colleagues are invited to taste the products and state their opinion. Let us consider one of these meetings, taking place a few months later.

At two o'clock in the afternoon, a group of people gather together in the canteen of the administration building of Viking Foods. The group includes several product managers, a marketing manager, Erling, Erik and myself. One of the tables is already set with plates, knives, forks, glasses and a huge pile of napkins. Several bottles of mineral water are placed on the table as well.[13] On another table there are six large trays with cuts of cold meat, all differing slightly in colour and appearance. We sit down, and Erik explains that the purpose of the meeting is to gather some responses to the product range, and to get some advice as to which varieties to develop further. Erling invites us to go ahead and help ourselves to the cold cuts, when Erik interrupts: '— *Hey, wait a minute, we've got to try the products one after the other to get some order out of this, otherwise it will just be confusing . . . '*.

He hands out a piece of paper to everyone, which contains a list of 17 different products, all numbered and briefly described, and suggests that we start out by comparing numbers one, two and three, which are: 'honey-marinated turkey', 'sauna-smoked turkey' and 'herbmarinated turkey provençale'. He then invites everyone to try the different varieties, and share their opinions. Below is an extract from the discussion:

Partic. A: *Compare three against one and two. I think the white colour looks sick.*
Erik: *But that is the natural one.*

Partic. A: *I know, but it looks sick . . . Pale . . .*
Erling: *It may be that the sugar in the honey-marinated variety gives a different colour. Only number two has nitrate. One and three don't.*
Partic. B: *Well, number one doesn't taste like honey. It shouldn't be called something with honey if it doesn't taste like honey.*
Erling: *Anyway, these cuts of meat are the kind that you would find in supermarkets in France and the USA. That's where they come really far on this.*

Every piece of food is served and tasted individually, followed only by mineral water or coffee to drink. Each item is thus removed from the context in which it is likely to be consumed, whether dinner or breakfast. This discontinuity between the items and their context contributes in making the event seem more like a laboratory experiment than a shared meal. Then turkey ham is introduced.

Erling: *This turkey ham contains some MUK. That makes it a little less expensive than the first varieties we just tried.*
Partic. C: *This tastes just like regular ham.*
Partic. D: *But is that an advantage or a disadvantage?*
Partic. C: *That's what I'm wondering . . .*
Partic. E: *It would be interesting to get out some attitudes on this.*
Erik: *Are you saying that we should go out and get another qualitative?*[14]

The cook announces that the hot marinated ratatouille is ready. He brings two different tin foil boxes to the table, one with whole chicken breast, the other with chicken pieces:

Partic. B: *This is good. I like this. But the whole cut is much nicer to look at.*
Erling: *Well, the reason I cut it, is that it is very difficult to find a piece that weighs exactly 180 grams, while when I cut it I can get the exact amount into the box . . .*

Then a variety of turkey sausages is placed on the table.

Partic. C: *We tried a low-fat variety of sausages ('pølser') once. We increased the meat content, reduced fat content, with no significant price increase. It didn't work.*
Partic. D: *Maybe it would work in a long-term perspective?*

Partic. C: *Maybe, but I think you get a problem of communication with healthy sausages. Sausages are perceived as being definitely not good for you.*

Partic. D: *I think you're right. We shouldn't try to jump the fence where it's highest . . .*

Erik: *All right, we'll drop the sausages for now.*

Hot chicken nuggets are presented.

Partic. A: *Why do they all have to look alike? Couldn't we make some different shapes? They look so . . . industrially produced.*

Erling: *That should be possible.*

The above discussion illustrates how the products at this stage are still extremely flexible, in terms of both symbolic and material features. It reveals the extent to which the material and symbolic dimensions of the product are closely intertwined. Furthermore, the discussion points to some dilemmas inherent in modern food manufacture, related to authenticity vs. imitation, and naturalness vs. artificiality. However, neither of the arguments seem to lead up to any final decision. Rather, the comments tend to switch abruptly from one theme to another, introducing a wide variety of criteria.

At the same time, we may read the entire sequence as a collective attempt at making order out of something which is, at this point slightly unfamiliar and highly 'unorderly' (Law 1994). Even though no final order is achieved yet, many of the comments categorize the material items in terms of overarching categories ('good' from 'bad') or seek to define the criteria that may be used for this purpose (defining what 'advantageous' implies).

The first comment, about the sick white colour, is clearly a subjective statement. When Erik interrupts, saying that the white colour is, in fact, the natural colour of the turkey, this is not so much an evaluation of the product itself, but rather a way of questioning the criterion that has just been applied. Being natural is implicitly something good; and may possibly serve as a point of reference that *justifies* a sick white colour. Erling makes it clear, however, that colours are the result of chemical processes that may be modified. Thus he reminds us that the products and their characteristics are still very much in the making. The comment on whether something that doesn't taste like honey should be called 'honey' emphasizes the interpretative flexibility even more. Neither names nor material characteristics are defined at this point. Erling's comment about similar products in France and the US suggests that the markets in those countries serve as another point of reference.

Still, the introduction of a new product inevitably brings up the question: What should turkey ham taste like? In other words: Which criteria ought to be applied? Indecision at this point makes someone suggest that they should 'get out some attitudes on this'. Consumers' attitudes may thus provide another point of reference from which to proceed.

However, consumers' attitudes are not only revealed by market research. Many comments imply a reference to consumers, even when this is not explicitly stated. For instance, the comment about the shape of hot chicken nuggets, which suggests that they should not look so 'industrially produced', makes little sense if it is interpreted only as a statement about subjective opinion. All the products are intended for industrial production, and all participants are fully aware of this. Rather, the statement should be interpreted as a response to the reactions that the product evokes in the participant *as a consumer*. It is as if the person temporarily switches out of the role of a professional in the food marketing business, and looks at the chicken nuggets from a consumer's point of view. What is in fact a subjective reaction to the shapes of chicken nuggets becomes a legitimate and relevant statement because it is interpreted as a reflection of the reactions that the product evokes in the person *as consumer*.[15]

But there is also a third way in which the consumers' opinion may be heard: namely, through previous marketing failure. Commenting upon the sausages, one of the participants shares her experiences with an unsuccessful attempt to launch low-fat sausages. According to the discussion, consumers perceive sausages as unhealthy, and low-fat (or turkey-) sausages therefore cause a problem of communication. Nobody claims that this cannot be changed, but it is no easy task, and might as well be avoided ('you shouldn't jump the fence where it's highest'). The final agreement that hot dogs should be dropped may thus be attributed primarily to the assumed opinions of consumers as they are expressed through a previous lack of demand. Previous experiences in marketing thus provide knowledge, which may serve as points of reference for future decision-making.

The product presentation meeting is an occasion at which persons with peripheral knowledge of the poultry project are invited to state their opinions. In the light of this, we should not be surprised that the applicability of the comments is limited. When I asked Erik, a few days afterwards, whether the meeting was useful to him, he replied:

> *Not at all. Nothing comes out of it. You just get even more confused. The only point, really, in having such a presentation is taking care of the information duties within the organization ('å ivareta informasjonsplikten internt'). You must at least give people a feeling that they have a say on the final outcome. And to some extent give in to their different wishes. Because it is necessary that people believe in the products. Otherwise there is no point . . .*

Phase 3: Confronting the Consumers: What do they Want?

> *[The Prince] must always be out hunting, . . . learning some practical geography: how the mountains slope, how the valleys open, how the plains spread out . . . If he obtains a clear understanding of local geography he will have a better understanding of how to organize his defence* (Machiavelli 1961:88).

As soon as Erik and Erling have narrowed down the range of poultry products, Erik starts planning a qualitative survey. But how is this achieved? How are the likes and dislikes of potentially four million Norwegian consumers translated into a useful tool for internal decision-making? Let us take a closer look at what happened.

First of all, there is an undisputed agreement in the marketing department that consumers must be approached professionally (see also Chapter 5). This implies that the whole task is going to be carried out by a commercial market research institute. The product manager mentions two market research institutes, and ends up selecting one that has previously provided him with services of this kind. He then writes a letter to the market research institute to suggest a strategy of implementation.

The letter informs them about the background for the poultry project, and the product development work that has been undertaken. Furthermore, it defines the general purpose of the qualitative survey as: *'our need for knowledge about general consumer attitudes ("generelle forbrukerholdninger")* to turkey and chicken products, including concrete attitudes to our prototype products that are new on the market'. Consumer attitudes are to be elicited from a target group consisting of: 'Women and men, ages 18–50, modern (urban) people, relatively open towards new products'.

In addition, a wide range of questions are suggested, including common ways of using chicken and turkey, attitudes towards nutrition and price, dissatisfaction with the poultry products that are already available, etc. The questions also touch upon an anticipated dilemma related to nutrition vs. battered and pre-fried products, and the extent to which industrial processing may destroy the healthy profile of the product.

This letter marks the beginning of a three-week period of negotiations with the market research institute, including first a preliminary meeting, then one at which a specified description of services and cost is provided by the market research institute, and finally a preparatory meeting in which details of implementation of the qualitative inquiry are discussed. During these negotiations it is decided that the survey will be arranged as group discussions with men and women separately. According to the market research institute, the traditional female role as an expert in the field of cooking might cause men to feel a need to demonstrate their capabilities, and thus distort the discussion into a competition of 'who knows best'. In addition, the women will be split according to age, yielding a final set-up of three groups: women aged 22–35, women aged 38–46, and men aged 24–50, each consisting of 6–7 persons, and all referred to as 'respondents'.

The preparatory meeting is organized as a combined discussion meeting and product presentation, and its primary purpose is to select products that are to be served at the qualitative group discussions. This takes place in the so-called VIP room, a room next to the Viking Foods canteen that is equipped as a dining room. Two female consultants from the market research institute attend, together with Erik, Erling, the assistant, two other product managers at Viking Foods who have an interest in the project and myself. One of the market research institute consultants presents herself as 'one who knows about qualitative methods', explaining later that she is a sociologist, while the other is 'on the consulting side'. Erling and his assistant prepare the dishes, while the others join the table.

Erling suggests that we try the products, one after the other, in order to decide which are best. He adds that we should not worry about details such as too much spice, as those things can be adjusted later, but wants us to focus instead on the major issues (*'de store linjer'*). Seventeen different poultry products are served, one after the other. Each dish is already described on a photocopy hand-out with its name and number, grouped according to whether it falls into the category of snacks, cold cuts, fancy dinners or inexpensive dinners. The comments touch upon practically all aspects of the dishes, from material content to anticipated consumer preference.

The debate focuses on why anyone would eat these products, such as for instance meat balls made of chicken: Because these are nutritious? Or because they like meat balls? After a while, the market research institute sociologist closes the argument by concluding that this raises a number of interesting issues, such as: *'Is this economical food? Is it convenience food? Or is the poultry content a benefit in itself?'* Going through the list once more, and reasoning back and forth a little, she finally picks out a total of fourteen product prototypes that will be presented to the consumers. Two of these will only be presented visually, while the other twelve will also be served.

A few days later, qualitative group discussions take place in the office premises of the market research institute, located on one of the busiest squares in the centre of Oslo. Most of the discussions are scheduled in the afternoon, after working hours. Erik and Erling are both invited to attend in order to watch the discussion through a one-way screen, but this time they do not take this opportunity. As the entire event is recorded, they will have the possibility of watching the discussion on video instead. According to Erik, the persons attending these group discussions are literally 'picked up from the street'.

A few days later, Erik receives a report of approximately thirty typed pages, called *'Report from 3 Group Discussions with Consumers: The Poultry Project'*. In the written report, the issue of recruitment is not touched upon. The samples are structured in terms of a strategic variation with regard to age, sex, civil status and parenthood. In the summary of the report we learn, among other things, that:

- *Chicken is primarily convenient, tasty, something everybody likes. Chicken is for some 'good housewives' considered so convenient that it doesn't even count as a proper dinner ('ordentlig middag').*

- *Turkey is first and foremost festive food, New Year's Eve, for big parties, hard to cut nicely, hard to find suitable trimmings for, and often dry. Some mention that turkey is hard to find in the stores when it is not Christmas time.*
- *Turkey would be more frequently used if it were sold in smaller portions.*
- *The general idea of new products and new (smaller) cuts of both turkey and chicken is warmly welcomed by the respondents. It is, however, hard for them to accept 'copies' of already existing meat dishes. Products of pure poultry (100 per cent meat) are very well received, particularly products of pure turkey meat. The expectation with regard to chicken seems to be closely linked to barbecued chicken.*
- *The idea of an inexpensive and convenient dinner that is also low on fat is very well received. Distrust and flavour are, however, also key considerations. Those who are 'sceptical towards sausages' are 'more sceptical towards chicken sausages'.*
- *The use of relatively large cuts (breasts and wings) raises some scepticism regarding hormones and unnatural methods of production. This is especially salient with regard to marinated chicken breasts.*
- *Breaded products are generally received with some scepticism, particularly with regard to amount of breading (compared to meat) and 'fatty' flavour.*

When Erik and Erling get together to discuss the report, Erling is quite surprised:

Erling: *I was proud when we made the sausage taste like pork even when it was turkey. But now, look, they react against imitations! Furthermore, they are sceptical towards large chickens, because they worry about whether they have been treated with hormones. But they don't have such worries about turkey.*

Erik: *This is important.*

Gradually, they are convinced that with regard to consumer attitudes, turkey seems to be more promising than chicken:

Erling: *It looks like people have a very special relationship to chicken. It seems like chicken is partly expected to be barbecued.*

Erik: *As for sausages, it is quite obvious that we cannot call it 'middag-spølse' (dinner sausage). And 'filet' is a better word than 'biff' (steak).*

> *I am surprised at the extent to which people seem to think in terms of products which already exist.*
>
> Erling: *There is a basic scepticism towards industrially produced foods all through this material. Well, this gives the industry something to work on. Because they are partly right, we have been squeezed on prices . . . ('vi har vært så presset på pris').*

While phase one implied an exploration of poultry raw material, the present phase may be analysed as a similar exploration of consumers. Just as 570 dead birds are expected to reveal some true characteristics of an infinite population of chicken and turkey carcasses, 19 invited persons are expected to reveal the opinions of a population of Norwegian adults. In this way, 'consumers' may be analysed as yet another primary ally whose interests and characteristics need to be explored.[16]

One could argue that the nature of these two primary allies differs fundamentally, one being alive and human, the other dead and non-human. I will contend, however, that from the perspective of the prime movers, the degree to which turkey meat will absorb a salty marinade is not in any significant manner different from the degree to which a female consumer aged 30 will accept chicken sausage as a proper dinner. This is not because they are similar *in themselves*, but because their respective characteristics are *translated* in a similar manner. Pieces of information regarding weight, texture, appearance and other characteristics of poultry raw material have been translated from crude numbers to complex calculations and evaluations. At the same time, the raw material itself has been transformed into a limited range of culinary formats that represent potential 'bridgeheads' to the consumers. Similarly, haphazard comments, likes and dislikes, from consumers who happened to pass by a busy square in Oslo at a certain time, are translated into a coherent extract that fits the format of a 'report', and even pinpoints some culinary concepts that seem particularly promising in aligning consumers' interests. Through these processes of translation, two primary allies have been transformed from something distant and unknown to something that may be mastered with the familiarity of experiences *already encountered* (Latour 1987). Primary allies may thus be defined as human actors or 'non-human actors' whose interests must be explored in order to ensure their future alignment with the poultry project. In both these processes of transformation intermediary translators play a central part. In relation to consumers, market research consultants are particularly important. Being responsible for the first-hand contact with consumers, their role is similar to that of the product development consultants in the first phase of test-production. While product development consultants served as intermediary translators between poultry raw material and the prime movers, the market research consultants serve as intermediary translators between consumers and the prime movers. The *network of allies* and intermediary translators is illustrated below (see Figure 6.1).

In accordance with Latour I use the term *network* to indicate the complex pattern of connections between allies that may be both human and non-human. Networks may be conceived of as *'knots and nodes'* that are connected with one another through processes of translation (Latour 1987:180). One of the key features of a network, in Latour's sense of the word, is that it crosses our conceptual division between nature and culture, or between the material and the social: *'networks as we have described them . . . are neither objective nor social . . . simultaneously real, like nature, narrated, like discourse, and collective, like society'* (Latour 1993:6).

As indicated in Figure 6.1, consumers and raw material are not the only primary allies involved. In addition, there is the advisory group, whose support must be secured in order for the project to proceed. We will return to this in the following section.

Phase 4: Towards a Stable Network

There are many ways in which the prince can win [the people] over. These vary according to circumstances . . . I shall only conclude that it is necessary for a prince to have the friendship of the people; otherwise he has no remedy in times of adversity (Machiavelli 1961:69).

Until now, the prime movers have been busy acquiring knowledge in the areas of product development and market research. They have implemented test production and carried out basic market research. In this way they have fulfilled part of the contract incorporated in the poultry project plan. During the first three phases (approximately 6 months) the advisory group has remained fairly non-existent as a group. Now the time has come for bringing the members of this 'sleeping ally' together, in order to present

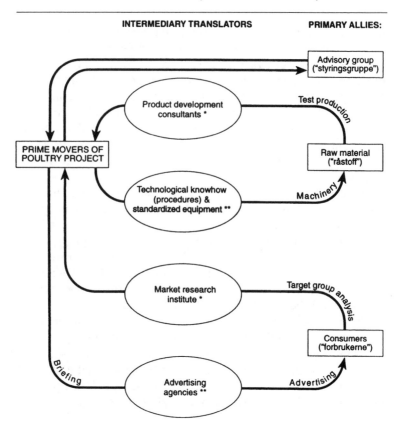

Intermediary translator whose main task is to explore and describe the characteristics of a potential ally to the prime movers.

** *Intermediary translator whose main task is to reaffirm (symbolically or materially) the prime movers' interpretation of the product vis-à-vis primary allies.*

Figure 6.1. The Poultry Project; Allies and intermediary translators

the current state of affairs and to secure further support. In other words: it is time for an internal presentation.

The fourth phase is initiated when Erik writes a so-called status report on the poultry project, addressed to the six members of the advisory group, but also circulated to six other persons, all senior directors. The status report consists of one-and-a-half typed pages detailing what main activities have been carried out so far, and a schedule of planned activities for the following year. We learn that:

- *Test production is implemented according to the project plan.*
- *We have established a good knowledge of all Norwegian actors.*
- *We have established a good relationship with one of Europe's major and most modern producers and suppliers of poultry . . . In order to challenge the authorities, we are ready to apply for import dispensation for the test sale of selected products.*
- *We have established a number of other foreign contacts with the supplier and machine delivery side and with other producers, which might give us valuable competence.*
- *We are beginning to acquire an overview of political preconditions and the legal framework ('politiske rammebetingelser') in the field, and the tactical manoeuvres that must be taken in this connection . . . a fairly incomprehensible matter ('uoversiktlig materie').*
- *Qualitative market research has been carried out in order to acquire knowledge about general consumer attitudes to poultry, and to obtain specific evaluations on our prototype products.*

The status report sets the agenda for the scheduled meeting with the advisory group, and sets the stage for realizing what, according to the project plan, is described as reaching detailed decisions about further implementation. The advisory group is invited to a meeting in mid-February with the following agenda:

8:00	Test production report
8:00–8:30	External consultant (Mr Biehl)
8:30–9:00	Price estimates, discussion
9:00	Qualitative survey report
	External consultant (market research institute) / discussion
	Legal and political framework
	Project status
	• What have we achieved so far?
	Suggested plan for future activities
	• Discussion
	• Conclusion

Focusing blindly on the formalities leading up to this scheduled event, we could describe Erik and Erling as neutral and disinterested implementers, who have now done part of their duties and will leave the final decision-making to their superiors. However, such a description hardly survives beyond the level of strict formalities. Erik and Erling are not only employees doing what they are told, they also want this project to be carried through! And even more, they want influence on the future course of events. Not surprisingly, therefore, during the subsequent weeks, many discussions seek to evaluate the pros and cons of various possible outcomes. And this is no easy task . . .

One day in early February, as I ran into Erling in a corridor, he exclaimed: *'It looks as if we are going to go for turkey!'* He then continued to explain the reasons for this, which were several. Most importantly, Mr Biehl had finished his cost–benefit analysis, which indicated that the profitability of turkey is far higher than that of chicken. Firstly, the size of a turkey carcass is about five times as large as that of a chicken, and because of this turkey requires less mechanical work. Secondly, Mr Biehl had measured the relative size of the breast fillets. These calculations demonstrated that turkey breasts represent 27 per cent of the total weight of each turkey, whereas the comparable proportion for chicken breasts was only 19 per cent. As breast fillet was the part of the bird most in demand, a high percentage of breast fillet was a clear advantage. Thirdly, turkey muscles are fairly large, which implies that they are easier to serve as whole pieces of meat, rather than as combined pieces. Erling considers this an advantage from a marketing perspective, because, as he says: *'people experience the meat as more authentic when it comes in whole (breast fillet) pieces'*. Fourthly, Erling adds that turkey generally seems to have a higher status than chicken – an assumption that was confirmed by the qualitative group discussions.

During earlier discussions, Erling had often argued in favour of chicken. He described his recent change of mind as follows: *'First I believed in turkey. Then we started test production, and I went into a phase when I was more positive towards chicken. Now I'm back with turkey again.'*

Before he leaves, Erling emphasizes the importance of studying the cost–benefit analysis by Mr Biehl more carefully, in order to elicit issues that will be particularly important for the presentation for the advisory group. Erling and Erik have scheduled a meeting with Biehl a few days later, and Erling describes his own task as having to *'translate Biehl's calculation into something that those "chicken brains"*[17] *are able to understand'*.

As it turns out, at the meeting with the advisory group Biehl presents the results himself, aided by blackboard calculations and overhead slides. We learn about weight percentages of the various parts (turkey yields 33.6 per cent meat, while chicken yields only 22.2 per cent, MUK not included), fat percentages of turkey and chicken compared to pork, time expenditure involved in cutting turkey and chicken (one hour yields 202 kg. of turkey meat, but only 53.2 kg. of chicken meat), price of purchasing turkey vs. chicken raw material compared with other kinds of meat (turkey costs 40 NOK/kg. while chicken costs only 35 NOK/kg.), and a recent food technology report that demonstrates that turkey has a greater capacity for absorbing marinade than pork.

After a brief discussion and some clarifications, Biehl leaves the room and the sociologist from the market research institute enters. She opens by saying that qualitative methods reveal a broad range of attitudes that exist among consumers, but does not indicate anything about the number of people sharing each of these attitudes. She then goes on to describe consumer attitudes, emphasizing that:

- Norwegian consumers are not used to large chickens, and therefore experience large pieces of chicken given them as unnatural, assuming that they have been manipulated in a suspect manner;
- turkey meat is expected to have a dry texture (when it does not, consumers are positively surprised);
- turkey is considered 'better' and 'more distinguished' than chicken;
- there is a negative attitude against imitations, or undefinable foodstuffs, and because of this, it is very important to find names that evoke trust and recognition; and
- consumers are used to chicken meat that gives a certain resistance upon chewing, so that when the breast fillet is very tender, they become suspicious whereas for turkey there are few such expectations.

At this point, Erling expresses his regrets that they have made some of the poultry products virtually identical to similar products made of pork. As the consumers feel it is 'too similar', and want more chicken flavour, they ought to change it. The sociologist does not quite agree. Again, she emphasizes the importance of hitting the right connection between the name and the product's flavour and texture. Instead of ham, they should call it turkey roll. Instead of steak, they should call it turkey fillet.

During the discussion, the sociologist often refers to what she calls USP (*'u-ess-pe'*). Asking Erik, I learn that she is referring to an English marketing term, the so-called Unique Selling Proposition.[18] She uses this term to underline the importance of bringing whatever are considered to be unique features of the product clearly to the front where they are easily recognized. Erling comments that they should not have added pork fat to the turkey products, which have a very favourable fat content in the first place. He concludes that making copies of other meat products is a cardinal mistake. But once more the sociologist disagrees, maintaining that the products may well *resemble* other products. The important point, however, is that they are given *the right name*.

Concluding the presentation, the sociologist recommends the development of a so-called *'brand umbrella'* that communicates *high quality, nutritious and lean*. A member of the advisory group then asks her about whether there was enthusiasm and curiosity in the group discussions. She replies that a group process tends to enlarge such issues, but her impression is that the consumers were positive, especially in relation to some of the product prototypes. After the sociologist has left the meeting, someone asks why poultry is so much more expensive in Norway than abroad. Erling explains that practically all other countries with a significant poultry consumption have what he calls a *vertical integration* of poultry production, i.e. the same company raises, slaughters and processes the birds, which implies lower cost. Terje (vice-president) suggests that high costs should not be considered a major barrier at this point, as the most important task now is simply to decide which products to go for, which market segments they should be aimed at, and then start pilot production. The main point at present, he claims, is not to make a lot of money right away, but rather to acquire know-how in a field that may become profitable in a long-term perspective. Erik mildly objects, saying that vertical integration seems necessary in order to make money. But another member of the advisory group emphasizes the previous point, saying that *'we are as yet only in the early learning phase'*.

Gradually, the discussion turns to activities in the near future. Pilot production will be started shortly, and will lead up to a pilot test sale of poultry products in some selected stores in the Oslo area. A member of the advisory group wants to know which products they will finally go for. Erik replies that they cannot say this for sure at the moment. But from a strategic viewpoint, he assumes that they should add as much as possible of what he calls 'processing value'.

Towards the end of the discussion, a member of the advisory group wants to know whether they should work only with turkey, or with chicken as well. Erik replies that he thinks they should do both. The staff director replies that much points in the direction of turkey. Erik emphasizes the importance of learning about both kinds of material, whereupon the staff director says: *'OK, I see your point, considering that we are in the stage of building competence'*, and several of the other members quietly agree.

Shortly after the meeting, as we are walking through the corridors, Erling asks me, half jokingly: *'Don't we work thoroughly?'* I agree, and when I ask him whether he was satisfied with the meeting, he complains that *'they are not willing to go into any details'*. Erik adds that he thinks it was a good meeting, except that he is worried that a few of the advisory group members take it all too lightly: *'There may be problems here that they are not willing to see . . .'.*

From the point of view of the prime movers, an important purpose of the meeting is to ensure extended support, both in terms of resource allocation and in terms of goodwill. Furthermore, the meeting represents an occasion at which anticipated problems may be presented and discussed, thus relieving the prime movers of carrying the burden of responsibility alone.

Finally, the meeting makes it clear that successful alignment of primary allies (poultry raw material and consumers) implies careful adaptation of the technical and the communicative aspects of the product. The sociologist stresses this point when she claims that a wide range of prototypes might work *provided they have the right name*. In other words, the prime movers should start thinking about the products as coherent entities, i.e. in ways that bring together the interests of the various allies. This implies keen attention to the issue of *semantic classification*. As we will soon see, the question of name will soon be a major focus of attention, and an issue of considerable worry.

Phase 5: Searching for a Brand Name

The struggle for order is not a fight of one definition against another, . . . it is the fight of determination against ambiguity, of semantic precision against

ambivalence, of transparency against obscurity, clarity against fuzziness
(Bauman 1991:7).

About a week after the meeting with the advisory group, Erik
meets with two of its members who are marketing directors. Until
now, turkey and chicken have been considered equally promising.
At this meeting, however, they decide to concentrate only on
turkey. This decision represents the temporary closure of a
controversy regarding use of raw material. (According to the
meeting report, chicken may still be reintroduced later.) At the
level of culinary concepts, however, the interpretative flexibility
is even greater than before. While the range of product prototypes
had previously been narrowed down to 21 varieties, out of which
only 8 were made of turkey, we now find a list of products attached
that includes as many as 25 different turkey products. Out of these,
they will pick out approximately 9–12 prototypes to be tried out
during test sale.

In the mean time, Erik has prepared a document that is
considered to be a crucial element in the process of creating brand
products: the so-called Brand Strategy, or, as they say in the
marketing department: 'the BS' (*'be-ess'*). The term Brand Strategy
(the English term is usually applied) is frequently referred to in
the marketing department. It was also the topic of a seminar that
Erik had attended a couple of weeks earlier, together with several
product manager colleagues ('The Brand Days', see Chapter 5).
At this seminar, the importance of a establishing a Brand Strategy
was emphasized. Thus, when Erik writes the BS for turkey
products, he applies a format that he has just been taught. The
format specifies eight different headings, each indicating different
aspects of the product that need to be defined, including brand
name, product characteristics, product advantages, target group
and price policy.

With regard to brand name, Erik writes that *'a common brand
name will cover all turkey products'*. He explains that this brand name
will function as a kind of umbrella, comparable to the American
'Mr Turkey', which covers a wide range of turkey products in the
US. Under the heading 'product characteristics', Erik writes that
*'with regard to flavour and texture, the products will resemble, as far as
possible, similar products made of other types of meat, without seeking
to eliminate the specific characteristics of turkey'*. When I ask him
whether this isn't slightly contradictory, Erik disagrees, explaining

that when the natural characteristics of turkey are readily apparent, they will be kept, as for instance in the case of turkey cold cuts. But when these are not so noticeable, as in the case of sausages, the product will be more like a substitute product. When it comes to 'product advantages', Erik emphasizes health, nutrition, convenience, and a minimum use of additives. Finally, we learn that prices to the consumer should not exceed 90 per cent of those for similar products made of other types of meat, yet the products should *not* be perceived as typical low-price products.

The Brand Strategy may be analysed as yet another level of translation, in the sense that both material and symbolic features of the product *and* sociological features of its target group are brought together in a way that demonstrates the coherence (or lack of coherence) between the three. In other words, as they write a Brand Strategy, the prime movers are forced to make some final statements about the product that demonstrate the simultaneous alignment of interests related to raw material, symbolic image and consumers. In this way, the Brand Strategy represents an important step in the process of closing controversies.

In addition, the Brand Strategy serves as a point of reference in future evaluations. For instance, once the Brand Strategy was prepared, it was distributed at all subsequent product presentation meetings. Furthermore, it served as an important piece of background material for the advertising agencies. In a sense the Brand Strategy is a way of imagining what will hopefully materialize itself as a brand product. Thus, with the emergence of the Brand Strategy, *'the assembly of disorderly and unreliable allies is . . . turned into something that closely resembles an organised whole'*, and we have what Latour might refer to as a *'black box'* (Latour 1987:130–1).

Once the Brand Strategy has been formulated, the main challenge for Erik is to find a brand name. Erik and his companions know very well that this part of the job is crucial. There are stories being told of high quality products that became total failures because the name wasn't right. He also knows that finding the right name is often difficult, and as we shall see, the poultry project is no exception.

The search for a name implies the entry of another intermediary translator: the advertising agency. While the market research institute translates interests of consumers *to the prime movers*, the advertising agency will work primarily in the opposite direction, translating the material and symbolic characteristics of the product *to potential consumers* (see Figure 6.1).

In March, Erik writes his first briefing to an advertising agency called Publicity,[19] explaining that *'we need a design concept for the Viking Foods turkey products'*, and that *'a general communication element must be developed as an integral part of this design, which must give a strong sense of recognition in all market communication'*. Enclosed with the letter is a copy of the Brand Strategy, and a copy of the qualitative survey report. Erik closes the letter with the following remark: *'A first response will be expected when the agency has thought for twenty thousand ("når byrået har tenkt for tjue tusen"), whereupon further budget negotiations may take place'*. This fairly abrupt mention of NOK 20,000 indicates that Erik has already discussed these issues (such conversations often happen over the telephone) and that a preliminary upper limit of NOK 20,000 is already negotiated. This is the beginning of a long and complicated process that lasted eight months, involved the consultancy of two advertising agencies, and cost an amount of money that Erik, in hindsight, would prefer *'not to even think about'*.

Six weeks later, Publicity invite Erik to a meeting in their office in which they will present some suggestions regarding name and design. In addition to Erik and Jon, another Viking Foods marketing manager, we are introduced to Nina and Peter, two Art Directors[20] (referred to as *'a-de's'*), Tom who is the account manager, Knut who is a creative director and the superior to Nina and Peter, and Grete, a project consultant who takes care of secretarial functions. The interior design is elegantly modern, combining high-tech design with the smoothness of wall-to-wall carpets and soft colours. Everybody gathers at a large table with chocolate and hot and cold refreshments. Cups and glasses are quickly distributed, people help themselves to what they want, and the meeting begins.

Tom opens on behalf of Publicity, structuring his presentation by a list of key words that are projected at an overhead screen. The list affirms some basic features of the poultry project and the current task. He then presents some aspects that he considers to be key requirements for a name that will serve as an umbrella for a range of present and future poultry products. One requirement is that the name should cover not only turkey, but also other kinds of poultry products that may be launched in the future. Furthermore, he refers to consumer attitudes to turkey, concluding that '*the existing turkey identity is different from what Viking Foods wishes to offer*'. This implies, he argues, that the advertising must change people's attitudes to turkey in order for the product to be perceived as good and trustworthy ('*troverdig*'). He concludes that the present target group for turkey products is not particularly relevant, and suggests that it should be more inclusive, including especially modern consumer segments.

At this point, Erik interrupts, saying that what they primarily want at this point is a name and a design concept. Tom responds by explaining how they have been through a long session regarding names. As it turned out, the chosen name happens to be among those listed in a document describing registered Viking Foods names. (Later, I learn that like other major manufacturers, Viking Foods has a list of names that they have already registered, and thus that they possess exclusive rights to use commercially. Many are not yet applied, and some will probably never come into use. Now Knut, the creative director, takes over: '*We decided that the name ought to signalize quality, and that it ought to be Norwegian. This lead to the elimination of many of the names on the list. Now we want to show you what we came up with*'.

At this point, Nina walks up to the board with a large placard folder. Knut adds that the question of exclusivity has been a difficult issue: '*How much exclusivity should be communicated? Even if the target group is fairly large, we believe it is important to signal a certain exclusivity . . . '*. Then Nina is ready, and in an atmosphere of quiet solemnity, she unfolds the placard and reveals a package with the name:

'*HERREGÅRD*' ('manor').

The package shows a red-checkered table cloth with a plate of food placed upon it. '*Herregård*' is written horizontally right across the package, '*Krydret kalkunkjøtt*' *(spiced turkey meat)* is written above, while '*100% kalkunkjøtt*' is written in small letters, forming an arc just above the dish. Nina leaves her placard folder open on a shelf, so that we may keep looking at it. Then Peter walks up with a second alternative. In a similar manner, he opens his placard folder, which reveals the same name, but with a slightly different design and different fonts.

As we look at the two alternatives, Knut comments that Peter's suggestion tends to emphasize product quality more strongly: '*it is more of what we might call a premium product'*. Peter adds that *'while Nina's alternative is **here'*** (with his right hand, he indicates a horizontal level in the air), *his experience of the product is **here'*** (he indicates a level somewhat above, implying that his impression of the product is slightly higher). Peter maintains that they need to consider which level of quality they want to be at. He then places his placard on the shelf next to the other one, and sits down.

Until now, Erik and Jon have mostly been listening. At this point they gradually become the centre of attention, as the others seem eager to hear their response:

Erik:	*I experience them as being very different.*
Tom:	*The name 'Herregård' was on your list of registered names. It was very favourably received in this house ('her på huset').*
Jon:	*But should a Wednesday product be called 'Herregård'?*
Nina:	*I don't think you should pull this down too much. It is high quality, isn't it?*
Erik:	*I like the concept. I just wonder whether we signal too much exclusivity . . .*
Knut:	*The second alternative, Peter's, shows the product name more clearly.*
Nina:	*But that can easily be changed in the first one as well. I think we should concentrate on which direction we want to go now . . .*
Knut:	*If you consider all the products in the retail discount stores that give a better impression than they deserve, I would not worry about aiming too high. I'd be more worried about aiming too low.*
Tom:	*I don't think we should promise too much . . .*
Knut and Peter:	*But it is all right! The product is good enough!*
Peter:	*The trend today goes in the direction of building brands, so we shouldn't underestimate all the time . . .*
Tom:	*Well, anyway, we need to test whether the package design is in accordance with the content. Because if you buy a Rolls Royce and get a Lada . . . (Addressing Erik:) Do you feel it would be better to continue with a combination of the two, or should we develop both separately?*
Erik:	*I think the important step at this point is concluding about the name.*
Jon:	*I think the name is quite all right . . .*
Erik:	*I didn't get any immediate negative reaction either . . .*

At this point, the discussion floats back and forth until they finally decide to go for Nina's design concept. The one that is perceived to be the less exclusive is thus selected, but will incorporate some details from the more exclusive one.

A few days later, Erik receives two new sketches of the package design. Instead of making a combination of the two alternatives, they have developed each of the concepts further. He shows me the two sketches (which appear to me as slight variations upon a familiar theme), saying that he wants to present them to the other product managers in the marketing department. At this point, Erik also expresses some uneasiness about the name:

> *I wonder whether 'Herregård' is the right name. Really, when you think of it, it signalizes neither poultry nor health . . . But that's the way it is, names are always so difficult. As I mentioned these things to Publicity last week, they sent me a list of suggestions to consider. But this is going to be expensive . . . So far, the design sketches have cost us thirty to forty thousand. Another round will cost a lot.*

As it turned out, the internal meeting strengthened Erik's scepticism towards the name 'Herregård' even more. A few weeks later, he therefore sends another briefing, much like the previous one, to an advertising agency called Promotion.[21] While Publicity was an old acquaintance, Promotion represents something new, and is strongly recommended by other marketing professionals in Viking Foods. Once again, the advertising agency is offered NOK 20,000 as an upper limit in order to come up with a name and a suggested design. This time, however, Erik is invited to an introductory meeting with the advertising staff in order to get acquainted and to explain about the project.

The meeting takes place in June in the offices of Promotion. It is a hot summer day, and the atmosphere is friendly and relaxed. A senior consultant called Sigurd opens with a brief presentation of the agency. The creative team, consisting of Monica (Art Director) and Olav (copywriter) are also present. Erik explains about the poultry project, and then he adds:

> *You might find it a bit strange that Viking Foods is going for a range of poultry products that are in fact going to compete with other Viking Foods products. But our philosophy is that such competition would happen anyway, and it is better that we do it than someone else. You could say that it is part of an offensive strategy.*

Monica and Olav ask a few questions about the underlying concept, and Erik explains: *'What we do, is we utilize our strength, technologically speaking. That means that many of the varieties of poultry products have in fact already been made, using pork. In other words, we know the technology behind it'.*

Erik continues by emphasizing that the name ought to cover a wide range of poultry products (including chicken), and that it should work in all of Scandinavia. Moreover, it ought to signalize something *modern.* Furthermore, he agrees with Olav, who believes that poultry products will appeal to men as well as to women, and maintains that the target group of the Brand Strategy should not be too narrowly interpreted.

Two months later, in early August, a meeting with Promotion is scheduled at the marketing department. The creative team will now present what they have come up with. (At this point, I had already followed the internal process at Promotion fairly closely, and was also familiar with the final suggestion. I had promised, however, not to reveal the name to Erik.) Sigurd, the senior consultant, arrives early, while Monica and Olav are delayed. Again, the actual presentation is left to the creative team. While Erik, Sigurd and I wait for the others to arrive, the discussion narrows in on the name.

Sigurd: *We have found a name that is firmly anchored in Norwegian food culture and Norwegian tradition, that will pass in Denmark and Sweden as well, and that arouses expectations of a good taste, and also something slightly new.*

Erik: *Well, that's just what we asked for! Sounds great to me . . .*

Sigurd: *We have also made some 'roughs'. It makes it easier to conceptualize than just the word.*

Erik [nods; then, jokingly:] *You are giving me sky-high expectations now.*

Sigurd: *Well, I'm enthusiastic, and so are my colleagues . . .*

Shortly afterwards, Monica and Olav arrive, and Olav starts their presentation:

Olav: *We thought that we needed to find a name that would serve as a basis for future communication. We thought about turkey, visualized landscapes, fiords and mountains, but decided that turkey should rather be associated with a countryside farm. Imagining this farm, we then conceptualized the kitchen. We imagined that inside this kitchen there would be some nice old women ('koner').*

And then we kept searching for such legendary female figures [he mentions figures from Scandinavian folklore, and talks increasingly in a suggestive manner . . .] and then we got it: Hanna Winsnes![22] *First we checked around some, to find whether this name evoked any associations, and it did! People immediately thought of all her cookbooks, or the recipe with all the eggs . . . Then we thought of 'Hannas Fristelse' ('Hanna's Temptation'), but we decided that it resembles 'Berthas Fristelse', which is a cookie brand. Then, finally, we got it:*

'HANNAS HEMMELIGHET' ('Hanna's secret')

[Olav pauses].

Sigurd: *We feel that we have found a name that signalizes something solid and Norwegian, something tasty and nutritious, and that we have a solid anchoring in Norwegian food culture.*

Then Monica starts presenting some sketches of design, explaining that these are only suggestions. The beige colour may be replaced by gold, depending on the degree of exclusivity. The design has a fair amount of blue, and Monica explains that this is not so common in food advertising, and it gives an impression of quality. When Sigurd asks Erik how he feels about what he has seen, he gives a rather vague, but positive, reply, adding that the only thing he misses is the nutritious aspect. Monica comments that nutrition can be communicated by other means, and besides, the fact that this is turkey indicates nutrition in itself. Finally, Sigurd asks Erik to 'chew on it' (*'tygge på det'*), and they part.

A few days later, I ask Erik how he feels about the new name. He says that he is basically in favour of it, but he is not quite sure. In order to get some help, he has already invited a bunch of people to a meeting:

Erik: *What I will do, is I ask people to come up with ideas, write them up on the board, and then we can discuss them. In the end, I will present the names from the two advertising agencies, and then we can compare all of them. If 'Hannas Hemmelighet' stands that test, I think we can go for it.*

At this point, almost NOK 60,000 have been spent, almost six months have passed, and according to Erik's time schedule, they should have decided on a name by now. However, as the following events will illustrate, the final name is still some time away.

In late August, nine men and women from the marketing department gather for a major 'brainstorming' on what is now generally referred to as Erik's poultry project.[23] Among them we find Erling, Erik, two marketing managers, product managers, product secretaries and the anthropologist. Some of the participants have, by now, attended several product presentation meetings, and are thus familiar with the poultry products. It is nine o'clock in the morning, and Erik has arranged for breakfast to be served, including rolls with turkey cold cuts, tea and coffee. As people help themselves to food and drink, Erik explains briefly the process he has been through. A lot of money has been spent, he says, but they are still not satisfied. *'That's why we want you to help us with some ideas'*. One of the product managers makes a joke about such processes being rather expensive, indicating that *his* ideas should be priced as well. The marketing manager picks up on this, and pointing to each participant, he mockingly adds up the cost of the participants, saying: *'300,000 for you, 500,000 for you'*, whereupon another product manager interrupts, saying: *'Hey, that's a lot! I guess I should think of renegotiating my salary . . . '*. While a humorous atmosphere is quite usual at internal meetings in the marketing department, it seems that the special assignment of acting as creative consultants lifts the spirit even more.

Then Erik distributes a hand-out of the Brand Strategy, emphasizing white meat, modern product, nutritiousness, good taste and convenience as the most important features, and reminding the others that the name must be in accordance with these principles. This leads to a brief discussion. After some negotiating back and forth on how to go about this, Johan, a marketing manager who is also member of the advisory group, positions himself by the blackboard with a chalk in his hand, much like a teacher facing a group of students. The others are now expected to come up with ideas, an expectation that brings about even more jokes, indicating a slightly distanced role enactment. Gradually, people start suggesting names aloud. Johan immediately writes the suggestions on the board, while some of the others occasionally murmur a friendly disapproval, or make some jokes about the suggested name. These comments lead to an almost continuous discussion on how such brainstorms ought to be implemented, to which Erik repeatedly insists that no critical comments are allowed at this point, as the main purpose of the meeting is to *'let ideas flow freely'*.

After an hour or so, 119 names fill up all the space on the

blackboard and on a few flipovers. The suggestions range from mere jokes, through a wide range of translations of poultry into other languages (*oiseau, usciella, pajaro, tasty bird*) to names that are possibly more realistic, including *Apollo* and *Fønix*. Then they go through the list again, crossing out the least serious suggestions, until they end up with a list of only 17 names. A product manager now suggests that each person should pick out two favourite alternatives among these, and then place their votes to decide which one comes out as the winner. Erik agrees to this, but first he introduces 'Herregård' and 'Hannas Hemmelighet', insisting that these must be included in the final vote as well. As it turned out, however, Herregård and Hannas Hemmelighet received only one vote each, while the winner was:

FØNIX ('Phoenix')

A few weeks later, Publicity makes a sketch incorporating the name *Fønix* in the package design, and Erik tells me that they are quite happy with it. But there are still some problems:

Erik: *We might have some problems using this name, especially in*
            Sweden, as it resembles 'Felix', which is a registered brand
            already. I've checked with our legal consultants, and they
            discourage us from using it.
Marianne: *So you are back at square one.*
Erik: *Yes. And we have used . . . I don't know how much . . . in getting*
            here. If 'Fønix' is out, I wonder if we shouldn't just settle for
            'Herregård'. I don't have a stomach to take this much longer . . .
            ('jeg har iallefall ikke mage til å fortsette stort lenger').

As it turned out, Erik sent another briefing to Publicity, this time asking for the design of an in-store campaign accompanying test-sale of '*Herregård*' turkey products. Shortly afterwards, however, Erik had to change his plans again, as he was informed that 'Herregård' was already a registered trade mark in both Denmark and Sweden. Later, Erik recalls:[24]

Erik: *We were quite empty and despondent at this point. There were*
            some discussions at which we considered whether we should
            simply use Viking Foods as a brand name, instead of building a
            new brand name. I was in favour of building a new brand.
Marianne: *Why?*

Erik: *Because this range of turkey products would represent something*
             new to the consumer, in terms of nutrition, flavour, and simply
             because such turkey products have never been on the Norwegian
             market before. Thus, I felt it was important to establish
             communications that emphasize directly the product advantages
             as different than in the other products. We are – as they say in
             the advertising trade – better at shooting with a rifle when we
             have our own brand name. The marketing manager has a
             different opinion, however. He thinks that meat is meat . . . But
             the marketing director, Aksel, agrees with me. He thinks that
             some of the value of Viking Foods in the future will be based on
             each brand that we produce. If we have several brands that are
             firmly anchored in consumers' consciousness, we will be better
             prepared when the competition in the market is more open. And
             in the mean time, we should build such brands.

             But then there is the Achilles' heel: we need to spend a lot of
             money to make this known. You don't build a brand just by
             giving the product a name. This costs a good many millions
             ('skikkelig mange millioner'). So the question is: are we willing
             to spend that kind of money?

Marianne: *I'm sure Aksel understands that.*

Erik: *Yes, Aksel does. But our budgets in the marketing department*
             are too small. So we have to raise more money, directly from the
             company, or through some special transfers . . . In other words,
             there must be willingness on top. So this is going to be a tough
             fight . . .

Marianne: *Isn't this a very common type of problem?*

Erik: *Of course. It is part of budget control. They don't let it all*
             flow . . . I went to a brand-building seminar recently, and then
             I asked these guru's on brand-building what we should do with
             these poultry things ('kalkungreiene'). They said that if we
             believe there is a potential, we ought to build a new brand. And
             we do believe in the potential . . .

Marianne: *So if the test sale is successful, that will be an argument for*
             spending more money on marketing.

Erik: *Yes, exactly.*

Marianne: *Tell me more about what happened with the name?*

Erik: *Well, when we were back at square one, I gathered some people*
             who are engaged in this, and we wrote down names from the
             last internal brainstorming that we thought might pass,
             including 'Apollo', which was mentioned there. Then we
             discovered that 'Apollo' was already registered, but by our sister-
             company in Denmark, so it is OK. And then we decided it was
             the least bad . . .

Marianne: *How do you mean?*
Erik: *Well, it gives no strong associations. I found out that pollo means chicken or hen in Italian and Spanish. Not that it really matters. The only other association is to space rockets, but I don't think that is very strong. So the name leaves us free to do what we want. But the latest news is that I've read a trade mark survey from Sweden, which shows that 'Apollo' is a registered margarine factory owned by Unilever. So maybe we're just as far away again . . .*

At this point of indecision, we will leave the poultry project. Phase 5 has revealed considerable difficulties involved in creating, evaluating and discarding brand names. Advertising agencies have been consulted, turned down and then consulted again, and a fair amount of money has been spent, all while the prime movers have felt increasingly uneasy about the whole situation. In the beginning, Erik expressed a certain ambitiousness regarding the importance of hitting the 'right name'. Nine months later he is far more pragmatic, and ready to settle for the 'least bad . . . '. Yet, as Erik insists: they still believe in the potential of the poultry project . . .

Phase 5 further demonstrates that the importance of ensuring internal support is not over just because the products have been launched. As Erik's final comments clearly indicate, building brand products requires more than a good product and a good name. Even if test sales are successful, a considerable amount of advertising expenditure is required. This implies that the support of an advisory group will continue to be crucial, even after the products are launched on the national market.

Dealing with Uncertainty: Summary and Discussion

I started out following this process with the aim of understanding how food products come to be as they are, expecting, rather naively perhaps, that I would be able to trace a logical course of events. What I encountered, however, was a long and complicated social process that, especially towards the end, twists and turns in ways that are increasingly hard to predict. While this should come as no surprise, what is more striking is the intense effort expended by the actors on creating order out of chaos in spite of this, and on continuously fitting their activities into a more or less predefined scheme of rational decision-making.

The poultry project demonstrates that the struggle for order is in large part a semantic struggle. Mostly, the closing of controversies implies the simultaneous production of a piece of written text. What makes the poultry project special, however, is the extent to which these pieces of text seek to incorporate material, social and ideological features into a logically coherent text (as in the Brand Strategy). In the field of food manufacturing, the struggle for order thus implies a strategy that is inclusive, in the sense that it subordinates entities that might otherwise have been kept conceptually apart.

In the beginning, while most efforts were directed at gathering knowledge, and controversies were still open, events could easily be described in a systematic manner (as illustrated in Figure 6.1). The first three phases indicate that the prime movers do their utmost to get to know their primary allies (especially raw material and consumers) and try very hard to translate these allies' characteristics in a way that makes this knowledge applicable. In the latter phases, however, when controversies need to be closed, we find that the final decisions are made in a far more haphazard and seemingly contingent manner. Partly, this may be attributed to the fact that, in spite of previous attempts at gathering knowledge, they are still aware that the information at hand is fragmented and incomplete, and that new information may change a previous decision at any time. Furthermore, final decisions are often based on an evaluation that goes far beyond the realm of rational deduction. This is most apparent in the search for names, when Erik and his companions accept or reject various proposals on the basis of fairly vague reasoning, until legal aspects literally decide it for them. Thus, in the final phase, decisions were made in a situation of considerable uncertainty.

This situation has many similarities with the situation of the netboss and the skipper as it is described by Fredrik Barth in his classical transactional analysis of actors on a Norwegian fishing vessel (Barth 1966). According to Barth, the netboss's decision on where to search for herring is the first and most vital decision affecting the chances of making a catch. In order to make this decision, various kinds of information are used, such as data relating to the sea and wind, weather reports, and radio conversations with other fishing vessels. But, just like the information gathered by the prime movers, *'when taken together, it is still very incomplete and fragmentary as the basis for a rational decision'* (Barth 1966:10).

While the netboss brings the expertise of 'feeling' the herring, the skipper makes decisions and takes full responsibility for the vessel and crew (Barth 1966:6). Barth describes the skipper's dilemma as continual: *'the vessel has to go or be somewhere always; so* **the decision can never be ignored or postponed***'* (Barth 1966:10, my emphasis).[25]

Although the present description of Erik and Erling is not directly comparable to Barth's analysis, a continuous pressure to make a decision within a situation conceived of as highly uncertain characterizes their situation as well. All key decisions are pushed up against a deadline: a name must be decided upon before the test-sale, and the test-sale must precede the national launch, which in turn should take place in due time before foreign competitors enter the market. Because the 'market' is always changing and unpredictable, the marketing department resembles, in a certain sense, the fishing vessel at sea – always on the move, continuously adapting to the shifts and changes of a floating environment.

According to Barth, this situation on board tends to produce a very special pattern of movements of the fishing vessels. Instead of spreading out over the vast, potentially bountiful sea, more than a hundred vessels *'constantly tend to congregate in small areas'*, devoting their attention mostly to discovering the movements of other vessels, and chasing them to a fruitless rendezvous (Barth 1966:10). If we consider the prime movers, we find that they too tend to 'congregate' in areas that are already explored by themselves or by others. Rather than exploiting the characteristics that make this particular raw material unique, there is a clear tendency towards treating poultry as if it were pork. And, if treated as poultry, the products tend to resemble turkey products that already exist elsewhere. Thus, in spite of an intention to align with interests of consumers who are described as 'modern', the final products represent continuity rather than innovation. Furthermore, the very decision to make something with turkey in the first place is argued for partly in terms of anticipated import liberalization, which is likely to imply an introduction of processed turkey products to the Norwegian market. As the innovation itself is thus justified by the anticipated movement of competitors, it may be interpreted also as a quest to 'get there first'. Finally, consumers' scepticism towards novelties is often interpreted as an obstacle that must be avoided (see Phase 2), thus preventing any even bolder attempt at innovation. Interestingly, this prudence on the part of the marketing professionals stands in stark contrast to current marketing ideology, in which innovations are generally considered an asset in themselves, and are considered to be crucial for a company's survival (see Chapter 5).

The most striking difference between the prime movers and the situation described by Barth, however, relates to the way uncertainty is handled. According to Barth (1966:8), the skipper on the fishing vessel: *'gives very few clues as to what he is thinking . . . he claims rationality without making the basis and logic of his decision available for critical scrutiny'*. Facing up to a situation in which he must make decisions in spite of great uncertainty, the skipper's silent posture make him appear as if uncertainty is not a problem. For Erik, on the other hand, whose role comprises both the expertise of the netboss and the responsibility of the skipper, uncertainty is a problem indeed. In fact, almost the entire process described above may be summarized as an effort to eliminate uncertainty – an elimination that, however, is never fully achieved.

We could have imagined Erling and Erik as two silent and confident decision-makers, whose years of experience and professional knowledge (which they obviously possess!) grants them the authority to 'cast their nets' without any further justification. Considering the contingency of the final outcome, we might even suspect that a few quick 'toss-of-the-coin'-type decisions would not have made much of a difference. Why then, do they have to subject their own decisions to such reflexive scrutiny? Why is uncertainty such a source of concern? In order to illuminate these issues, I will elaborate upon discontinuity between the semi-scientific gathering of knowledge on the one hand and the notion 'creativity' on the other. I will suggest that these issues and this discontinuity may be better understood in the light of general theories of modernity. I will return to these considerations in Chapter 10.

Notes

1. The term is inspired by Callon's term *'primum movens'* (1986). Callon uses this term to refer to the actors that he chooses to follow in his description of the domestication of the scallops and fishermen of St Brieuc Bay.
2. While Erik is granted the primary responsibility for the project, the two will work as close collaborators throughout. As will be demonstrated, their different fields of competence also imply a certain division of labour between the two.
3. 'Lørdagskylling' (*'Saturday Chicken'*) is a frozen, marinated chicken product, ready to heat in the oven.
4. MUK (*'Mekanisk utbenet kjøtt'*) is a residual category, consisting of that which is left over when breasts, thighs, skin and bones are removed.
5. This is in accordance with statements by marketing managers in Viking Foods, who emphasize the salience of copying in food manufacture, maintaining that 'most of what we do is photocopying' (*'det meste vi gjør er blåkopiering'*).
6. The term 'system' here refers to the internal structure of the organization, covering all internal decision-making that will be required for the project to proceed. Applying the term 'selling the ideas', the product manager evokes a metaphor related to the market, indicating that good ideas are, in fact, exchanged for continued support and resources.
7. English term used.
8. English term used.
9. English term used.
10. English term used.
11. According to Norwegian food legislation, both 'wiener sausage' and 'hamburger' are protected names, i.e. the products must contain a minimum quantity of meat, usually specified as beef or pork.
12. Hokksund is a small township in eastern Norway. In the present context, it represents something traditional and conventional, and is used in a slightly prejudicial way.
13. This arrangement resembles that of qualitative group discussions in market research institutes.
14. By the time the meeting took place, one qualitative survey had already been undertaken.

15. The term 'consumer' denotes a role that is situation-specific: everybody is a consumer part of the time, but no one is a consumer all the time (Lien 1994). Because of this duality, it is perfectly possible for anyone (even in the marketing profession) to claim to give their opinion on behalf of the consumers. In fact, we may argue that it is this very duality that makes the product presentation meeting seem possible or worthwhile.

16. Interestingly, these explorations imply that each individual consumer is removed from the context in which he or she normally eats. Instead s/he is placed in a room together with five or six strangers whose only common denominator is that they are of the same sex and (for women) approximately the same generation. In this experimental setting, the consumers are as much removed from their ordinary social context as the food items are removed from their culinary context.

17. 'Chicken brains' refers in this context to members of the advisory group with little competence in the field of product development.

18. This term's initials are always pronounced in English.

19. 'Publicity' is a fictitious name. This agency is frequently used, and Erik is well acquainted with persons there.

20. The English term is always used.

21. 'Promotion' is a fictitious name.

22. Hanna Winsnes is a woman who lived around the turn of the twentieth century and is famous in Norway for her cookery books. Wife of a priest, she represents the upper middle class, and is known for her extravagant recipes.

23. In the invitation, this meeting is referred to as a *'Kreativt Forum'*, a term most often reserved for the creative team in advertising. In the present context, the term is used slightly ironically, as the subsequent paragraph indicates: *'The purpose of gathering this hand-picked bunch of highly qualified marketing professionals is that we wish to have an internal brainstorm effort in order to find THE right brand name for our range of poultry products. Our advertising partners have now burnt such a significant portion of our budget, without any useful result, that we will try to find the NAME through an internal effort instead. Enclosed you will find the bureau briefing and the BS. If we decide to use one of your suggestions, we do not exclude the possibility that the source will receive an attractive award'*.

24. At this point, my fieldwork period was basically over, and I had to follow up the poultry project through telephone calls and the use of written material.

25. If the crew cast the nets at the right place and moment, they may make a considerable amount of money; if not, hours of hard labour may be wasted. Barth argues that the whole interaction between the three types of actors 'depends on and maintains relations of trust; the prestations on the bridge are in a sense *token* prestations'. This must be so, he maintains, because the transactions involved are not about stipulated amounts of value, 'but about the *chances* of catch' (Barth 1966:7–8).

Chapter 7

Reaching the Average Norwegian: The Pizza Superiora Film Project

The present chapter describes the creation of a TV commercial promoting pizza. This implies a shift from a case in which product development was heavily involved (Chapter 6), to a case that involves the production of advertising only. In the first part of the chapter, models, concepts and recommendations inherent in consumer segmentation are presented. The second part of the chapter describes how these conceptual models are 'translated' into an advertising commercial.

The promotion of pizza products exemplifies the application of consumer segmentation strategies. Unlike most other products, pizza is referred to as a highly differentiated brand product. Consequently, information about the life styles and values of the various target groups is considered very important, and is carefully incorporated into the final product. Such information derives primarily from consumer segmentation strategies, of which *Norwegian Monitor* is the most important. A marketing manager puts it this way:

> *The Norwegian market is too small to really use consumer segmentation systems such as* Norwegian Monitor. *If we are going to segment ourselves right to the bottom ('hvis vi skal segmentere oss helt ned i bånn') the costs will quickly exceed the earnings. That's what I think. But I may be wrong . . . It is different in the States. They can market Budweiser to three categories of blue-collar, out of which one will be the kind who drinks 'a case a day'. Here in Norway (with a population of 4 million), physical properties and price are often enough . . . Pizza is the only market which is large enough for us to enter with consumer segmentation. We are now going to promote three different brands without cannibalizing. One locomotive, Pizza Superiora, and two others.*

The categorization of pizza as a highly differentiated brand product is partly normative, in the sense that it implies that consumer segmentation profiles *ought to* be taken into account. At the same time, it may be seen as a reflection of the current state of affairs; the wide range of pizza products on the market do differ in ways that might be considered significant. For Viking Food's marketing professionals, the promotion of pizza therefore represents an interesting challenge, in the sense that it offers a good opportunity to practise brand differentiation.

Before moving on to the course of events, I will first summarize some key characteristics of pizza consumption in Norway, and then trace the emergence of the present product range as it is described in consumer segmentation target group analyses.

A Brief History of Norwegian Pizza Consumption

Pizza was introduced in Norway by the establishment of a well-known pizza restaurant in Oslo named Peppe's in 1970. Quickly adopted as a popular meeting place for youth in the city and the suburbs, the American-inspired restaurant was very successful, and two other Peppe's restaurants were opened within the first few years. Since then, the number of pizza restaurants and take-away services has steadily increased. In 1993, there were more than 30 restaurants and/or take away services *explicitly marketing pizza* in the yellow pages of the Oslo phone book, and a much greater number of restaurants with pizza on the menu. In fact, pizza is the dish that is most frequently referred to in this list of Oslo restaurants. A similar tendency may be observed in other Norwegian towns and villages. Driving through the Norwegian countryside, there is hardly a community that does not have its local pizza restaurant.

The popularity of fresh pizza in Norway is only surpassed by the popularity of frozen pizza. In the mid-1970s, when Peppe's was well established, a major food manufacturer launched frozen pizza on the Norwegian market. Within the next few years, two other manufacturers followed suit. Still, the popularity of frozen pizza did not really take off until the early 1980s. Since then, the total sale of frozen pizza has steadily increased until it reached a total of approximately 14 million frozen pizzas sold in 1991. According to marketing professionals in Viking Foods, this gives Norway the *highest per capita sales of frozen pizza in the world!*

The popularity of frozen pizza in Norway has, to some extent, also granted manufacturers the privilege to define what a proper pizza should be like. In parts of Norway where no freshly made commercial pizza was yet available (and the familiarity with Italian cuisine was still fairly limited), frozen pizza sometimes set the standard of what a proper pizza should be like. Thus, in a Northern community in the mid-1980s, people who would prefer home-made to pre-prepared foods, would try to make their home-made pizza in a way that closely resembled the frozen manufactured kind (Lien 1989).

During these processes of appropriation, pizza has been transformed, both at the material and at the symbolic levels. First of all, the material product referred to as pizza in Norway is materially quite different from its original Italian counterpart. Most importantly, a Norwegian pizza usually contains meat, an item that is rarely a key ingredient within the Italian culinary concept. Furthermore, in Norway, as in the United States, meat often implies beef, an ingredient that is rarely found in Italian pizzas. In this sense, the Norwegian pizza concept is closer to that of the US than to the Italian concept.

Secondly, since it was introduced in the 1970s the symbolic properties of pizza have also undergone a gradual change. From being first considered something foreign and exotic, pizza has become something fairly trivial and common. This is partly due to its wide dissemination. As pizza is incorporated into everyday domestic consumption, its original 'foreignness' will be likely to be replaced by a sense of familiarity, at least among its users. At the same time, there seems to be enhanced awareness among Norwegians (through travel and global exchange of culinary knowledge) of the difference between manufactured pizza varieties and pizzas as served in Italy.[1]

Such awareness is closely linked to a culturally defined appreciation of *authenticity* as an independent quality. But in addition to this almost inevitable process of 'routinization' through everyday use, the changed symbolic properties of pizza in Norway may also be due to deliberate marketing strategies. The interplay between statistical popularity and qualitative characteristics will be an underlying theme of the present chapter.

Who eats pizza in Norway? Market research information available at Viking Foods in the spring of 1992 indicates that 76 per cent of the population eat pizza (i.e. only 24 per cent do not eat pizza at all). Furthermore, although the majority of the users are between 15 and 30 years of age, there is also a considerable portion of consumers who are between 30 and 49 years. The majority of consumers are resident in the eastern part of the country, and have an average aggregate household income above NOK 160,000 (source: Briefing Pizza Superiora).

In 1992, more than 20 different pizza brands were available on the Norwegian market, while four food manufacturers (including Viking Foods) held more than 90 per cent of the total market share, with several brands each. Of these, Viking Foods was the most important, with a total market share of more than 60 per cent in 1992.

Italian or American? The Emergence of the Present Product Range

In spring 1992, Viking Foods manufactured six pizza products on the Norwegian market. Pizza Superiora was by far the most important, with a total market share of approximately 50 per cent. The other Viking Foods pizza products had market shares of less than 10 per cent each. According to the Brand Strategy for frozen pizza, the various products and target groups are described as follows:

- **PIZZA SUPERIORA** (cheese, tomato sauce, meat and red paprika)
  POSITIONING: *Superiora is a quality pizza priced above the average in the market. It shall be a safe and good ('trygt og godt') alternative for the majority of the market. The flavour shall be adapted to as many as possible, and it is therefore not a 'niche product'.*
  TARGET GROUP: *A pizza for pizza-lovers. Superiora is 'folkepizzaen' ('the people's pizza') that everybody likes regardless of age, but most users are within the age group 10 to 30 years.*
- **PIZZA ROMANO** (cheese, tomato sauce, pepperoni and green pepper)
  POSITIONING: *Pizza for the more advanced ('erfarne') eater. Romano has a distinctive flavour and character. The quality is high, and the product is priced considerably higher than the market average.*

TARGET GROUP:	*A more adult and selective ('kresent') audience. The majority of users are young people. This is a pizza for those who prefer a slightly stronger taste.*

- **PAN PIZZA** (pizza with a thick crust, cheese, tomato sauce and ham)

POSITIONING:	*High quality at considerably above average price. Pizza with a thick crust. Shall be as similar as possible to the original 'pan-pizza'.*[2]
TARGET GROUP:	*The pizza is adapted to modern young people between 15 and 30 years of age. The target group is open to new products and eating habits, and to quality.*

In 1992, several million NOK were budgeted for promotion purposes. These were apportioned with some 49 per cent to Superiora, 25 per cent to Romano and approximately 20 per cent to Pan Pizza. The remainder were distributed on minor pizza products. While Superiora and Romano have both existed for some years, Pan Pizza has been on the market for just a few months, and is the first and only pizza on the Norwegian market that is promoted as 'American', rather than as 'Italian'.

In addition, there are three other pizzas that are less heavily promoted. Out of these, we should mention:

- **PIZZA PRECIOSA** (wholemeal crust, cheese, tomato sauce and vegetable topping)

POSITIONING:	*Preciosa shall be a variety adapted to the low-fat trend ('lettbølgen'). Reduced calorie content and topping with vegetables only makes it a healthy alternative.*
TARGET GROUP:	*Women aged 15–40 focusing on health, body and appearance. Vegetarians.*

The emergence of the present product range is a result of careful considerations of the characteristics of real and potential target groups. An important source of information is the consumer segmentation target group analyses. In the case of pizza, *Norwegian Monitor* target group analyses have been purchased twice, in May 1990 and in May 1992.

A *Norwegian Monitor* target group analysis provides a complex and fairly detailed description of the characteristics of the target group. The underlying dimensions of the sociograph appear as vertical and horizontal axes, labelled modern–traditional and materialist–idealist respectively. These axes provide four different quadrants, which are referred to by product managers as '*upper left*' (modern and materialist), '*upper right*' (modern and idealist), '*lower left*' (traditional and materialist) and '*lower right*' (traditional and idealist) (see also Chapter 4).

According to the 1990 target group analysis, consumers of frozen pizza tend to be located primarily in the upper left quadrant of the sociograph. They belong to a segment sometimes referred to as 'live-for-the-present', and are characterized as modern, materialistic, younger, status-oriented and consumption-oriented.

The 1990 target group analysis stated two possibilities with regard to target-group-oriented promotion. One possibility was to focus on the 'heavy users' ('*storforbrukerne*'). According to the analysis, this strategy would be suitable for situations of intensified competition, in which case 'capturing market shares from competitors' would be the key strategy. Another possibility would be to try to reach consumers who do not normally eat frozen pizza in an attempt to transform them into users. This strategy is more relevant for manufacturers who already dominate the market. In the present case, as Viking Foods was in strong competition with several other manufacturers, a primary focus on 'heavy users' was recommended.

As a second strategy, an attempt to reach non-users was recommended. One way of doing this was through a more diversified product spectrum. On the basis of these considerations, a twofold communication strategy was recommended, in which the first part implied:

1. An emphasis on convenience, modernity and American symbols to strengthen the alliance with consumers located in the upper-left.

Segments 1, 3 &4 [upper left] are pleasure-oriented. This means that they are more concerned with whether food tastes good, and less with whether it is nutritious, has a high caloric intake etc. It is also important to be aware that the meal pattern of this group is breaking down. They let activities govern meals, and not the other way around. They often skip a meal, or substitute dinner for cold food or fast food. This is one of the reasons for the high use frequency of frozen pizzas in these segments. Their emphasis on convenience makes them use a lot of all kinds of 'take-away' food and fast food. In general, they are oriented towards American ideals and lifestyle.[3]

On the basis of this characterization, the following promotion was recommended:

> *If we relate this to frozen pizza, it implies that symbols emphasizing convenience and modernity will have appeal. Examples are names like 'King Size' and the use of 'square American letters' ('kantete Amerikanske bokstaver') with 'stars and stripes' elements, contra varieties like 'Pizza Italiano' and a focus on Parisian baguettes and red wine.*

This strategy of Americanization was later pursued through the launch of the American 'Pan Pizza' in 1991. The concept of Pan Pizza corresponds closely with the recommendations regarding 'King Size' and 'stars and stripes'. On the package, which is decorated with stars and stripes, we find the silhouette of the Statue of Liberty, surrounded by the text: 'Real American[4] Pan-Pizza'. On the back, there are drawings of a cowboy on a bucking bronco, two jazz musicians, and an American football player, all common symbols of the US in Norwegian popular culture. The text goes:

> *American pan-pizza represents a new trend, and Viking Foods with Pan Pizza follows up on the Scandinavian market . . . Everybody knows that pizza is originally from Italy, where it is practically a national dish. Pan Pizza, however, was created ('så dagens lys') in America and has now become a concept for pizzas with a thicker crust, even in Scandinavia. Pan Pizza is that kind of pizza, tasty and more filling than ordinary pizzas.*

As Pan Pizza was a fairly new concept, no target group analysis of its users had yet been carried out, but it is generally assumed that the target group is firmly located in the upper left segment.

The secondary strategy recommended by the 1990 target group analysis was an attempt to reach consumers who were not using pizza, a strategy which implied:

2. An emphasis on health, authenticity and Italian symbols as an attempt to establish an alliance to consumers located in the upper right.

> *Persons in segments 5, 6 and 10 [upper right] are cosmopolitan, while they are also interested in food and cooking . . ., they are in favour of French cuisine, and frequently read about gastronomy and the art of cooking. Food is a way (for many) of realizing themselves. They frequently have good*

knowledge of what they are doing, including cooking. They are interested in culture . . .

On the basis of this, an emphasis on authenticity and 'Italianness' was recommended:

Consequently it will be correct to focus upon the origin of pizza through a focus on the product characteristics, Italian name, etc . . . 'Preciosa' is in our opinion based on a correct concept for segments 2 & 6 [upper right] . . . Through an emphasis on contents, including exotic vegetables like aubergines and squash, it will automatically be attractive to this type of consumer . . . We think Pizza Preciosa is 'a good weapon' to ensure Viking Foods' market shares also in this part of the population . . . The challenge for Viking Foods in order to maintain the use frequency in the upper right segment is thus to promote a pizza which is as distanced as possible from the factory-produced pizza.

However, as it turned out, the attempt to reach the 'upper right' was not very succesful. In 1992, a second target group analysis concluded that the heavy users of frozen pizza were even more materialistic and slightly more traditional in 1992 than two years earlier, and that frozen pizza was even less popular in the upper right segments. Pizza Preciosa, a variety intended to appeal to the upper right, had not been very succesful. In an analysis of the new situation, statements that previously provided the background for promoting Pizza Preciosa now served to explain its lack of success:

The cosmopolitan persons who are interested in food and cooking have increasingly reduced their use of frozen pizza. They are in favour of French cuisine, and frequently read about gastronomy and the art of cooking. Food is therefore a way (for many) of realizing themselves. They often have good knowledge of what they are doing, including cooking. They are interested in culture and often seek background information for what they are doing, including cooking. Because of this 'machine-produced factory-pizzas with soy meat fall right through' ('maskin produserte fabrikk pizzaer faller tvers igjennom') (Target group analysis 1992).

The overall conclusion goes right back to the material quality of mass-manufactured frozen pizzas. No matter how Italian or healthy-looking, a manufactured frozen pizza is necessarily 'machine-produced', and there is a certain segment of the population for whom this particular product will 'fall right through'.

Pizza Romano is referred to in 1992 as another candidate for emphasizing 'Italianness', but according to the target group analysis, it would need a more distinct profile:

According to our information, Romano is a variety which was supposedly 'more Italian'/stronger taste/more 'feinschmecker' directed than Superiora. However, it does not seem to be perceived this way. These two [Superiora and Romano] compete heavily right in the middle of the pizza market. The reason is probably that Romano has not managed to attain a distinct profile. It has become very similar to all other manufactured pizza.

On the basis of these experiences, in 1992 a policy of enhanced emphasis of product differentiation was pursued. This implied extensive promotion of both Superiora (the market leader), Romano (the authentic Italian) and Pan Pizza (the American). Through advertising, the distinctiveness of all three products would be emphasized. Differentiation was further achieved through a division of labour that implied that three different advertising agencies would get involved, one for each pizza product. This was the general state of affairs when a new Pizza Superiora TV commercial was about to be produced.

Case 2: The Pizza Superiora Film Project

We enter the project in March 1992, when Kristoffer, a product manager responsible for pizza products, has just written a 'briefing'[5] to Tom, an account manager at the advertising agency Publicity, regarding plans for a new TV commercial for Pizza Superiora. This event took place at a time when the use of TV commercials was still fairly new in Norway. Owing to recent liberalization, a number of commercial channels had become available through cable television, but (because of the limited dissemination of cable TV) their audience was still fairly limited. However, this situation was expected to change fairly soon, as TV2, a national commercial TV channel, would start broadcasting in about six months, independently of the cable system. For the first time, national broadcasting of advertising would become possible through television (see Chapter 3). Anticipating this new media option, several advertising campaigns were now being produced as TV commercials, and the Pizza Superiora film is one of them.

Pizza Superiora is already a very succesful product. With a market share of approximately 50 per cent, it contributes significantly to making Viking Foods what Kristoffer refers to as 'decidedly number one' (*'den desiderte ener'*) in the pizza market, a position which is achieved through a total share of 63 per cent of the frozen pizza market in March 1992. This position reflects a relative growth during the previous year in the sales volume for Pizza Superiora that exceeded the growth of 'the frozen pizza market' as a whole.

The purpose of the commercial is therefore not to introduce anything new. Rather, the commercial is a typical example of what is generally referred to as 'product maintenance', activities that arouse some attention and contribute to preventing an expected decline of demand (cf. Chapter 5). For similar reasons, the project does not involve product development. The material properties of Pizza Superiora are already defined, and only the symbolic and communicative dimensions of the product are now the focus of attention.

Writing the briefing for Pizza Superiora, Kristoffer draws upon information both from the target group analyses based on the sociograph and from a so-called profile analysis of the target group. He delineates the target group for the new commercial as the 'heavy users', i.e. 'those who eat manufactured pizza 2–3 times a month or more'. Drawing on information from the target group analysis, Kristoffer describes the heavy users by the following terms: consumption, emotions, hedonism, mobility, optimism, risk-taking, control, individualism, novelty and spontaneity (Source: Briefing, Pizza Superiora).

Phase 1: The Emergence of 'Folkepizzaen'

For Kristoffer, who is responsible for the entire range of Viking Foods pizza products, the challenge is not only to increase market share for Pizza Superiora, but also to do this without 'cannibalizing', i.e. to sell more Pizza Superiora *but not* at the expense of other Viking Foods pizza brands. Theoretically, this may be achieved either by introducing pizza to those who are not yet users, or by strengthening alliances to present users (either through increased use, or at the expense of other manufacturers' products).

As already mentioned, a previous effort to reach the 'upper right' was not very successful. In the 1992 target group analysis, these experiences are summarized as follows:

> *It could seem as if frozen pizza was in the process of acquiring heavy consumers among the more food-knowledgeable, inner-oriented, slightly more health-conscious and cosmopolitan consumers towards the end of the 1980s . . . However, this seems not to be the case. We maintain that segments 5 and 6 [upper right] are not significantly large to go for, even if in 1990 this seemed to be an alternative third strategy.*

Another possibility for expansion is represented by consumers who are located in the lower left quadrant, slightly below the horizontal axis:

> *A possible further conquest ('erobring') of heavy consumers should be directed towards segments 7, 8 [lower left] and maybe 9. Here, it is important to be aware that price is increasingly important the farther down in the sociograph (and to the left) one proceeds. Inexpensive pizzas find a ready market in these groups . . . Somewhat jokingly, we often say that it is in segment 7 and 11 we find 'the real rebate Indians' ('de ekte tilbudsindianerne'). Price may therefore be an important entry in the lower parts of the socio-graph, where we absolutely do not find the same conflict between 'manufactured food and authenticity' that we find in the right segment of the sociograph.*

Except for a possible expansion towards the lower left by means of price cuts, a significant transformation of non-users into users is not very likely.[6] For Kristoffer, this implies that communication must continue to be directed towards those who already constitute the target group, i.e. *persons located in the upper left segment*. This strategy will definitely represent a threat to other manufacturers of pizza, and it might even make the users eat pizza more often. But how can it be achieved without 'cannibalizing' other Viking Foods pizza products?

A major strategy for avoiding this is *product differentiation*. Instead of promoting a range of pizza products that are more or less the same in terms of material as well as visual design, each product must be designed in a way that makes it recognizably different from the others. According to marketing theory, this will make the products less prone to substitution. In addition, such differentiation will enhance and strengthen the brand properties of each product, thus contributing to the general aim of brand-building in the marketing department.

Consequently, Pizza Superiora must be promoted in a way that makes it different from other Viking Foods pizza products, and particularly from Romano and Pan Pizza. Still, this differentiation must be achieved within the general framework of values defined as characteristics of the upper left segment of the sociograph. The communication ought to be directed towards the upper left segment, but stay away from the 'spaces' occupied by the target groups of Romano and Pan Pizza (products that target the 'authentic Italian' and the 'American' markets respectively).

This point is emphasized by Stein, the marketing manager, at a product development meeting some weeks later. Explaining the positioning of Pizza Superiora, Stein draws the following figure of the upper left segment in which the two asterisks pointing up and to the left represent Romano and Pan Pizza, while the asterisk pointing towards the sociograph *origo* represents Pizza Superiora (see Figure 7.1 below):

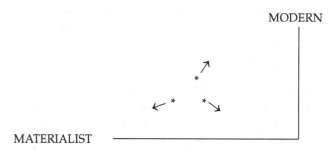

Figure 7.1. Marketing strategies for three leading pizza products (hand-drawn illustration; arrows indicating product differentiation strategies by reference to the target groups).

Keeping these considerations in mind, we are now better able to understand why Kristoffer, emphasizing the unique characteristics of Pizza Superiora, mentions neither 'American' nor 'Italian'. Obviously, he must come up with something else, which is neither of the above. Elaborating the brand strategy in the briefing for Pizza Superiora, Kristoffer writes:

> *Superiora is the pizza for pizza lovers. In addition it is to be positioned as Norway's clearly most popular ('mest solgte') pizza. This is the pizza that*

everybody likes, regardless of age, sex and other demographic data. Superiora is the people's pizza ('folkepizzaen') in Norway. It is basically Superiora that comes to mind, when one thinks of frozen pizza. When you buy a Superiora you know what you get . . . The pizza must be presented as a good-quality product that is convenient and easy to make.

The stress on quality should, however, not be too strongly emphasized. Describing the 'brand personality' ('*merkets personlighet*'), the briefing continues: '*Superiora is perceived as the qualitatively best pizza of the market. This is obviously closely connected to the product's market share.[7] We want this situation to be maintained, but the film should not communicate that this is the best pizza in the market.*'

According to general requirements of brand-building (heavily emphasized by the marketing manager), brand positioning and brand image should be coherent with the target group definition and the general market situation. Conceptualizing Pizza Superiora as '*folkepizzaen i Norge*' (the people's pizza in Norway), Kristoffer establishes a certain *sameness* between product position and the product target group. Stein makes a similar statement through his hand-drawn sketch (Figure 7.1), in which he locates each product precisely at the point of gravity for its respective target group. Visually, the product and its consumer tend to merge.

This *sameness* is, however, simultaneously a result of a deliberate effort to create *difference*. More than any other pizza product at Viking Foods, Superiora is consumed by 'nearly everybody', and Superiora is given its distinct characteristic precisely through the image of being the Norwegian people's pizza.

In addition, the concept '*folkepizzaen i Norge*' introduces a second dimension that is not immediately apparent through English translation. Conceptualizing Pizza Superiora as '*folkepizzaen i Norge*', Kristoffer simultaneously recontextualizes this particular pizza as something very Norwegian. In general discourse, the prefix '*folke-*' has connotations of egalitarian values that are deeply rooted in Norwegian society. In her description of central themes in Norwegian culture, Marianne Gullestad emphasizes what she considers to be the typically Norwegian notion of equality *defined as sameness.* Highly apparent in Norwegian discourse, the egalitarian tradition involves '*not necessarily actual sameness, but ways of under-communicating differences during social encounters*' (Gullestad 1989:85). This theme is reflected in a wide number of ways, including social institutions whose primary purpose is to ensure equality through sameness. Such sameness may be conceptualized in economic terms, as in the social security system (*'folketrygden'*), or in terms of a shared system of knowledge through a common schooling system, both at elementary level (*'folkeskolen'*) and at higher levels (*'folkehøyskole'*). Often, these institutions are referred to in terms of the prefix 'folke-'.

Consequently, when he reconceptualizes Pizza Superiora as 'folkepizzaen i Norge', Kristoffer locates his product conceptually right at the heart of Norwegian notions of equality and social democracy. Most importantly, perhaps, he transmits a notion of a pizza that is non-pretentious in terms of a social hierarchy (social stratification). Something which is termed *'folke-'* is almost by definition *non-exclusive* in terms of social class. In Norwegian discourse, the term *'folke'* and notions of high culture, élite or upper class are almost mutually contradictory.[8]

The fact that Kristoffer chooses the term *'folkepizzaen'* to describe his product does not necessarily imply a deliberate effort to link the product to the values mentioned above. Drawing on a shared cultural repertoire of concepts and metaphors, he may simply have come across one that seemed to fit. He needed a concept that would cover the average Norwegian, not exclude anybody, and not evoke the notion of the traditional, nor the very modern. Furthermore, the product should symbolically be differentiated from communication that was simultaneously being produced for other products such as the more 'advanced' Romano and the 'Americanized' Pan Pizza. Consequently, Kristoffer conceptualizes the average Norwegian, the person for whom no describing characteristics apply, except for 'ordinariness' – being just the same as everybody else. This is exactly the notion that the term *'folke-'* conveys.

Phase 2: Promoting Pizza Starring 'Ordinary' People (The Fate of a Bad Idea)

Until now, Kristoffer has relied primarily on the expert interpretations of consumers offered by market research institutes. These institutions have served as *intermediary translators*, passing on detailed information about consumer interests, preferences and differentiating characteristics to the decision-making unit at Viking Foods. Such knowledge has, in turn, been incorporated into the briefing, so that in its final version, the Pizza Superiora brand ideally bears some features that somehow resemble those of its future consumers. The briefing thus provides a *closing of controversies* regarding the communicative properties of the product.

As Kristoffer sends the briefing to Tom at Publicity, the process moves from the phase of consumer interpretation to the phase of planned communication. This implies a simultaneous shift of social relations: from relying upon the written interpretations of market research institutes, Kristoffer now consults a set of intermediary translators who specialize in transmitting messages *from* the Viking Foods marketing unit to consumer target groups. In other words, we are entering the arena of professional communicators: advertising agencies and film production.

A few weeks after the briefing has been sent, Kristoffer receives a letter from Publicity with three roughly sketched 'storyboards' enclosed, each illustrating separate ideas for Pizza Superiora commercials. Each storyboard includes a series of 5–13 sketches with an accompanying text. Much like the format of cartoons, the sketches emphasize some key situations, and together they give a certain idea of what the film might look like. Having discussed the three suggestions with Stein, Kristoffer decides that he prefers the first one, and passes the message to Publicity. This storyboard depicts a room with people waiting: we see a man and a woman who keep checking their watches; a teenage boy enters, sits down with his parents; they check the time again; and suddenly there's the sound of a timer ringing . . . Then, as the woman bends down to look at something cooking in the oven, the camera closes in on her face as it would look from inside the oven. Finally, the pizza appears with a 'voice-over' saying: *'Those who wait for Norway's most popular pizza do not wait in vain'.*

During the next few weeks, the creative team at Publicity develops this idea further, contacts a company that specializes in film production, and invites Kristoffer and Stein to a meeting at 'Film Makers'.[9]

We meet outside the Film Makers building one sunny early morning. The location turns out to be an old, renovated factory building, recently equipped for film production. When I park my car, Tom and Kjell (account manager and copy writer) from Publicity have already arrived. As Tom and I have already met on many different occasions, and Kjell is well informed of my fieldwork, no presentation is necessary. We are slightly ahead of schedule, and as we wait outside in the sunny parking lot, Tom points to an old car, and makes a humorous comment about some assumed characteristics of the owner. Then Stein (the marketing manager) shows up in a brand-new Toyota Carina. He explains that he is only trying it out, and doubts whether he'll buy it, and pretty soon the discussion focuses on the various advantages and disadvantages of this car, and of other cars. The meeting is not mentioned yet.

As we enter the building, we search around for quite some time through stairs and hallways still in the process of being remodelled. Finally, we enter a large hall with a high ceiling, and notice a conference table where Kristoffer, Knut (creative director at Publicity) and a third man whom I assume must be the film person, are already seated.

The atmosphere of the building is quite different from that of an advertising agency. While the advertising agency appears to be fairly stylish and aesthetically up to date, the present location has a bohemian originality, partly achieved by incorporating elements of the old factory halls, and partly due to the various collections of film accessories stored in different places. Taken as a whole, the physical atmosphere seems flexible and highly dynamic, although not in the 'spotless' and efficient sense of the advertising agency.

As we sit down, everyone who hasn't met before shakes hands, and the film person presents himself as Richard. Tom opens by stating the purpose of the meeting:

> Tom: *We wanted to give Kristoffer some more information about how we conceive of the film, and about the way we have adapted and improved the initial idea.*

According to Tom, Kjell and Richard have considered various characters (*'personer'*) for the different roles, and Richard explains that he has prepared some portraits to give an idea of the model standard that is to be used.

> Kjell: *Film-making is a matter of trust ('film er en tillitssak'). We want you to feel safe about this part. So as Film Makers is new to you, we feel this meeting is important.*

Richard suggests that they start by doing a tour of the production premises and looking at some specimen films. Soon afterwards, we are led around an impressive labyrinth of sound studios, scenes (some of us recognize the background of other commercials), camera rooms, TV studios, hallways and staircases. Except for a carpenter working in the sound studios, and a man who appears to be a technician in the TV studio, the premises are practically empty. As we pass through, single file, Richard keeps explaining the various possibilities of the studios:

> Richard: *Here, we can film, edit and finish for broadcasting, send it to London and then get it on the air via satellite all within a few hours. Of course, one should never be that short of time, but you know how it is . . .*

We listen politely to his description of the technical equipment, most of us probably too ignorant to really understand the implications, or to even ask questions. After a while, Tom jokingly comments to Kristoffer in a low voice: *'I wonder if they have any TV games'*, whereupon Stein exclaims to those of us who stand right next to him: *'The more I see of this, the more I realize that I'm better off using a pencil . . .'.*

Entering a room with TV screens covering an entire wall, we are asked to sit down. Obviously, this room is for viewing, equipped with chairs facing the screens. Richard now starts talking about 'Cedelmayer', a film producer who has been awarded a number of prizes at Cannes, and with whom Richard apparently has some affiliation. Appraising the work of Cedelmayer, Richard explains that this guy does not use models or film stars, but rather the man in the street, 'ordinary people with character' as he puts it.

He illustrates his point by showing us sequences of videotaped Cedelmayer commercials from the US, mostly in black and white, showing rather ordinary and not particularly attractive people, who are placed in a context that is sometimes funny. Obviously, this is the latest trend, but I don't quite understand what this has to do with our meeting, and I realize that I'm not the only one when Stein interrupts to ask: *'Is this Cedelmayer coming here or something?'*

It might have been a silly question; anyway, Richard replies that the trip alone would cost a million, more than twice the budget for the present project. Gradually, I understand that Cedelmayer serves only as a kind of inspiration, and that these commercials illustrate Richard's ideas about the film he wants to make.

All through the show, Richard does the talking while Kristoffer and Stein are rather quiet. I feel that some affirmative response is required, but withhold my urge to say something when I notice their blank poker-faced expressions. Suddenly, Stein interrupts: *'I thought we were invited here to select the characters for our commercial? And then, all we do is watch the commercials of somebody else? This isn't getting us anywhere at all.*

He goes on, explaining why he feels that they have to decide on the characters before they can proceed: *'They must not by any means be unattractive. People with greasy hair who drivel are **not** OK. The wrong people can ruin the whole thing.'*

Tom claims that there must have been some misunderstanding. He maintains that he made it very clear that he invited Stein and Kristoffer to present the further development of the idea, and to present Film Makers, but *not* to present the actual models. The importance of trust and confidence is mentioned again. Finally, Kjell and Richard add that casting is very expensive. They cannot start that process before they have a final 'go' from Viking Foods. Kristoffer and Stein seem to accept this argument, but still emphasize their doubts. Is Richard really serious when he says that he is going to 'pick the models from the streets', and what does that imply? Richard explains that, of course, the expression should not be taken literally. In fact, they have already established an archive of some 1,000 models from which to pick and choose. The point is that they are not going to use famous actors.

But Stein is not convinced. He still expresses worry that an unattractive person might ruin the whole film. Richard reassures him that no characters will be selected until Viking Foods has approved; in fact, they might select them together. Richard then insists on showing some other food commercials that Film Makers has produced. Half-heartedly, Stein makes an attempt to talk him out of it, saying that such reassurance is unnecessary, but finally gives in: *'Tom has chosen you, and that's all the guarantee I need. It's the **other** bit I'm worried about. I just want to make that clear . . .'.*

A few minutes later we are all back at the conference table where the meeting first started. Small talk seems to smoothen the previously tense atmosphere, but no final decision is yet made. The importance of trust is frequently mentioned:

> Kristoffer: *I don't know, I don't feel quite sure about this. But then, I guess it would have been a bit strange if I did.*

Tom mentions a marketing manager at another major client, who during the initial phases of a now very successful commercial production felt exactly the same way. Someone adds that this does not mean that feeling unsure about something is a guarantee of success. Obviously, everybody can agree to that. As the question of the target group is brought up, Tom maintains that the commercial will not appeal equally to everyone: *'That's simply not possible. The problem with commercials like this Superiora film is that the target group is practically all of Norway. And if we try to reach everybody, we reach nobody.'*

Gradually, the discussion closes in on the content of the film, and Kjell and Richard start presenting their latest development of the idea:

Richard: *We have these people sitting there, you know, waiting for the pizza, and then, at the very back we see old grandpa* [he stands up], *shaky hands, walking towards the camera* [he starts walking towards the table, mimicking the short-stepped, shaky way of walking that the elderly sometimes acquire]. *This man keeps reappearing in the picture, each time a little closer. This is how we indicate that time is passing. Obviously, he is walking towards something. But does he reach it in time? No. When the bell rings, everybody else is immediately right there, grabbing the pizza. He tries to grab the very last piece, we focus on his hand real close, but then – whoops, somebody else takes it just in front of him. Too late . . .*

Kjell: *This adds the notion that someone is really waiting to get this, it is popular stuff, people are really anxious ('folk er på alerten') to get their hands on these things.*

Stein: [slightly sceptical] *I just feel kind of sorry for him . . .*

Richard: *Exactly! You see, this introduces something else. You get a social thing in this, more engaged ('det har en mer sosial greie i seg').*

Kristoffer: *But can you really do this within 30 seconds?*

Richard: *Yes, of course . . .* [slightly ironical] *No, we've discussed this part. Obviously, the commercial will be far better if we go out to 40 seconds . . .*

Kristoffer: *That's what they always say . . .*

The discussion zeroes in on the time available. Richard and Kjell maintain that they will be able to do this within 30 seconds. But they still feel it would be a good investment to go up to 40. Kristoffer says that showing a 40-second commercial costs a whole lot more, and someone suggests two versions, one long and one short . . .

> Tom: *Compared to other advertisers, you people at Viking Foods operate mostly within the lower half as far as investments go . . .*

Shortly afterwards, Stein looks at his wristwatch. The meeting has lasted more than an hour already, and he needs to go. Kristoffer concludes the meeting, saying that now they feel they need to take all of this back, chew on it, and then give a message back to Publicity before the end of the day. Stein quickly leaves, and shortly afterwards I am out in the sun.

Instead of calling back the same day, Kristoffer and Stein present these ideas at an internal marketing meeting a few days later. After the meeting, Kristoffer tells me that they have decided not to accept the idea. The main objection, according to Kristoffer, is that it is too 'tame' (*'tamt'*), too boring, and that the story is not good enough, particularly as it lacks what is referred to as a 'Big Idea' (for further explanation, see below).

> Kristoffer: *Even though the characters were to be selected very carefully, you cannot expect these people to carry the whole story.*

Kristoffer will give Publicity this message, and ask Tom to come up with a new idea, possibly by means of a different creative team. A week later, Stein puts it this way as he explains to another marketing manager why they turned the idea down: '*First of all, the people are ordinary, they are not supposed to be beautiful, this means that they might be disgusting ("ekle"). This, to me, is risky, particularly when you're talking about advertising food. Secondly, the story would really require good actors in order to be funny. That was taking a chance as well . . .'.*

The meeting at Film Makers differs from meetings with advertising agencies described previously in that a third party is involved. When printed advertising is to be produced, the creative team is part of the advertising staff. When advertising implies film production, professional expertise is usually sought outside the advertising agency, and external actors get involved. In this situation, the advertising agency holds the position of a broker. In the present case it was Tom, the account manager, who took on the responsibility of leading the meeting, clarifying potential misunderstandings, and standing security for the competence of Film Makers *vis-à-vis* his client. Still, while acting as a broker, Tom was clearly leaning towards his client, rather than towards the film-makers. This was particularly apparent when, during the grand tour, he took part in establishing a back-stage atmosphere of low-voiced joking, an act that also expressed a certain opposition to the technological show-off. Yet this does not restrain him from feeling critical. Obviously, Tom is in a position in which he has no choice but to put up with the likes, dislikes, and unpredictable twists and turns of his clients. Especially, in relation to major clients with considerable budget portfolio, any discontent must be exposed very carefully, if at all. In the present case, we may assume that Tom most of all wants to get things going swiftly, and in a manner that ensures the continuation of a good relationship.

Phase 3: Promoting Pizza Starring 'Beautiful' People (The Fate of a Better Idea)

Three weeks later, in June, Publicity has come up with three new ideas for Pizza Superiora commercials. This time, the ideas are not illustrated by storyboards, but by a sequence of texts describing each shot in short sentences. Kristoffer meets with Publicity for a more thorough presentation of these new ideas. A few days afterwards, a marketing meeting gives Kristoffer the chance to discuss the ideas with his product manager colleagues once more.

In the meantime, the so-called 'ten commandments' (*'de ti bud'*) have frequently been mentioned by product managers in the marketing department. The ten commandments is a list of ten principles for good advertising, and introduces as its first commandment (and the most important) the term 'The Big Idea'.[10] The concept is well known to most product managers, and was a central theme at a seminar about the production of TV commercials half a year earlier. Written hand-outs from this seminar have since been photocopied and distributed among some of the product managers, and is now frequently applied as a check-list for evaluating advertising ideas.[11] The concept of 'the Big Idea' is elaborated as follows:

CONCENTRATE ADVERTISING AROUND THE BIG IDEA. (1) First, identify the consumer benefit. The big idea – if there is one – is the core advertising idea used to communicate that benefit. (2) Lifestyle, humour and entertainment are not in themselves big ideas. (3) The core advertising idea might not appear as big when you just see it. It is particularly difficult to identify in a layout, script or storyboard. (4) Each execution should be seen as an opportunity to breathe new life into the core idea, not a carbon copy of the first commercial. (5) A property is not in itself a big idea; nor is a consumer benefit on its own a big idea (Hand-out from seminar).

As Kristoffer presents the three new Superiora film concepts at the Marketing meeting, the ten commandments and the concept of the Big Idea serve as criteria for evaluation. At the meeting all three concepts are favourably received by the other product managers. The final choice is a concept presented with the working title: 'Rendezvous'. The draft is written as follows:

TV-SPOT, PIZZA SUPERIORA, 'RENDEZVOUS'[12]
We see a young, beautiful woman put on lipstick in front of the mirror. All the time, we hear beautiful, romantic music.
Cut. A young, handsome man walks out of the bathroom of his apartment with an open shirt; he runs his hand through his hair.
Cut. The woman opens the door to the freezer and bends down.
Cut. The man knots his tie.
Cut. The woman turns on the oven. The romantic music keeps playing.
Cut. The man steps into the driver's seat of a red Corvette.
Cut. Through the door of the oven, we see the pizza being cooked, warm and delicious.
Cut. The man turns a corner in his Corvette and parks.
Cut. The woman opens the oven door, and looks in.
Cut. The man closes the car door behind him.
Cut. The woman takes a bite of the pizza to try it out, approvingly lifts her eyebrows, nodding . . .
Cut. The man runs along the pavement in slow motion.
Cut. The woman opens the door, he throws himself against her, she places her arms around his neck and kisses him.
Cut close-up: 'Are we eating at your place dear?' he asks, smiling with glittering white teeth and intense blue eyes.
Cut close-up of the couple: They are standing cheek to cheek, holding each other. We see her face, and his back. She opens her mouth, burps and says: 'No.'
Cut to the kitchen counter: There's an empty Superiora package and an oven tray with just a bit of dark crust left.

However favourably this was judged at the marketing meeting, there were still some important objections. On the basis of these, Kristoffer sends a telefax to Publicity with the following recommendation:

- *Eliminate the lifestyle image. Playing on lifestyle we are competing with a range of other companies with considerably higher budgets than ours. We want to stand apart, not fall through.*
- *Strengthen the fact that she doesn't need to go out to eat – she has already enjoyed her favourite dish. Thus strengthen the point that Superiora is the pizza for pizza lovers.*
- *Avoid old clichés like running in slow motion, etc.*
- *Make the film a bit more down to earth.*
- *The burp is appalling. It should be exchanged for another effect.*
- *As a concluding sequence: Pizza Superiora – pizza for pizza lovers.*

Reading through the list, I ask Kristoffer what he means by eliminating the lifestyle image.

Kristoffer: *Well, this looks almost like the concept of a Coca Cola commercial. Very cliché-like. I want it more down to earth, more ordinary, I don't want to emphasize any glamour, I'm just afraid it will fall right through, as others with more money to spend are doing that part better than we are . . .*

Marianne: *This concept is really different from the previous one, with people more beautiful than most and driving Corvettes?*

Kristoffer: *Sure, they can be beautiful and drive Corvettes. It's just this running in slow motion that I don't like.*

No progress is made on the Superiora commercial project until mid-August, when an afternoon meeting is scheduled in the new offices of Publicity. (In the mean time, the advertising agency has changed its name and organizational structure and moved its offices to new and more fashionable premises.) Once again, Kristoffer and Stein represent Viking Foods, while Tom, Knut (creative director) and a female consultant, Hege, represent Publicity. In addition, another film producer, Marius, has been invited.

I arrive early, and having ascended to the 6th floor in an elegant elevator with a view of the entire building, I am seated in a soft couch near the entrance. Tom hurries by, stops for a moment to ask how my work is going, and quickly sits down. Aware that I am by now also participating in meetings at another competing advertising agency, he asks me whether I notice much difference in the way they work. I tell him that I think they're quite similar, and then we have to go.

The conference room is situated in the centre of the offices, separated from a surrounding corridor by glass walls. Glass walls also serve as divisions between the offices and the corridor, but our view of the surroundings is diminished by metal shades, which also prevent passers-by from looking in. As usual, we may help ourselves to mineral water, coke and coffee, and, instead of the usual chocolate, there is a tray of Danish pastries in the middle of the table.

Tom opens the meeting, saying that he assumes that everybody present is familiar with the suggested concept, and with the present disagreement. Referring to Kristoffer's latest fax, he briefly mentions the main objection, which is the lifestyle image, especially as it is expressed through the running in slow motion. The other objection relates to the burp at the end, which Kristoffer feels is too disgusting (*'ekkel'*). The other issues mentioned, he says, are immediately agreed upon by the creative team at Publicity, and are unproblematic. The remaining problems thus relate to the lifestyle image and the burp.

Then he leaves the floor to Marius, the film producer, who maintains that this is no lifestyle commercial at all; rather it is a *parody* of the lifestyle commercials. This is precisely the reason why he wants to do the running in slow motion. And that's why he wants the characters to be so incredibly handsome and successful. For the same reason, the final burp is more than an indication that the woman has had a pizza; rather, it is supposed to serve as a direct break from the lifestyle image, kind of a hint to emphasize the parody. Listening to him, I realize for the first time the ironic intention, and I wonder whether Kristoffer has been misunderstanding it, just like me. (I get the feeling that the advertising people wonder about the same thing, but this is no occasion for finding out.) The film producer concludes: *'If I eliminate the lifestyle image and the burp, as you suggest, what's going to be left of it? Whatever it is, it is certainly not a good commercial.'*

As soon as he finishes his presentation, the discussion closes in on the burp. Various questions arise, such as: Is it really disgusting when a beautiful woman burps? Does it have to be? Are there different kinds of burps, and does it have to be so explicit? After about half an hour, someone suggests that the burp is primarily a sound effect, which can be added on or eliminated afterwards. The same goes for the slow-motion running, which is really no more than a special effect. Both elements may be eliminated, and thus do not have to be decided upon at this point. The main thing now is that Viking Foods give an approval that enables Publicity and the film producer to proceed. In other words, the possibilities of technically adding or eliminating elements after the actual shooting imply that the process may proceed in spite of unresolved controversies.

Then Stein (the marketing manager), who has expressed considerable scepticism during the discussion, maintains the need to hit 'right at the centre of the sociograph origo'. This is not easy, he says, and it is especially difficult with such disgusting elements as burping. Trying to summarize, Hege, who has been busy taking notes, concludes that there is an agreement in principle to proceed with the production of the film, and that the unease regarding certain elements will be considered as the process goes along.

Going down in the lift as we leave, Kristoffer, who is usually quite cheerful, looks tired. He says it's been a horrible day. And besides, they are selling so much Pizza Superiora that they have problems with delivery . . .

A few days later, Publicity submits a report from the meeting, stating that: 'the elimination of slow-motion running is considered, but . . . the exaggerated lifestyle image should be kept. Further it was agreed that the content of the final sequence is to be decided upon when the sound is added'. Receiving this report, Kristoffer cannot accept the conclusion regarding the lifestyle image, and sends a protest to Publicity to make his objections clear. I ask how he feels about this idea of making a parody of lifestyle commercials.

Kristoffer: *I don't mind, it's just that I want it more down to earth, and I want 'pizza for pizza-lovers' to be more strongly emphasized. And the burp is absolutely out of the question . . .*
Marianne: *So you feel that this irony is kind of a side track?*
Kristoffer: *If he wants to use it as a means to get the promise of the product across, I don't mind, as long as it is the product promise that is important.*

In spite of Kristoffer's objections, in its final version the Pizza Superiora commercial is rather close to Marius's first concept. The couple is elegantly dressed and with the air of high class, and we see the man running in slow motion from his red Corvette. In the end, and quite surprisingly, we hear the low sound of a burp and then the sound of the woman laughing, slightly embarrassed. None of Kristoffer's objections seems to have been followed up.

Postscript

Almost two years later (as I am writing up a draft of the present case study), I call Kristoffer to borrow a copy of the Superiora video. Unable to recall having seen it on TV, I feel I need to take another look at the final result. Kristoffer, who has now been promoted to the position of marketing manager and is no longer in charge of pizza products, refers me to Trond, a previous product secretary who is now brand manager for the pizza products. Trond tells me that they have now made some new films, as the earlier one turned out not to be very successful.

Trond: *No, we were not happy with it. The commercial was taken off ('tatt av plakaten') just a few weeks after it had been released, and will never be shown again.*

Marianne: *What was wrong with it?*

Trond: *Well, there were several things, such as for instance the burp towards the end. It was not very well received. The film producers actually did some testing before it was released, and got very positive figures. But in hindsight we've been kind of sceptical of those results . . . Anyhow, we decided to run the film, hoping that it would be perceived as 'folkelig',[13] and that people would see the irony. But like I said, the response was almost entirely negative. Most people did not see the irony, and the burp was distasteful ('usmakelig'). The guy who made the film does not work for that advertising agency any more. All in all, it was not a very good process.*

Marianne: *How was it bad?*

Trond: *Well, especially the way some ideas were just pushed through, in spite of objections. Today we use the film as a horror example of how things go when you don't have a very clear idea right from the start.*

Marianne: *Are you satisfied with the new commercials?*

Trond: *Well, they are definitely a lot better. But whether we are really happy with them, I don't know . . . Not really. You know, there's always something . . .*

Summary

The present chapter illustrates how an image of the consumer target group (derived primarily from consumer segmentation) is applied and incorporated as part of the final product image. Pizza may be conceived as a foreign dish in Norway, a culinary concept that originated far from the local cultural context. During the processes of incorporation, and through the application of marketing theory, pizza has been domesticated and has been recontextualized in accordance with Norwegian cultural values. As such, the case of Pizza Superiora indicates that global dissemination of culinary concepts does not necessarily lead to a cultural homogenization. In fact, as the ideology of brand-building clearly demonstrates, marketing implies a celebration of diversity.

Pizza Superiora is also an example of a case in which, in spite of detailed target group analysis, consumer interests remain elusive and undefined. This is due partly to the fact that the pizza target group is located fairly close to the *origo* of the *Norwegian Monitor* sociograph in the first place, but also to the strategy of product differentiation, which requires the act of symbolically 'pushing' Pizza Superiora significantly closer to the *origo* than its Romano and Pan Pizza counterparts. While Romano remains 'advanced', and Pan Pizza is designed to be 'American', Pizza Superiora is stuck with the notion of the average Norwegian. Perhaps for lack of a better word, the product is recontextualized as *'folkepizzaen'* and thus linked to basic Norwegian notions of sameness and ordinariness, of what in French would be termed *'le moyen'*, a term which in French also entails the notion of mediocrity.[14]

Ironically, it is the very popularity of Pizza Superiora that provides the rationale for such conceptualization. Obviously, with a market share of more than 50 per cent, the distinguishing criteria of its consumers are likely to be rather similar to the distinguishing criteria of frozen pizza users in general, and the target groups will largely overlap. Consequently, the construction of a distinctive image is difficult. In addition, the seeming 'ordinariness' of Pizza Superiora might also be a result of the operational characteristics of the sociograph itself. The sociograph is constructed on the basis of 60 operationalized values that are, in themselves, arbitrarily reflecting an indefinite number of potentially distinguishing characteristics within the Norwegian population. These values are relevant for distinguishing some consumer behaviour patterns, while they may be irrelevant for others (Lien 1993). Consequently, when a target group is located at *origo*, it may simply be because the distinguishing characteristics of the target group are *not* among those included in the *Norwegian Monitor* value base. In other words, an *origo* location might be an indication of the failure of the sociograph in describing the particular phenomenon at hand. The latter possibility seems, however, not to be taken into consideration by the product and marketing managers involved. According to their interpretation, the image of Pizza Superiora should be directed simply to the average consumer.

As it turned out, addressing the average was not easy. The characters may be ordinary, but not in a negative sense. They may be beautiful, but not in a too exaggerated lifestyle sense. Like the prime movers of the poultry project, Kristoffer is in a position where he constantly has to make up his mind about something he feels uncertain about. But his role leaves little room for doubt – Viking Foods' acceptance or refusal is continuously required, and it is Kristoffer's responsibility to provide this. Consequently he collects all the information he can get, and tries his best to apply it. In the present case, this also implies the application of guidelines for judging TV commercials.

The case also highlights potential conflicts between the creative (advertising agencies and film-makers) and their clients. The former depend on selling their ideas, which are by definition more 'creative' than any idea that their clients could come up with by themselves. (Though as is illustrated in the poultry project, this proposition does not remain entirely uncontested.) However, in the present case, the Viking Foods' product manager is totally at the mercy of agencies possessing specialized knowledge in the field of film production. In spite of this dependency, the 'creative' are not free to do as they please. Each little detail must be approved by their client, and is thus liable to disapproval, often for reasons that – from the perspective of the advertising profession – may seem unreasonable or hard to accept. While my close connection (and assumed loyalty) to the marketing department usually prevented me from backstage encounters with the advertising profession, one may reasonably assume that the experience of having one's ideas disapproved of or even misunderstood may give rise to some frustration. Especially when new ideas are repeatedly discarded by product managers, whose judgemental criteria may be quite different from those of the profession itself, there is considerable potential for conflict.

The present case highlights these conflicting views, and also reveals that the seemingly friendly relationship between advertising agency and client is more complex than it appears on the surface. This is indicated especially through Tom's final comment regarding Viking Foods' general low payment and high expectations. Rather than being surprised at his critical comment, we should perhaps be surprised that such comments do not enter discourse more often. From the perspective of advertising agencies trying to survive during a period of enhanced competition, long-term relationships to major clients are clearly too precious to be jeopardized by any uncontrolled outburst of frustration. In the light of this, the outward layer of friendliness may be a precarious social condition, carefully maintained by the social 'fingerspitzgefühl' of persons such as Tom, whose position is that of a broker between the client and the creative. In this particular case, the use of jokes and humour may serve to maintain the atmosphere of informal sociability. The fact that it tends to be Tom who takes on the role of a joke-maker substantiates this interpretation, and indicates that the ambiguous relationship between the advertising consultant and his client may (sometimes) be handled by means of humour, thus constituting the phenomenon often referred to as a joking relationship.

The present case also introduces explicit reflections on the part of the various actors over the notion of disgust. This is brought up first during the consideration of character types, and secondly during negotiations of the meta-narrative function against the potential disgust evoked by a woman's burp. The fact that the notion of disgust enters into the negotiations of a food commercial is hardly surprising. Anthropological literature on food and eating repeatedly documents how cultural separation between edibles and inedibles often entails simultaneous reference to the notion of disgust (for instance Fischler 1988; Lien 1989). In the present case the notion of disgust relates not so much to food itself as to persons, either through appalling behaviour, or through their unattractive looks.

Finally, this discussion of disgust is also a gendered discourse. In the commercial, the woman is the one who triggers the shift from exaggerated lifestyle image to parody. Through her burp at the end, she effectuates a swift 'falling from grace' – an event that in turn yields a rather ambivalent message with regard to the initial status of the couple. This act is, at the same time, a negation of general notions of feminine behaviour. In a sense then, we might argue that the swift descent from grace is effectuated through an abrupt break with a stereotype gender role pattern. We may also interpret this story within a framework of a Norwegian ideology of sameness, and argue that the commercial serves simultaneously to ridicule those who appear to strive for status.

Notes

1. Italy is the most relevant country of origin. In spite of the fact that Peppe's pizza set a standard for pizza that was already highly 'Americanized', this reinterpretation is rarely acknowledged among Norwegians, and pizza is generally conceived and referred to as Italian.
2. The English term is used.
3. In Norway, fast food (*'gatekjøkkenmat'*) is often associated with an American lifestyle. This is probably due to the fact that fast food outlets have increasingly included on the menu since the late 1970s hamburgers, a dish that is strongly associated with the US.
4. In Norwegian, the term 'American' is frequently used to denote the US, rather than to the entire American continent. Reference to parts of the American continent other than the US are usually specified, by terms such as South America, Latin America, Mexico or Canada.
5. The English term is used.
6. A target group expansion that requires significant price cuts is hardly compatible with the strategy of brand-building. Brand products are, by definition, products that consumers are willing to pay a bit more for. Consequently, trying to reach the lower left quadrant by means of considerable price cuts would not only imply less profit per product sold, but also weaken the image of Pizza Superiora as a quality brand product.
7. This is confirmed through market research, which indicates that consumers give Superiora a top score in terms of quality; but it

is not in accordance with Kristoffer's own judgement of relative qualities, as expressed during interviews.

8. Incidentally, the Norwegian *'folkemuseum'* is a collection of farmers' and peasants' houses, each reflecting the specific building traditions in various parts of the country, and thus the historical traditions of ordinary people. Similarly, we find the term *'folke-'* right at the core of democratic institutions, in which the elected politicians are referred to as *'folkevalgte'* (literally: publicly elected), or through the Norwegian term for a referendum: *'folkeavstemning'*.

9. 'Film Makers' is a fictitious name.

10. The English term is used.

11. The origin of these principles is rarely mentioned, but, according to the written hand-out from the seminar, they were developed by two men named Peter Sheldon and Dennis Saunders at the multinational corporation, Unilever.

12. The French term is used.

13. *'Folkelig'* is another example of a common term that is derived from the prefix *'folke-'*. It is an adjective referring to something that is popular in the sense of being well received among 'ordinary' people, being appreciated by 'the man in the street'. Popularity within the higher social strata would, however, not imply *'folkelig'*, but rather the opposite. Often, the term *'folkelig'* is used to characterize a certain kind of humour.

14. In French, there seems to be a more immediate connection between the concept of the average, *'la moyenne'*, and a somewhat degrading notion of mediocrity. Feldman maintains that there is in French what she calls an irreducible residue of condescension: *'"Moyen" apparait en fait très souvent comme une litote pour "médiocre", qui, lui, signifie clairement: "au-dessous de la moyenne" . . . La plupart du temps, être dans la moyenne signifie poliment: être affligé de quelque médiocrité'* (Feldman 1991:22).

Chapter 8

Offering Convenience and Culinary Appeal: The Bon Appétit Project

In the present chapter we will follow the fate of a range of convenience foods over a period of two years. During this period, considerable resources are spent on promoting the product, which is considered promising, but not yet very successful. The efforts involve product development, the elimination and introduction of different product varieties, and, most importantly, two major advertising campaigns, one through the printed media, and the other through film.

According to a definition launched by the Viking Foods' product development director at a seminar, *'ferdigmat'* includes not only complete meals, but also meal components that the consumers combine with other industrially produced or home-made components to constitute a meal. In general discourse, however, *'ferdigmat'* usually refers to fairly complete meals, and especially to *industrial products that combine elements that have previously been put together in the home*. For instance, a package of dry spaghetti is usually not referred to as *'ferdigmat'*, as the possibility of making spaghetti from raw materials is generally not considered. Once the pasta is purchased in a mixture with a pre-prepared sauce (dried or hermetically sealed), the product is more likely to be referred to as *'ferdigmat'*, as the preparation of pasta sauce in the home is fairly common.

The concept of *'ferdigmat'* may thus be conceived of as a relative, rather than an absolute term. Its meaning derives not only from industrial processing, but also from the *absence of culinary elaboration in the household*. 'Ferdigmat' and 'hjemmelaget mat' (home-made food) thus represent the opposite poles on a continuum, in which the most significant dividing line appears at the point at which a product could have been, but *is not*, put together in the home. An increase in the consumption of *'ferdigmat'* would thus indicate a transfer of certain household activities from the private sphere to the industrial domain.

Convenience Foods in Norway: Fertile Ground for Growth

By the end of the 1980s, food manufacturers in Norway observed the following paradox: On the one hand, market research into changes in eating habits, demography, and family structure predicted a significant and increasing demand among consumers for convenience foods. On the other hand, the actual consumption of convenience foods in Norway was still relatively low, especially when compared with mainland western Europe and the US.

With regard to changes of eating habits, the most important source of reference in the marketing department is consumer segmentation surveys and a recent survey on eating habits. According to the latter, recent changes may be described as follows:

1. Destructuration. During the late 1980s there was a consistent tendency towards 'destructuration of meal pattern and eating habits'. An increasing number of people are eating at irregular times, persons in the same household to not eat together as often as before, and do not always eat the same. This is documented by data that show that the percentage of the population eating breakfast at home daily has dropped from 81 per cent in 1986 to 76 per cent in 1990. Concerning dinner,[1] there is a similar drop from 76 per cent eating dinner daily at home in 1986, to 64 per cent in 1990. According to the market research institute, this tendency provides fertile opportunities for convenience foods.

2. Simplification. There is a parallel tendency towards simplification. People substitute hot dinners for more simple meals. In 1986, 34 per cent of the respondents reported that they replaced dinner with a cold meal to make things simple ('often' or 'now and then'). In 1990, this category had increased to 42 per cent.

During the same period, there had been a dramatic increase in the number of households with a microwave oven, from only 3.7 per cent in 1986 to 26.9 per cent in 1990.[2] It is expected that the spread of microwave ovens will continue. In addition to these changes there is also a steady tendency towards more single-person households, and more families in which both parents work full-time. According to information available in the marketing department, approximately 60 per cent of the population were living in households consisting of 1–2 persons in 1990, and this proportion was assumed to be increasing. For marketing managers at Viking Foods (and for market research consultants), all these tendencies indicate a considerable *'potential for growth'* in the area of both frozen and chilled convenience foods.

This potential is also substantiated by sales figures indicating a considerable increase in the consumption of convenience foods during the late 1980s. According to Viking Foods sales statistics, the total volume of ready-made dinner products doubled from 1988 to 1990. When broken down into specific product groups, however, figures indicate that this is primarily due to a dramatic growth in so-called *'panneretter'*, i.e. frozen mixtures of various meats, vegetable and potato components that are to be heated directly in the frying pan. When it comes to dishes that are suitable for microwave ovens, there has also been a considerable increase, while for other convenience dinner products the increase is negligible.

The emphasis on convenience foods is also reflected in advertising. According to an analysis of printed Norwegian food advertising collected during fieldwork, 8 per cent of the adverts were promoting dinner products normally referred to as 'ferdigmat', whereas 9 per cent promoted raw ingredients usually prepared for dinner (meat, fish, poultry, rice, potatoes, dry spaghetti). A quantitative content analysis of the same material revealed that the concept of convenience (*'lettvint'*) appeared in 18 per cent of all adverts, and thus ranked among the terms most frequently encountered in food adverts (Lien 1995).

In spite of this recent increase, the total consumption of convenience foods is still considered to be fairly low in Norway, compared to countries in the European Union and in the US. This discrepancy is often explained by economic constraints related to the size of production series. At a seminar in 1990, the Viking Foods product development director put it this way:

> In Scandinavia the total sales of ready-made, complete [dinner] meals has been low up until now. This is due to several factors. The market in each

country is limited, and consequently production levels are limited, resulting in high costs of production. This leads to a purchase price which the customer thinks is too high. With a market as small as Norway, and only 4 million potential customers, the marketing resources are also limited. It takes time to establish a considerable consumption level of new products. In countries within the European Union, however, the high sales potential allows for investments in far more effective product lines. This leads to far lower wage costs per portion. When, in addition, raw materials costs less, and there is lower taxation on foods, we see prices in England, France and Germany that are about half of what they are in Norway. This is the reason why, during the next five years, we will surely experience an increase of the import of frozen or canned convenience foods in Norway.

In addition to these indications of increased consumer demand, convenience foods also represent a considerable potential for so-called 'added value'. In a market that is considered to be saturated in terms of food supply, the most important potential for economic growth lies in the manufacturing process (Fine and Leopold 1993:164). When Viking Foods launches convenience foods, it may thus be seen as a strategic adaptation to a saturated and stable consumer demand.

This situation broadly sets the stage when Viking Foods starts formulating a strategy in the area of ready-made frozen convenience foods.

Case 3: The Bon Appétit Project

Bon Appétit is a range of frozen, processed dinner products generally referred to as 'ferdigmat'. I first entered this project in October 1991, when I joined Henrik and Sissel (both product managers at Viking Foods) at an international food fair in Cologne. The biannual ANUGA *'Weltmarkt für Ernährung'* (World Market for Nutrition) is famous within the area of food manufacture and food import. Featuring more than 5,000 firms from more than 80 countries, the fair is considered one of the major international events in the European food business.

While an overview of the entire exhibition area would require the full five days of the fair, Henrik and Sissel are more selective, spending their two-day visit separately, focusing on specific themes only. For Henrik, this implies, among other things, a good look at convenience foods in general, and meetings with potential exporters to Norway, most of which were scheduled ahead of time.

Within the areas defined by the main product categories, we stroll along the hallways with convenience foods, where each firm is represented at a separate stand, individually designed and equipped with sales personnel, pamphlets, computers, video screens, food displays and foods to taste. Totally unfamiliar with food manufacturing at this early stage, I find myself suddenly immersed in a world of professionals that is both curiously strange, and somewhat familiar. On the one hand, I am an ordinary female consumer, excited about the wide range of possible culinary experiences that unfold as we are walking down the aisle. On the other hand, I am an unprofessional outsider in the constant stream of food business professionals, a 'consumer in disguise' in premises where ordinary German consumers are not allowed to enter. Even more, I am a woman in a world predominantly inhabited by men – mostly men in suits, men in business, men in an environment in which the male dominance is, as far as I can judge by the hundreds of people passing by, a ratio of approximately 5:1. The women present are generally dressed-up, many in elegant female versions of the male suit-and-tie. Suddenly, and in spite of my sore feet, I feel relieved that I replaced my comfortable sneakers with a pair of high-heeled shoes.

In this environment of male dominance, Henrik is a good companion. Our shared Norwegian language offers a space for backstage privacy, and allows for questions and direct comments that in a *lingua franca* would have been withheld.

As we stroll through the hall, Henrik stops here and there to take a closer look or to try something out, and sometimes he puts a few questions to the sales personnel, who are usually more than eager to answer. Through these discussions, I only occasionally reveal my role as a researcher. Mostly, I am immediately received as Henrik's silent colleague. This odd position poses no problems at all, as most of the people he talks to seem immediately to place me in the role of a secretary or an assistant, and need no further explanation. For Henrik, the main purpose of the visit is to see other products that might give him some ideas, and to get a general update on what's going on. In addition, he seeks to make some contacts both with potential suppliers of ingredients and with foreign manufacturers from whom they might purchase ready-made products in the event of future import liberalization. In that case, the products might well be sold under the Viking Foods brand name. Not yet familiar with the business of food manufacturing, I am surprised to learn that the actual manufacturer and the company brand name do not always coincide. Henrik explains that this happens all the time, as major manufacturers may deliver their product to different companies, each of which will market their product under a different name.

As we stop to look at German manufacturers of convenience foods, Henrik spends a long time looking at the varieties of ethnic convenience foods offered, many of which I have never encountered in Norwegian food stores. I notice that, while some dishes catch his interest, others are immediately discarded. It seems to me that these judgements are made intuitively, and when I ask him about what he's actually doing, he replies:

Henrik: *I'm just picking up some ideas. A lot of these are not relevant for the Norwegian market. It is simply too unconventional ('sært'). Like for instance 'Deutsche Knödeln'. This is food for the Germans. But then there are other things that are interesting.*

Marianne: *Like what?*

Henrik: *Lots of things. Italian dishes, obviously. And spring rolls as well. I think spring rolls have now reached a point which is suitable in terms of a launch . . .*

Marianne: *How do you know?*

Henrik: *I guess it relates to an overall knowledge of the Norwegian market . . .*

This foreign experience marked the beginning of my fieldwork period, and the beginning of my involvement in what was referred to as the 'Bon Appétit project' as well. At this time, the product range had already been on the market for more than a year, and subsequent decisions were mostly legitimized by reference to major strategic decisions that had been made within the preceding months. In order to obtain a more comprehensive understanding of the long-term strategy involved, I therefore collected all the material that had been filed by the product manager on the Bon Appétit product series since it was first presented to the advertising agency, eighteen months earlier. Let us first take a look at what had happened.

Phase 1: Towards a Formulated Strategy

In February 1990, Henrik had written a letter to Tom, account manager at the advertising agency Publicity, headed 'Package design for a new convenience-dish series': *'On the basis of the experiences we have had with various concepts during recent years, market research surveys, studies of concepts in other countries, and repeated internal and external discussions, we have now formulated a strategy for directing our efforts towards building up ('satse på'[3]) frozen convenience dishes.'* He enclosed a document that was referred to as the Marketing Strategy, and asked Publicity to develop package design on the basis of this. He further informed them that the assortment would consist of 14–15 different products, and would replace all the convenience foods currently on the market except for Lasagne, which would remain unchanged. The other products were not yet finally decided upon.

He also enclosed a short note about the market situation, which referred to changes in family structure and eating habits and pointed to a *'strong potential for growth in the sales of all kinds of convenience foods in the future'*. Discussing various types of preserving methods (cooled, frozen and sterilized), it was further claimed that in Norway, *'with our long distribution distances and low population density, frozen foods are likely to have the greatest potential'*. The product range was defined as *'one- or two-portion package[s] which can be heated in the inner package either in an oven, microwave oven, or hot water'*. Furthermore, they are complete meals or basic components to be served with a side dish, and are characterized by *'high quality, good taste at a reasonable price (compared with competitors), and as healthy and nutritious as possible without interfering with the taste experience'*. The main idea behind this marketing effort was to *'gather all the frozen convenience-dishes as one brand'*, which will be given the name Bon Appétit. The target group was defined as:

modern, busy, urban people with high income; men and women aged 20–55; internationally oriented, with an interest in design and good taste; active leisure time; individual, unstructured meal pattern; eat conveniently during weekdays, but do not give up on taste or quality requirements for that reason. Taste is most important, but the products may well have a healthy image as well.

During the following months, Publicity developed suggestions for a package design. In the mean time, the results of a *Norwegian Monitor* target group analysis for convenience food were submitted to Henrik from a market research institute.

In July 1990, Henrik wrote a new letter to Publicity. On the basis of the concept that was now established, he needed a slogan, a brochure and printed advertisements for information and promotion towards the retail business, in-store advertising material and suggestions for an advertising campaign to be released both through TV and for the press. This time he enclosed a so-called Brand Strategy (BS), which resembles and replaces what was previously referred to as the Marketing Strategy. In the Brand Strategy for the Bon Appétit product range, consumer segmentation is repeatedly referred to. We learn that the product will be positioned so as to reach primarily the *'upper left segment of the sociograph'*, and secondarily, the *'upper right segment'*. The primary target group is described as modern, busy, urban people with a high income, eating conveniently during weekdays and having an individual, unstructured meal pattern. Furthermore, they *'are engaged and active both at work and in their free time, willingly pay if the quality is satisfactory, and are not a marked gourmet group'*. The secondary target group, who are to be found in the *'upper right part of the sociograph'* are described as the *'"feinschmecker" segment'*, who *'focus more upon health, nutrition and natural products'*. According to the Brand Strategy, the latter category is hard to please, but is still an important target group for selected products. Under 'product characteristics' we find a strong emphasis on time-saving, convenience and a wide range of choice. Under the heading 'consumer advantages', Bon Appétit is described as a: *'qualitative food experience, a convenient and healthy meal that gives good conscience ("god samvittighet"), although it is not health-food or slimming-food. It gives time to spare, releases time for other activities.'*

The target group analysis commences with a comprehensive description of those tendencies that we have previously described in terms of destructuration, simplification and increased use of microwave ovens. We learn that the tendency to simplify meals correlates with the modern–traditional axis, indicating that, the more modern one is, the greater the likelihood that dinner will be replaced by a cold meal. When it comes to the use of convenience foods, the picture is less clear, but there is still a tendency for people who consume convenience foods to be located in the 'upper left quadrant'. The analysis thus offers a market research 'rationale' for Henrik's choice of the 'upper left' as his primary target group.

On the basis of a recent shift of convenience food consumers depicted as a movement downwards and to the left in the sociograph, the target group analysis concludes that Viking Foods should put a greater emphasis on the upper left quadrant of the sociograph, at the expense of the 'upper right'. This implies a general accentuation of the more materialistic and practical advantages of the product, at the expense of an emphasis on nature, health and gourmet appeal. Furthermore, the emphasis on ethnic specialities is no longer considered as important: *'Convenience food is in the process of getting a foothold among persons without the apparent taste for foreign foods or food in general, for that matter. This coincides with the spread of the microwave oven just described. The motivation for buying this kind of food is first and foremost time-saving . . .'.*

The report also refers so-called '*ad hoc* surveys' that indicate a tendency among consumers to assert that convenience food 'is not proper food' (*'er ikke ordentlig mat'*), and that the more 'ready-made' the food (defined as: the less labour investment in the household), the less proper. The market research institute observes that this tendency is stronger towards the right side of the sociograph: *'Convenience food has a credibility problem ("troverdighetsproblem") in appearing as a natural product precisely because it is pre-prepared at the factory, especially among well-educated, food-interested persons on the right side of the sociograph'* (Target group analysis, May 1990).

Consequently, when Henrik decided to address the 'upper left' as his primary target group he was right in line with the target group analysis recommendations. In spite of the difficulties described with regard to reaching the 'upper right', Henrik selects this category as his secondary target group, but recognizes the difficulties involved and considers this a relevant target group for *'selected products only'*.

We see here how the attempt to align the consumers as a future ally involved the consultancy of intermediary translators who specialize in 'knowing' the consumers. On the basis of interpretations offered by a market research institute, Henrik is better able to formulate a rough description of his convenience food product range, a task which he completes within the format provided by the Brand Strategy. As we shall soon see, this will provide a framework for judging the results of product development, and will also serve as a basis for subsequent negotiations regarding the material features of the product range. In addition, as it is submitted to the advertising agency as well, the target group analysis will provide a framework for evaluating the communicative and aesthetic aspects, and serve as a point of reference for negotiations regarding advertising message and advertising design.

Phase 2: Getting the Dishes Right: Technology and Taste

Unlike the poultry project, in which the material products were to be developed practically from scratch, the Bon Appétit product range consists mostly of products that have been on the market for some time. It also features new additions – some of which may appear after the product range has been reintroduced. In other words, Bon Appétit may be conceived as a flexible concept, to which single products may be added or eliminated as time goes by.

When Henrik wrote the first Brand Strategy, the dishes of the product range were not yet decided upon. Even after the launch of the Bon Appétit product range in March 1991, certain problems still remained with regard to material features of some products. This is reflected in written documents passing between Henrik and various branches of the product development staff. These documents reveal a continuous process of product development, a process that only occasionally coincides with marketing efforts. For Henrik, however, who has to keep an eye on both processes, these two areas come together in the sense that they are both crucial to the success of the product range. In October 1991, a letter from Henrik to Arne, who is responsible for the product development of convenience foods, describes 'high-priority development projects'. Under this heading, six different products are listed, followed by comments as to what the problem is, and what remains to be done. Most of these dishes are new products that, according to present plans, will be included in the Bon Appétit product range in the near future.

The difficulties are mostly related to specific details regarding combinations of ingredients, flavours, or packages, which Henrik insists on getting solved. The comments are partly phrased as actions that Arne needs to undertake, and partly as descriptions of the state of affairs. For instance, in connection with a complete salmon meal (*'Laks i Hollandaise'*),

> *Arne to undertake production experiments ('produksjonsforsøk') with rice and the vegetable dish [broccoli] in order to find out how much we can put into the form without getting problems with welding the tinfoil.*

In connection with a popular reindeer dish (*'Finnebiff'*),

> *the mixing of wild rice is very successful, and Arne will confer purchase . . . of ready mixture wild rice/white rice – check price.*

Regarding a fish casserole for microwave oven (*'Fiskeform'*),

> *Out of the four different toppings presented, we will continue development of a combination of cheese and sliced carrots.*

Regarding a pasta dish (*'Torsk Tagliatelle'*)

> *The presented product is not satisfactory. The sauce is too thick. There is too much cayenne – very strong aftertaste. Must add more taste that is experienced immediately. Drop the broccoli. Make two varieties, one with green onions, the other with vegetable stock.*

Regarding a fish and potato casserole (*'Torsk Hollandaise med potetskiver'*)

> *The potato slices from supplier G are quite good. Must discuss at some point how hard the potatoes are to be deep fried. New test with 5-millimetre potato slices – placed as thinly as possible, full 'cover'. More varieties with different amounts of sauce. Make one series of cod en bloc, and one series with grated fish.*

We see here how Henrik establishes a dialogue with product development regarding fairly detailed matters. Moreover, the document reveals that to some extent it is Henrik who defines the further choice of direction, specifying to the product development expert what to do, and in what order of priority. These negotiations over material characteristics occur at a level of detail that is quite far removed from the abstract product concept defined in the Brand Strategy. Negotiations about the right amounts of cheese and carrots and the correct viscosity of a particular sauce can hardly be closed by referring, for example, to the degree of modernity of the target group.

Henrik's task may thus be perceived as the work of translation between the abstract level of general consumer characteristics, and the very concrete level of material composition (and vice versa). Clearly, the Brand Strategy provides no manual of how to go about this. How then, does Henrik manage these translations? How does he know that the pasta sauce is too thick, and on what basis does he select the combination of cheese and carrots out of four possible toppings?

Faced with such questions, Henrik uses the expertise that is most readily available: himself, his wife, and a few colleagues in the marketing department. Right in the middle of the marketing department office area, there is a tiny kitchen. Fully equipped with a microwave and an ordinary oven, it allows for certain experiments. Sometimes the smell of hot food spreads into the office area, whereupon Henrik, mostly without any previous notice, gathers whoever is present to try something out. At other times, during discussions of various products, he jokingly refers to recent test results from '*Edvard Griegs vei 54*', referring thus to his private address, where he tries dishes out together with his wife. Thus, while the written documents mostly reflect professional market research, informal, *ad hoc* testing is part of decision-making as well, although it is not always referred to as such.

A few months later, in February 1992, three of the six products listed above are launched. The others are either discarded owing to difficulties in product development, or will be launched in the near future. None of the products launched have been formally tested by consumers. Henrik replies: '*It is risky, but then, there are also many fiascos that **have** been tested*'. He adds that the development process has largely taken place on the product development side, and the inclusion of the three new products in the product range will take place without any advertising effort.

Phase 3: A Sudden Need for Reassurance

The negotiations on product development reveal considerable doubt about the final material characteristics of the dish. From the perspective of the product manager, there are nearly always possibilities for improvement, and Henrik makes some serious attempts at discovering such possibilities and so contributing to such improvement. Still, these efforts do not imply a total elimination of risk. Even after the products are finally launched, Henrik does not know how consumers will respond. This is partly due to the fact that they have not been tested. But then again, no test can totally eliminate the possibility of a fiasco, as Henrik points out. In other words, in spite of ambitious efforts at product development, and some consumer testing, there is always an element of doubt involved.

Still, there are times when such doubt must be replaced by a more certain and enthusiastic expression. This was the case in late October 1991, following an incident that was assumed to have attracted unfavourable public attention, and thus some internal worries as well. The trigger of the event was a range of articles, published simultaneously by local newspapers throughout Norway, regarding a taste-trial of microwave convenience foods. The test had been carried out by a cooperative retail and producer chain, and came to a conclusion that did both Bon Appétit and competing products little honour. A significant characteristic of media coverage of such taste-trials is the use of a very direct and often exaggerated language. In the article mentioned, the description of a competing pasta product opens as follows: *'Yucky, doughy things – inedible. Discussion whether the beef really was meat. Almost impossible to remove the plastic . . . a great mess with the scissors'.*

Obviously, such descriptions are not only formulated for informative purposes, but for entertainment as well. For the producer, however, such descriptions may be detrimental both in terms of reduced sales, and indirectly through the effect they might have upon the general attitude towards the product within the organization. Following the publication of the newspaper articles, Henrik produces a written comment that he distributes widely within the organization, to the departments of product development and marketing and to the regional sales managers. He refers to the articles in which Bon Appétit and a few competitors did fairly poorly, and then goes on to criticize such tests in general:

> *This is another one of those tests where a small panel of experts 'elevate' themselves to represent the Norwegian grass root. I do not doubt that the taste panel are expressing their sincere opinion, but the point is that the judgments are based upon the subjective taste of the food experts. They express their opinion on the basis of a very limited number of tests of each variety,*

and accidental quality deviance may therefore have an enormous effect on the total judgement. Such a test is absolutely not statistically valid . . .

As an example, he compares the results of the present test to the results of a similar trial conducted by another national newspaper, and finds that a product that was judged to be almost inedible by the former expert panel was given a vary favourable score by the latter. As for the quality of Bon Appétit, however, his main argument relates to recent sales figures: *'When it comes to Bon Appétit, we can feel sure that the average "Ola and Kari convenience food-eater" are satisfied with our products, even if this test claims something else. . . . The first and most important argument is, obviously, our sales and market share development.'*

He then goes on to describe the sales figures, which indicate a steady increase. In fact, from early winter 1991 to late summer, the market share tripled (as measured by sales figures to the retail chain). This increase coincided with the launch and promotion of the new Bon Appétit concept, and is thus seen as a proof of its success. Henrik concludes: *'The target group perceives our products as fully satisfactory.'*

Finally, Henrik refers the results of an in-home test recently conducted for Viking Foods by a market research institute, which indicated that 88 per cent of the respondents maintained that *'Bon Appétit products are as good as or better than comparable products from other suppliers.'* Henrik concludes the document as follows: *'With this, I hope you have got some good arguments should you be confronted with the [referred] newspapers' consumer taste-trial. KEEP ON GOING ("STÅ PÅ"), THERE ARE STILL "VACANT" MARKET SHARES TO FIGHT FOR!'*

This enthusiastic expression of confidence on the behalf of Bon Appétit products should not be interpreted simply as a reflection of Henrik's present opinion. As other conversations indicate, Henrik's attitude to the quality of his products is far more moderate. Rather, we should see this note as an indication of one of the roles he has to take as part of his job as a product manager; namely that of the product's unyielding supporter. Like the coach of a soccer team, Henrik must stick with his products, through victory as well as through defeat. In the present case, a supportive attitude was needed in order to fend off worries and lack of enthusiasm among other actors involved in the development and promotion of Bon Appétit: worries that – if granted a certain legitimacy – might lead to less wholehearted efforts of promotion. This is in accordance with another ethnographic account of marketing practice, in which the author emphasized the importance of enthusiasm, as expressed by sales personnel (Prus 1989).

Interestingly, in his attempt to ensure internal support, Henrik refers directly to the consumers. We should, he argues, *not* listen to the panel of food experts who have 'elevated' themselves to represent the Norwegian grass roots. Instead, we should look at the actual purchasing practices of consumers. Fortunately for Henrik, he is able to substantiate his arguments by means of quantifiable sales results. As stated above, these are more 'trust-worthy' than those of 'food experts'. Through these statements we may note a certain ambivalence related to the value of what Henrik refers to as 'subjective taste experts' and methods that are 'not statistically valid'. While in some instances such evaluative methods provide necessary bridgeheads for translating consumer preferences into product recipes and vice versa, in the present situation, such an approach is judged as invalid. Equipped with sales figures, Henrik thus holds a position from which the 'subjective' opinions may be discarded for what he considers to be a more valid source of information.

Through sales figures, Henrik depicts an alliance to the consumers which is already established, and which is taken as a proof of consumers' acceptance of (or preference for) Bon Appétit products. This alliance is presented as a proof of the material quality of the product, which, in turn, serves to ensure internal support.

Phase 4: Constructing a Testimonial: Fame and the 'Ordinary'

The strategy of establishing the Bon Appétit brand also includes the production of a commercial. Thus, while Henrik is busy denouncing the validity of the newspapers' taste-trial, Nina, an Art Director at Publicity, makes the very first sketches for a commercial for Bon Appétit products. (According to Henrik, no briefing was produced for this particular film, and most initiatives and agreements have been reached informally, over the phone.) The concept of the commercial is therefore based upon a previous Brand Strategy and target group analysis.

In October 1991, Henrik receives a storyboard from Publicity for a Bon Appétit commercial, conceptualized as a testimonial by a public character who is well known, in Norwegian: a so-called *'kjendis'*.[4] Testimonials may be defined as a variety of the personalized format that shows a consumer using the product in the visual while explicitly stating that this is so in the text (Leiss *et al.* 1990:275). In the present storyboard, a famous middle-aged sports commentator, especially known for his knowledge of alpine skiing and soccer, Jon Jonsen, is the main character.

> *The storyboard starts by introducing Jonsen together with the image of some sports accessories (soccer ball, shoes), and then focuses on his face. We see him as he opens the freezer, we see him watching a clock on the wall which also features the picture of an alpine skier. Then the camera zooms in on his hands, cutting something,[5] and shortly afterwards we see a tray of food inside the oven, and the face of the main character as he opens the door. Then there is a sudden shift to pictures of tomatoes falling. The scene shifts to winter, and we see Jonsen through a window surrounded by snow; then we see an alpine skier, camera zooming in on his feet; and then we see Jonsen again inside the kitchen and with the living room in the background. He holds a glass in one hand and turns on the oven. The scene shifts again, with the picture of spaghetti being poured into boiling water. Back to Jonsen seated in his living room, with candle lights and ready to eat. Finally there is the so-called packshot, showing the Bon Appétit package and the dish.*

A few days later, Henrik sends a letter to Publicity, clarifying issues related to budget, time-schedule and media channels (the films will be shown on TV and in the cinema). Regarding the films, he repeats the main idea behind them: he wants to emphasize the concept of a dinner that is ready at any time of day, and what he calls *'activity-governed eating situations'*. Furthermore, he wants to select a *'kjendis'* in such a way that *'the target group . . . experiences identification with spokesman, milieu and not the least, lifestyle'*. He also wants attractive food shots within what the available Norwegian film technology can offer. Considering the suggested storyboard, Henrik comments: *'Film no. 1: In my opinion the storyboard indicates too many sequences, something which may contribute to a lack of coherence in the film. Must find alternative food shots as London is no longer relevant. End with a wider range of products'*.

Then he comments on suggestions for a Film no. 2, which is going to feature a female *'kjendis'* and a different dish. Briefly discussing two possible women, he asks Publicity to *'come up with suggestions for more suitable ("brukbare") women in occupations that appeal to our target group'.*

Two weeks later, in November 1991, I join Henrik at a meeting at Publicity. Other persons present include Johan, a Viking Foods marketing manager, Tom, who is account manager at Publicity, Knut, the creative director, Nina, the Art Director, and Grete, a consultant whose main functions are secretarial.

The meeting starts with a video presentation of recent Publicity commercials. Afterwards, while we wait for a film director to appear, the conversation focuses on possible characters. As for the commercial with a female spokeswoman, a decision seems to have been reached already: Maria Mortensen is the primary choice, a pop-singer in her early thirties who was successful in the Eurovision song contest a few years back. Jon Jonsen is obviously out, I don't know why, and I realize that these agreements must have been made informally over the phone in the mean time.

Then a process of verbal 'name-dropping' starts, and Tom keeps writing names on the board as they keep coming up. Each name releases spontaneous comments, most of which relate directly to the target group. Pretty soon a simple sociograph is sketched on the board, featuring the two main dimensions (modern–traditional, idealist–materialist). Tom locates the present target group by means of an amoeba-like figure on the left side of the vertical axis, and with a movement downwards he indicates that the target group is more traditional than they had originally thought.

The comments go approximately as follows:

Karl Kristoffersen[6] (Soccer commentator on the National TV broadcast): *'Cut him out'.*

Hans Vik (actor): *'He's too unknown for most people, and too expensive.'* (Someone mentions that he costs NOK 40,000.)

Morten Liland (musician, pop/rock, affiliated with a famous band): *'He lives at Lillehammer, and has played with band x, but do people really know who he is?'*

Vidar Frantzen (singer-songwriter, country/roots): *'Who's that? Oh, him with the ponytail.'* [Tom:] *'He looks just like a film-director. All film-directors have pony-tails, don't they?'*

Ivar Svendsen (singer-songwriter, folk-rock, politically to the left): *'Yes, he has appeal. But he belongs slightly over to the*

> *right side of the sociograph, doesn't he? He does have a*
> *wide appeal, but . . .'*

Fredrik Røed (comedian, satirist and singer):

> *'He's too controversial. But he probably needs the*
> *money . . .'* (According to popular press coverage,
> Røed has had some economic difficulties.)

John Sortland (singer-songwriter):

> *'I'm sure he's ready* [laughter].' (Like Røed, Sort-
> land's financial difficulties have also received
> recent coverage in the popular press.)

Until now, comments have been largely negative, and each suggestion is quickly discarded, until someone mentions a national broadcast programme director called Kjell Gregers. For the first time, as the following comments indicate, they seem to have found a appropriate candidate:

> *'He's known. He's ordinary ("vanlig"). Not controversial. He's in*
> *"Se & Hør"*[7] *almost every week. He gets a lot of attention. And he*
> *goes to all first night performance parties ("premièrefester"). It seems*
> *like he's on the way up.'*

Tom: *'And besides, he just bought a new car. I read in an article that he*
> *was crazy for cars.'*

Then, the film director and his secretary arrive, and the film director becomes the centre of attention. He immediately suggests a person whom he considers to be the right male character, Vidar Sande, a well-known racing driver from rural Norway, who is known both for his speed driving talent, and for his rough and outspoken behaviour. It seems as if the film director had made up his mind before he entered the meeting, and he spends most of his presentation defending this choice:

> *A lot of people like him. He may be a bully ('røver') and a reckless driver*
> *('råkjører'), but he's a good guy. And one can easily understand that he has*
> *little time for cooking. Things must happen fast. And he has a charming*
> *dialect. He is likely to appeal to the segment we are talking about. There's a*
> *lot to play upon, film-wise.*

According to the film director, Sande has already said that he's willing to participate. He costs less than some of the other candidates, and has asked a price that is considered reasonable.

Gradually, a consensus is reached, and shortly afterwards Grete leaves the room in order to try to call him and make an appointment. She returns a few minutes later, saying that he'll be home in an hour.

The film director continues explaining his concept. He wants pictures of Sande returning to his home in the evening, he wants flashbacks from his busy day and the sound of car tyres against gravel, and he wants Sande's voice all along. Now and then, he wants to interrupt this sequence with delicious pictures of raw food material. Henrik is a bit worried that the film might introduce too many different sequences; but the director reassures him that it won't. Towards the end of the film, the voice and image will be synchronized, and we will see Sande speaking directly to camera. Then there will be so-called pack shots, and a voice-over saying something about Viking Foods.

The discussion leads up to a general agreement to go for the present idea. A week later, Henrik comments on the meeting in this way:

> *Now, after a while, I'm starting to feel comfortable about ('har slått meg til ro med') these plans for using Vidar Sande. I was more sceptical at first as to whether he lacked a kind of . . . nice and likeable ('sympatisk') appeal. But then, on the other hand he might just appeal to the target group of slightly 'rough men' that we are thinking of, so then it's OK . . .*

Henrik's last comment indicates the extent to which he differentiates between his own subjective likes and dislikes and the assumed preferences of his target group. As the discussion at the meeting indicates, the main criterion for selecting a character is his or her appeal to the target group, a feature that is partly grounded on his or her presumed ability to evoke feelings of identification within the target group. Thus, the singer-songwriter Ivar Svendsen, who is considered to be a nice guy, is unsuitable, as there is a suspicion that he might appeal more to the 'right' than to the 'left' part of the sociograph. Furthermore, the person should not be too controversial. Fredrik Røed, the comedian, whose performances are often quite satirical, is discarded for this reason, while the programme director Kjell Gregers is a possible candidate, precisely because he is an ordinary guy, and *not* controversial. Still, the concept of ordinariness must not imply a publicly low profile. Morten Liland is a person that 'nobody really knows'; consequently he is out. In other words, a certain level of fame is required. But at the same time, there is a consistent trade-off between fame and financial cost. Obviously, there are many persons who are more famous than the ones mentioned whose charges would exceed the budget.

Being ordinary and non-controversial, but yet famous are thus among the most important criteria for the selection of a main character for the testimonial. In addition, the main character should not be too different from the target group. Except for the issue of fame, all these criteria play upon a notion of sameness. Previously we have seen how the notion of sameness serves as a key principle for negotiating material products in the making, sometimes causing the descriptions of material product to blur with those of the target group (see also Chapter 7, in which Pizza Superiora was practically located at the sociograph *origo*). In connection with the present film case, the notion of sameness operates primarily between the main character and the target group.

The purpose of the testimonial is to ensure a steady alliance between the product and the target group. Ensuring this alliance, the spokesman (spokeswoman) may be seen as a temporary metaphor, substituting for both the product (through testimonial: 'I like it, so it must be good') and its future consumer (through sameness: 'I like it, so you must like it too').

Another interesting feature of the discussion is the inherent contradiction between the criteria involved. The spokesman (spokeswoman) should be famous, but yet ordinary. These criteria may be interpreted as mutually exclusive (Leiss *et al.* 1990).[8] In the present case, the aim is to make these two characteristics come together in one and the same person! Obviously, this is not an easy task, as fame tends to be based on some personal trait or activity that makes the person stand apart as different, un-ordinary. However, as the comments about Kjell Gregers indicate, the criteria are not always incompatible. Television (and to a lesser extent, radio) is important in this respect. Owing to his frequent appearances on radio and television, Gregers, a fairly 'ordinary' person, has become publicly known. His fame is *not* based on any trait that makes him stand apart as different, but is rather a function of frequent exposure. In this way, national broadcasting provides possibilities for fame even for persons who are not talented or outstanding in any particular way. In a sense then, a national broadcast constructs a '*kjendis*' out of the person next door. In this way, television contributes to producing person images in which the criteria of fame and 'ordinariness' are reconciled. Not surprisingly then, the use of the so-called 'TV-kjendis' is quite common in Norwegian advertising and TV testimonials.

While television provides an answer to the question of *how* fame and ordinariness may be reconciled, the question *why* still remains. Especially, in the light of frequent references to the term 'ordinary', we may ask: why does the spokesman (spokeswoman) have to be so ordinary? Attempting a closer description of the three male candidates who were seriously considered (the sports commentator, the programme director and the racing driver), they all possess a certain 'ordinariness'. The first two are both middle-aged men whose fame rests entirely upon their ability to handle successfully their roles as leading figures in television programmes. The last is famous for being a racing driver; but his popularity seems to be more related to his ordinary appeal. The fame of the spokeswoman, Maria Mortensen, is definitely based on her abilities as a singer; yet she leaves the impression of a person who is straightforward, 'natural' and unpretentious, thus contributing to a public image of an ordinary Norwegian woman. To the extent that these tentative interpretations are valid, they all indicate the importance of ordinariness as the single common denominator that all four candidates share.

The fact that the requirement for ordinariness seems so important may be analysed in the light of what Gullestad (1989, 1992) refers to as the typically Norwegian notion of equality as sameness. She writes: *'Because sameness (being alike) is a central value, it is problematic to demand prestige and recognition. Norwegians are no less interested in recognition than others, but for them an initiative to attain recognition must be inscribed in the ideal of sameness. Modesty is a virtue, and self-assertion is seen as bragging'* (Gullestad 1992:192). This is also confirmed by other studies from the Nordic region (Graubard 1986).

Searching for a character who is famous, but yet ordinary, may thus be interpreted as a way of ensuring recognition while at the same time under-communicating social difference. As mentioned above, one way handling this delicate balance between public fame and ordinariness is through the use of a 'TV-kjendis'. But what about the situations in which fame stems from the demonstration of talent? When fame must be inscribed in the ideal of sameness, rendering any explicit claims for extraordinary talent somewhat illegitimate, how then is public popularity achieved? Looking more closely at the racing driver and the female singer, we find that they share one important characteristic: namely, a direct way of expressing themselves that is readily conceptualized in Norwegian as natural (*'naturlig'*) or honest (*'ærlig'*). For the male character this is expressed through a rough and unpolished way of speaking (which also includes a rural dialect); for the female character, it is expressed more subtly through a nice and ordinary image, which makes her similar to any girl next door. When Maria Mortensen comes off as ordinary and natural, what we see may be a certain avoidance of artificiality in social encounters that serves to substantiate an implicit claim of being yourself, i.e. of being authentic. By emphasizing a certain naturalness and authenticity in their behaviour, both of these persons succeed in presenting their extraordinary talents within a context of ordinariness. It seems reasonable to suggest that it is precisely this ability that makes them both stand out as more popular than many others (who may be equally talented), and thus also preferred candidates for a commercial. This interpretation is in accordance with Gullestad's assertion about the concept of nature as a central cultural symbol in Norway: *'Artfulness and style are often experienced as unnatural and artificial and therefore as negative oppositions to the natural'* (Gullestad 1992:206).

The salience of the notion of the ordinary in the present context bears some resemblance to the idea of ordinariness described in Chapter 7, in which Pizza Superiora is reconceptualized as 'folkepizzaen i Norge'. These issues will be further elaborated in Chapter 9.

A few months later, a Bon Appétit commercial with the racing driver eating lasagne appears on commercial cable TV channels and as a trailer in cinemas in the four largest cities in Norway. However, its female counterpart is still not released. In the mean time, Maria Mortensen had been replaced with a female actress, Greta Granfoss. This change was made very quickly, when the former suddenly revealed a change of schedule that implied that she would be off to the Canary Islands on vacation. The actress agreed to replace her at short notice, and after some changes in the narrative, a commercial with Greta Granfoss eating tagliatelle was produced.

Some weeks before the commercial release, however, Henrik informed me that the Greta Granfoss commercial will have to be withheld. The decision was reached because of some problems with the food product involved.

> Henrik: *We're having some problems with the tagliatelle – there's too much water in it, so they've had to temporarily take it out of production. This means that the film with Greta Granfoss, which was going to be released together with the one with Vidar Sande, cannot be released. Hopefully, the problems will be solved and the film will be released by next autumn.*

Five months later the tagliatelle commercial was released, along with a repeated exposure of the commercial with the racing driver. This final incident illustrates once more a point of intersection between the spheres of material production and those of communication. Before leaving the present case, let us return for a moment to the seemingly endless negotiation of product development – and to its symbolic connotations.

Phase 5: Pasta or 'Finnebiff'? Norwegianness as a Competitive Advantage

In January 1992, ten months after it was first launched, the Bon Appétit product range consists of *'lasagne'* (two varieties), *'biff stroganoff'*, *'tagliatelle'*, *'chop suey'* and *'spaghetti bolognese'*. These dishes had all been on the market during the previous year, together with three dishes that had recently been omitted from the product range (*'tortellini'*, *'orientalsk gryte'* and *'lapskaus'*). Taking a closer look at the figures, we find that lasagne makes up as much as 45 per cent of the total amount of the Bon Appétit products sold. Other pasta dishes based on an Italian culinary concept (tagliatelle, spaghetti bolognese and tortellini) constitute 22 per cent of the total volume, making Italian dishes by far the most important, constituting approximately two-thirds of the total volume sold. Dishes claimed to be of oriental origin (chop suey and oriental stew) constitute 15 per cent, while the dish that reflects a more typically Norwegian and traditional culinary concept (lapskaus) makes up only 4 per cent of the total amount of products sold.[9] In addition, there is *'Biff Stroganoff'*, a popular meat stew that accounts for approximately 15 per cent of the total sales volume.

We see here how the Bon Appétit product range consists of a combination of foreign and domestic culinary concepts.[10] Why are references to Italy so frequently utilized? And how can we explain the combination of convenience and foreign reference? In order to illuminate these issues, let us take a closer look at the process of eliminating and adding new products to the product range, as it is experienced by Henrik.

In early March, just about a month prior to the release of the racing driver commercial, Henrik makes several attempts at improving the Bon Appétit product range. Partly, he seeks to improve the material quality of products that are already included in the product range, such as tagliatelle. Partly he is considering the possibilities of introducing new products. On the basis of informal and frequent discussions with product development and others, he decides to carry out a so-called 'in-home' taste trial of four new products that are not yet released.

In March 1992, three new Bon Appétit products are launched: *'Laks Hollandaise'* (Salmon Hollandaise), *'Fiskegrateng'* (oven-baked fish casserole), and a variety of *'Fiskegrateng'* that includes cheese.[11] All these dishes contribute to a shift in the general impression of the Bon Appétit product range, from that of one based almost exclusively on foreign foods, to one of a more varied selection, also including Norwegian dishes.

This shift is hardly coincidental. When Henrik orders the 'in-home' taste trial, he also wants to include a typically Norwegian product based on reindeer meat: *'finnebiff'*. In addition, he wants to test a new and improved variety of the tagliatelle, and two varieties of spring rolls.

A similar shift towards Norwegian dishes may be registered in relation to new product development. In addition to the tagliatelle and the *'finnebiff'*, which will be launched in September, Henrik wants to try to introduce *'reinsdyrkaker'* (reindeer meatballs), another dish that is generally classified as typically Norwegian. In a summary of the present state of affairs addressed to the department of product development, he announces the following dishes to be launched the following year:

- *A lasagne variety, 'chilli with green and white pasta plates'. Approximately 400 g., for microwave oven.*
- *A new pasta variety for the oven (tortellini has been used up).*
- *Cod in hollandaise with potato slices for the oven.*

- *Fish soup for micro.*
- *New fish variety for micro, cod in light sauce (lobster sauce) with rice and vegetables.*
- *'Norwegian casserole' ('norsk gryte'), with meatballs or baby sausages in sauce, with vegetables and mashed potatoes for micro.*

Of these six concepts, all the fish dishes are based on ingredients commonly used in Norway. 'Norwegian casserole' is an attempt at creating a new product on the basis of a Norwegian culinary format, while the two remaining dishes are Italian pasta products. Under the heading *'Special project, side dishes'*, Henrik suggests:

— *Quality improvement of boiled potatoes*
— *New alternatives:*
  - *gratinated potatoes*
  - *mashed potatoes w/flavour /mixed with vegetables*
  - *rice w/variations of thinly sliced vegetables*
  - *macaroni*

The potato dishes are all accessories to main dishes that usually consist of a meat or fish basis. Finally, Henrik states the need to improve the current lasagne, claiming that the flavour must be modified – it is too sweet. He also suggests one more layer of pasta plates, and that the layers with meat sauce should be as thin as possible; and finally asks what the cost will be.

A few days after this summary was distributed, I had a chance to discuss these priorities with Henrik. I was particularly interested in the balance between Norwegian and foreign foods in the Bon Appétit product range, and the apparent shift towards a more Norwegian product range:

Marianne: *There were already quite a few pasta dishes in the product range. Yet you plan to launch two new ones. Why do you do that?*
Henrik: *I believe it is right to go for ('satse på') pasta products. That is primarily based on the recent survey of eating habits, which shows that among ethnic foods, Italian food is rated as no. 1.[12] In addition, pasta is the kind of dish which may taste good even when there's not a lot of meat in it. In other words, it is cheap to produce, and we avoid some of the problems related to high costs of production.*

Marianne: *In addition to these foreign dishes, the new product development plans seem to reflect an idea of launching more Norwegian dishes? Is this a deliberate strategy?*

Henrik: *Yes, it's deliberate. It is also included in our initial strategy for convenience foods. Part of our product strategy goes kind of like this: In order to protect ourselves against foreign competitors, our only possibility (on the actual product side) is to develop typically Norwegian dishes out of Norwegian raw materials. Here we have a competitive advantage compared to the foreign competitors, while on international dishes, we are more equal. I don't mean to push Norwegian food down people's throats. But the idea is that if we can develop such Norwegian dishes which sell fairly well, then that's a good thing. In addition, there are signals from the sales corps. They often ask why there aren't any more Norwegian products in the product range. Especially from peripheral areas of Norway, we tend to get such signals . . .*

Marianne: *I would assume that it is precisely in such peripheral areas that you'd find consumers who rather cook such traditional dishes themselves, and are less ready to accept convenience foods?*

Henrik: *We've thought about that. That's why we deliberately do not launch 'fårikål' and 'kjøttkaker'.[13] Instead, we try to make other things, like for instance 'finnebiff'. I believe in that. And 'rensdyrkaker' [reindeer meatballs]. I don't know if that will work, whether people will want it. But if it works, it is something we might compete on. 'Norwegian casserole' is another attempt: something which is Norwegian, but which is not prepared exactly in the households already.*

Marianne: *Why did you choose 'fiskegrateng'?*

Henrik: *Because it sells so well! Our major competitors have it already, and convenience foods made of fish are also included in our long-term strategy . . .*

Marianne: *How about the new side-dish varieties?*

Henrik: *Boiled potatoes don't come out very well. And if there's something that people know the proper taste of, it's potatoes . . . we had boiled potatoes as part of a previous convenience food product range, but we don't have it now. That's why we try to raise the quality of some other side-dish varieties.*

As the above sequence indicates, the Bon Appétit product range is a flexible concept, whose material content and symbolic connotations are continuously negotiated. Unlike products like Pizza Superiora, which represented a 'closed controversy' with regard to material content, the concept of Bon Appétit refers to a range of convenience dinner products continuously in the making.

Because the Bon Appétit concept is so flexible, each new launch may be interpreted as an act of negotiation in which 'real' consumers are confronted with 'real' products that they may or may not choose to buy. To the extent that 'flops' may be prevented by purchasing the services of market research institutes (such as for example the 'in-home' taste trial), it is apparently worthwhile. Nevertheless, the fact that a single unsuccessful product may be quietly removed without seriously altering the basic concept of the product range (as exemplified by the tagliatelle) allows for a certain trial-and-error, and may explain why Henrik relies to some extent on intuitive knowledge (gut-feeling) and on his private home as a 'test-institute'.

During the process of finding a balance between foreign and domestic culinary traditions, several voices of interest may be identified. First of all there are the consumers, whose attitudes and interests are voiced directly through aggregate purchase behaviour, or indirectly through feeding into market research interpretations, or through the success of competitors. When Henrik 'believes' in introducing two new pasta varieties, he refers explicitly to consumers' preference for Italian foods, as it is reflected in market research surveys. In addition, his decision is in accordance with Viking Foods' and competitors' sales figures, which indicate that pasta is being purchased.

In addition, the wide dissemination of foreign dishes in general, and of Italian dishes in particular, may also be explained in terms of material advantages involved. Convenience foods are generally perceived as expensive by consumers, and, according to Henrik, controlling costs, and thus keeping the prices down, is of key importance. Consequently, dishes that consist of relatively inexpensive raw materials will be at a definite advantage. Pasta, which is filling, but yet inexpensive compared with meat – according to Henrik it: *'tastes good even when there's not a lot of meat in it'* – fulfils this requirement. As an additional quality, pasta is a culinary concept that may be varied endlessly, thus giving rise to a wide variety of different products (tortellini, spaghetti, lasagne, etc.). These features may partly explain the dominant emphasis on 'Italianness' in the Bon Appétit product range, and also in convenience foods in general. This thus exemplifies how certain material characteristics of product components contribute to shaping the symbolic connotations of a product range.

An additional explanation of the dominance of foreign foods may also be considered. Elaborating a culinary format, the product manager strives to achieve a certain coherence between the material product (in terms of taste, texture, appearance), and the anticipations evoked by a product's name and visual design. Put more simply, there is an expectation among the consumers that the product should be what it claims to be. Such judgements of coherence are based upon knowledge and previous experience on the part of the consumer, and imply a certain sharing of the cultural repertoire between producer and consumer. This, I suggest, is why Henrik deliberately avoids the inclusion of certain popular Norwegian dishes such as 'fårikål' (mutton casserole) and 'kjøtt-kaker' (meatballs) – dishes that most consumers make at home, and for which judgements of coherence are likely to be rather distinct and defined. Almost intuitively, Henrik 'knows' that 'fårikål' is not going to work. His first-hand knowledge of Norwegian culinary formats allows him to differentiate 'finnebiff' from 'fårikål' on the basis of distinctions that he assumes might make a difference.

Similarly, when Henrik decides that they need to try out new potato side-dishes, his judgement is based upon a tacit knowledge about Norwegian consumers' knowledge and expectations of potatoes. More precisely, in light of the assumed sensitivity among Norwegian consumers with regard to the quality of potatoes, the material changes in the potatoes that occur during industrial processing and preservation (especially freezing) cannot be overlooked.

When it comes to foreign culinary concepts, the knowledge possessed by most Norwegian consumers is generally far more limited, and consumers are thus likely to be much less predisposed with regard to what to expect. Consequently, creating new products based on foreign culinary concepts, such as, for example, Chinese Chop Suey, the producer, to a much greater extent, is *free to define the product in a way that suits the various requirements and conditions of industrial mass production.*

In light of these difficulties, why then does Henrik strive to include more Norwegian dishes within the Bon Appétit product range? As he points out, this partly reflects the fact that the potential demand for more Norwegian dishes has been trans-mitted from the sales corps. An equally important explanation, however, refers directly to strategic documents, according to which

Norwegian dishes are to be developed out of Norwegian raw materials. This is a fairly new strategy, and it is grounded as part of the general strategy for protecting the company against enhanced foreign competition in the future. These considerations may be analysed as a way for Henrik to align his project with the interests of a group of decision-makers who are responsible for the long-term strategy of the company as a whole, interests which are made explicit through various internal documents that serve both to guide and to legitimize day-to-day decisions. These guidelines reflect, in turn, normative models inherent in marketing theory. For instance, the emphasis on 'Norwegianness' as a competitive advantage reflects the general ideology of product positioning. According to Kotler and Armstrong (1987), product positioning may be defined as: *'the way the product is defined by consumers on important attributes – the place the product occupies in consumers' minds relative to competing products'* (Kotler and Armstrong 1987:225).

Positioning is often visualized in two-dimensional space, by means of a figure in which horizontal and vertical axes represent different product attributes. According to the marketing textbook, a company has two choices: One is to position the product *next to* one of the existing competitors and fight for a market share (the introduction of 'fiskegrateng' into the Bon Appétit product range may be seen as an example of this strategy). The other choice is to develop a product that will be located *at a space which is not yet occupied,* or, as Kotler puts it: to *'discover a "hole" in the market and . . . move to fill it'* (Kotler and Armstrong 1987:223). In any case, *'When setting a positioning strategy, the company should look at its competitive strengths and weaknesses compared to those of competitors, and select a position in which it can attain a strong competitive advantage'* (Kotler and Armstrong 1987:223). As Viking Foods anticipated the challenge of foreign competition in the early 1990s, a strategy that included Norwegian culinary concepts within a convenience food product range was entirely in accordance with the general idea of product positioning inherent in marketing theory.

Summary

Convenience foods represent a significant transfer of labour investment from the private sphere of the household to the professional sphere of industrial production. In advertising, this feature is usually presented as an advantage of the product, implying less time and effort spent on cooking by the consumer. At the same time, this transfer of labour is also fraught with consumer scepticism.

Partly, this may be related to the inherent gaps, both in space and in time, between production and consumption that are a key characteristic of modern food provision. The food industry is characterized by concentration, intensity of production, and to some extent multinational ownership and marketing. These features imply redistribution of raw materials (transformed as food products) on a large scale, and processes of storage, handling and transportation that imply the passage of time. As processes of decay are partly a function of time, the struggle to retain an impression of freshness is thus a considerable challenge in the sphere of food manufacturing.[14] When the target group analysis concludes that *'convenience food has a credibility problem in appearing as a natural product'*, it may in fact refer to a general understanding among consumers of the conditions of industrial food production.

The Bon Appétit case illustrates the complex set of interrelations between the material and the symbolic properties of the product. Sometimes these links are merely accidental, such as for instance when a sudden material imperfection in a specific product caused the commercial with the actress to be withheld for about half a year (thus causing a far more male-oriented promotion of the product range than what was originally intended). At other times, the interrelations are due to a more consistent dynamism, such as when certain material advantages of product components (pasta) contribute in strengthening the foreign (Italian) image of the product range as a whole, or when the normative models of marketing theory (as it is reproduced in Viking Foods' strategic documents) force Henrik to try out 'Norwegian' raw materials (potato, fish) that might otherwise not have been considered.

Finally, a comment on the notion of sameness is required. Sameness appears to be an overarching requirement in the selection of a proper spokesperson for the testimonial. As the negotiations of 'ordinariness' revealed, one of the key features required of an actor was that he or she, in spite of obvious differences related to talent or fame, was still similar to the target group. This mediation of sameness echoes the negotiations of Pizza Superiora, in which sameness was mediated through the material product itself, in terms of a location of both target group and product at the sociograph *origo* (see Chapter 7). Thus a consistent mediation of sameness occurs throughout the various communicative efforts, contributing to the coherence between the package's visual design, the image of its consumer target group, the testimonial character and the material properties of the product.

This consistent notion of sameness represents a contrast to the parallel processes of negotiating difference: the coherent definition of the Bon Appétit product range is simultaneously an effort at setting Bon Appétit apart, an effort at constructing a brand product that the consumer may differentiate from other brand products. This feature is perhaps less salient in the present case than in some cases described previously, and is even contradicted through mere attempts at copying. Yet I contend that, as an underlying premiss of the entire endeavour, there is the ambition of establishing the Bon Appétit product range as a differentiated brand product, one that stands apart from its competitors in a favourable manner.

Notes

1. In Norway, dinner is usually served around 5 p.m. It is the most ritualized meal of the day, and the only meal that usually consists of hot food. In this respect, it differs markedly from lunch, which in Norway (in contrast to neighbouring Scandinavian countries) usually consists of cold sandwiches, often brought to school or to work in a paper wrapping (*'matpakka'*). A tendency to skip dinner in Norway would thus for most people imply an elimination of hot meals altogether.
2. Source: Internal market research document.
3. In Norwegian, 'directing our efforts towards building up' is expressed very briefly by the term *'satse'*. Frequently used in such documents (and in oral discourse), this term is far more encompassing than the English translation. Literally, *'satse'* refers to the deliberate movement of the body just before a jump, something close to the English term 'take-off'. When transferred to the present context, the term refers to the deliberate effort of directing a wide range of available resources towards a common

goal. The term implies more than a pragmatic allocation of resources, however, as it also indicates a certain enthusiasm and a will to succeed.

4. The term *'kjendis'* is originally a Swedish term that has gradually become part of Norwegian discourse. It refers to a person who has become publicly known through repeated mass media coverage. The term points especially to those for whom mass media coverage implies that the traditional separation of the private sphere and the public role tends to blur.

5. Each picture of food is accompanied by the following comment from the AD: *'Table top, slo/mo highspeed Studio London'*. According to Erik, this refers to a special film technique that gives a clear and detailed image of miniature details, frequently used for table-top food shots. However, the equipment is only available in London.

6. Karl Kristoffersen is a fictitious name, as are all of the following names of possible characters.

7. *'Se & Hør'* is a so-called gossip magazine that features extensive material on famous persons. In the present context, being a topic of *'Se & Hør'* signifies the *'kjendis'* status.

8. According to Leiss *et al.* (1990:269), testimonial appeal may be broken down into *expert appeal* (explicitly addressing the credibility of the claims), *star appeal* (emphasizing an aspect of the relation between testifier and audience in terms of fame), *popular appeal* (emphasizing an aspect of the relation between testifier and audience in terms of an ordinary person), and *status appeal* (emphasizing an aspect of the relation between testifier and audience related to differences in social class, the testifier being 'above').

9. *'Lapskaus'* is a traditional Norwegian dish, usually prepared as a casserole combination of meat, potatoes and carrots.

10. This is quite in accordance with a tendency documented in the analysis of Norwegian food adverts, in which claims of foreign origin and convenience are frequently combined. Furthermore, the analysis also indicates an emphasis on Italianness: in fact Italy scored as the most frequent term among the foreign references appearing in the adverts (Lien 1995a).

11. *'Fiskegrateng'* is a very common everyday dinner in Norway. Salmon Hollandaise is a more elaborate meal, which tends to be associated with festive occasions.

12. According to a 1991/2 survey available in the marketing department, 54% of the respondents report that they are interested in Italian dishes (only 49% in 1989/90), while as many as 61% report an interest in Nordic foods (only 56% in 1989/90). These are followed by Chinese food (45%), South American/Mexican food (35%), Greek food (29%), Indian food (20%), American dishes (20%) and East European dishes (18%).

13. *'Fårikål'* and *'kjøttkaker'* are both traditional Norwegian dishes, frequently described as the most typical Norwegian dinner courses. *'Fårikål'* is a mutton and cabbage casserole, while *'kjøttkaker'* is the Norwegian word for meat balls, and usually consists of ground pork meat.

14. Among the top ten food science innovations during the last fifty years, six relate directly to methods of preservation whose primary purpose is to prolong the freshness of manufactured foods by counteracting the processes of decay (Fine and Leopold 1993:164).

Part III

Discussions

Chapter 9

Articulating Difference Within a Global Format

*I believe that it is probably true that **fortune** is the arbiter of half the things we do, leaving the other half or so to be controlled by us* (Machiavelli 1960:130).

The notion of marketing as warfare permeates much of the information provided to Viking Foods product managers from intermediary translators. Such images are also evoked by product managers themselves, when discussing products and strategies. The current chapter commences with a brief summary of the extent to which the various performative consequences indicated in Chapter 5 are reflected in day-to-day practice. This summary provides a starting-point for a more thorough discussion of the ways in which product managers enable themselves to *'act at a distance on unfamiliar events, places and people'* (Latour 1987). This implies a consideration of the interplay of sameness and difference inherent in the notion of a brand, and of the role of marketing as a global grammar for articulating local differences.

The image of marketing as warfare is frequently referred to. We may recall Erik, when, upon emphasizing the importance of a brand name for his poultry product range, he says: *'We are – as they say in the advertising trade – better at shooting with a rifle when we have our own brand name'* (Chapter 6). Similar metaphors are applied in the target group analysis of frozen pizzas, in which notions of *'competition'*, *'conquest'* and the importance of *'capturing market share from competitors'* are emphasized (Chapter 7). Finally, we find the notion of marketing as warfare in Henrik's letter of reassurance about a newspaper taste trial that paid Bon Appétit scant respect, when he concluded with the exhortation: *Keep on going! There are still vacant market shares to fight for!'*, and also when he talked about Norwegian dishes as a way to *'protect ourselves against foreign competitors'* (Chapter 8). Several other examples could be cited.

To the extent that the four cases allow for certain generalizations, it seems as if the notion of the market as battlefield appears primarily within the context of normative or persuasive discourse. If we consider the actual day-to-day activities of product managers, however, these are more aptly described by terms like uncertainty, contingency and doubt. As all four empirical cases illustrate, product managers devote a great deal of time and attention to meticulously gathering and interpreting information, incessantly doubting whether the evaluations are correct, and reluctantly making decisions that can neither be ignored nor postponed. In spite of references to marketing as warfare, the entire poultry project may be described as a chain of efforts at classification, legitimized within the overall purpose of reducing uncertainty in marketing decisions (Chapter 6). Similarly, Kristoffer's relentless attempts at communicating with the average Norwegian, a category that in spite of detailed target group analysis remained elusive and undefined (Chapter 7), may be seen as an ongoing effort at creating a category. In the Bon Appétit convenience foods, no material improvement could ever eliminate what Henrik conceives of as an element of risk (Chapter 8). As a general impression, each case demonstrates contingency and doubt, rather than offensive action. In the light of the pervasiveness of an offensive warfare image within much marketing literature, and also the salience of such images in certain types of discourse, we may suggest a certain discontinuity between discursive images and day-to-day action. Thus, considering the day-to-day activities of marketing practice, the marketing-as-warfare image is slightly misleading.[1] Trying to grasp marketing practice, the metaphorical assertion suggesting that the 'market is a flux of constant transformation' is the one that most aptly describes the daily activities of product managers. Especially when combined with the image of the market as a 'pie to be shared', the performative consequences serve to describe a great majority of the roles and activities involved in the development of products and advertising.

The metaphorical image of the market as an environment of natural selection is primarily reflected through visual models (see Chapter 6), in *post hoc* explanations of why things went wrong, and in general discourse about products as 'dead' or 'alive'. Furthermore, the image implies a notion of adaptation (of the product to the market) that is quite central to target group analysis. To the extent that this notion of adaptation is reflected in actual activities of product managers, it is, however, in a much more active manner than the metaphorical image itself would imply. Rather than the fatalist acceptance of a product's destiny, the product managers work very hard to control (or at least have an influence upon) the future.

The contrast between the fatalism implied in the notion of the market as an evolutionist environment, and the strategic analysis implied in the notion of the market as a flux of transformation resembles what Giddens (1991) describes as the historical shift from fatalism to modernity, as it is foreshadowed by Machiavelli. One salient feature of this transition, is what Giddens refers to as the *colonialization of the future*. He writes:

> *[Machiavelli] foreshadows a world in which risk, and risk calculation edge aside* fortuna *in virtually all domains of human activity . . . The 'openness' of things to come expresses the malleability of the social world and the capability of human beings to shape the physical settings of our existence. While the future is recognised to be intrinsically unknowable, . . . that future becomes a new terrain – a territory of counterfactual possibility. Once thus established, the terrain lends itself to colonial invasion through counterfactual thought and risk calculation* (Giddens 1991:11).

We may conceive the product managers' struggles and considerations as truly modern in Giddens's sense of the term. To the extent that a more archaic, fatalist rhetoric may be identified, it appears primarily within a context of *post hoc* explanations. Furthermore, to the extent that the metaphorical image of the market as a battlefield occurs, it operates primarily at the level of normative and persuasive discourse. Consequently, we are left with a general impression of product managers' activities as critical and self-reflexive, as they constantly struggle to create products and messages that adapt to a market that they themselves can never fully know. Thus, in spite of a rich array of metaphoric structures (which potentially legitimize a wide range of actions and interpretations), I contend that the performative consequences implied by the metaphor of the market as a flux of transformation are the most suitable description of marketing practice.

Approaching food products as carefully designed to 'hit targets with great precision', we may ask: What are the general features of such processes of design? And: What are the basic principles by which the product managers adapt their products to the market?

Adaptation through Sameness – Conquest through Difference

The task of the marketing professionals may be described as two processes of *translation*: one by which interpretations of consumers' needs and preferences (as detected in consumer research) are literally 'materialized' in terms of a physical product, and another by which selected characteristics of the material product are visualized and textualized in packaging and advertising material. Together, these two sequences of translation make up what I refer to as the food product.

During both sequences of translation, the notion of *sameness* is central. As demonstrated by all cases, the material and symbolic properties of the product are defined so as to achieve an optimal match with the selected consumer segment. Recall, for instance, how Erik, upon selecting the package design for poultry, carefully tried to achieve a certain resemblance between the exclusivity conveyed in package design and what he conceived as the exclusivity of the product. In the selection of characters for a testimonial (cf. the Bon Appétit case), a principle of sameness between character and consumer target group was aimed at.

Yet brand-building implies differentiation (see Chapter 5). The challenge for the product manager is to create or emphasize a difference that makes the product stand apart, and enables the consumer easily to distinguish it from other, competing products in the market. In this sense, brand-building may be described as active and *conscious work of differentiation for commercial purposes*.

Differentiation may be achieved in two ways: by constructing a difference of degree, or by constructing a difference in kind. Marketing Pizza Romano as more authentically Italian than other pizza products is an example of differentiation based upon advantages that are a matter of degree. The introduction of pizza in Norway and the first introduction of poultry products on the Norwegian market are both examples of new product launches that had the advantage of being qualitatively unique at the time, thus representing a difference in kind. However, the latter are exceptions rather than the rule. Generally, most products launched in Norway in the 1990s seem to be merely new varieties on familiar themes.

Together, the principles of sameness and difference may account for the careful precision with which products are designed. The notion of difference implies that the product will occupy a space that is *not yet filled*. On an aggregate level, differentiation may ultimately imply a diversification that – referring to a market metaphor – may serve to enlarge the pie to be shared, by constantly giving rise to new subcategories of products – and thus also of visualized markets. The notion of sameness implies that this particular space, niche, or newly constructed market corresponds in some significant manner with a subcategory of consumers.

This is the core of the normative discourse, which, according to current models in the marketing department, would be true if things were done right. However, as the cases clearly show, things aren't always done 'right', and, more importantly, there are no simple and straightforward criteria by which informants may separate the 'right' strategy from the wrong one. Not surprisingly, then, product managers frequently express feelings of doubt. I will return to this in Chapter 10. At present, we may simply conclude that notions of sameness and of difference serve as overarching principles, informing and guiding many of the decisions that product managers need to make.

Marketing as 'Totemic Classification'

As a system of classification based on simultaneous principles of sameness and difference, marketing shares a common base with most human systems of classification in general, and *totemic systems of classification* in particular. Totemism denotes a classificatory correspondence between social groups and natural species. This correspondence implies a notion of similarity, and may also give rise to rituals of avoidance. A full account of the debate on totemism in anthropology goes beyond the scope of the present chapter. For the present discussion, I will rely on Lévi-Strauss's definition, according to which totemism denotes '*a classificatory device whereby discrete elements of the external world are associated with discrete elements of the social world*' (Lévi-Strauss 1963:7). Two aspects of totemism are important: First, following Durkheim and Mauss, totems may be conceived as *emblems of group membership* (Durkheim and Mauss 1963 [1903], or the *'sign by which each clan distinguishes itself from the others'* (Durkheim 1961[1912]:236). Secondly, totemism as a classificatory device may be approached as a structure of *corresponding differences* between human groups and natural species (Lévi-Strauss 1966), or even between human groups and culturally manufactured objects (Lévi-Strauss 1963). According to Lévi-Strauss, the differences between totem animals provide a model for conceptualizing differences between human groups. For Lévi-Strauss, totemism is thus an example of a universal tendency to classify one domain by modelling it on another.

The resemblance between brand-building inherent in modern marketing and totemism in traditional societies is quite apparent.[2] *Sameness* serves as a key principle for establishing a link between product and consumer in marketing practice, parallel to the way in which sameness (of origin or characteristics) connects a totemic animal to a significant social group. Simultaneously, in both instances, these linkages are *based upon notions of difference* between products, between natural species, or between social groups. Thus, in both instances, the peculiar alliance is founded upon a simultaneous recognition of sameness and difference.

A similar observation of the resemblance between traditional totemism and modern manufacture was made by Marshall Sahlins (1976) in his contribution to a cultural account of production. Rather than making a sharp distinction between the material and the social, Sahlins brings attention to the *symbolic appropriation of nature through production of manufactured objects*. Thus, the significance by which we distinguish between different manufactured objects is, he argues, both constituted by and constituter of the cultural order. Production of manufactured goods is thus a realization of a symbolic scheme. It is precisely this power to demarcate and classify even their individual owners that makes manufactured objects resemble 'totemic operators' (Sahlins 1976).

Following Sahlins, we may argue that modern consumption of manufactured goods represents totemism of a modern kind. However, there is a significant difference: in 'modern totemism', natural species have been replaced as a model for classification by items that are highly manufactured. By this distinction, I do not imply that the natural species that provide the emblems of traditional totemism are not also a matter of cultural interpretation. Obviously, the selection of totemic emblem is necessarily based upon *cultural perceptions of difference.* Nevertheless, we may reasonably assume that in cases of traditional totemism these differences tend to appear as if they are part of a natural world order. To the extent that this natural order is taken for granted, it implies that totemic emblems also appear as 'given', as part of the natural environment. In the case of 'modern totemism', however, the manufactured world appears as an arena in which the number (and variety) of potential totemic emblems is open-ended and highly dynamic, swiftly changing so as to reflect significant differences in the social world. This has two important implications:

Firstly, it implies new orders of social differentiation, as the power to shape manufactured goods is unequally distributed. In metaphoric terms, it implies that some of us are taking up the position next to the Creator, while the rest take up the more passive position of recipients, selectively appropriating whichever manufactured products have been made available to us.

Secondly, the changeability of modern signifiers is likely to challenge seriously any 'taken-for-grantedness' regarding the relationship between the signifier and its sign. These changes, which may be referred to as processes of re-codification, occur when a social meaning is no longer appropriately expressed through an 'old' artefact, or when a manufactured good gradually ceases to be endowed with the connotations it once had. The gradual transformation of pizza from being perceived as something exotic and Italian to something far more trivial is a case in point: 'pizza' has acquired a new meaning, while 'Italianness' must be conveyed by other means. As the success of a product depends on the maintenance of stable relationships at every level of signification, such discontinuities may also threaten the alliance between the food product and the consumers. Thus, while traditional totemism implies that members of a certain social group may trust their symbolic kinship to be part of a 'natural order', modern consumers experience a world of manufactured objects in which most totemic emblems turn out to be arbitrary and eventually obsolete. As a totemic emblem, each product is therefore 'unfaithful' in the sense that we can never know when it will cease to exist, or how its connotations will change on the way. This arbitrariness is perhaps the most significant difference between totemism as Lévi-Strauss describes it and the similar totemism in modern consumption.

The present comparison also confirms that an attribution of meaning to food is neither particularly modern, nor particularly traditional. Food is 'good to think', regardless of whether it comes pre-packaged from the manufacturer or is killed by a hunter's arrow. However, as empirical examples demonstrate, the social mechanisms by which meanings are attributed to food are very different. Most importantly, in modern manufacture the 'totemic emblems' have already been shaped and transformed by a particular group of professionals to *adapt to their image of consumer preferences.*

Considering these issues, we may ask: What are the basic dimensions by which the construction of modern 'totemic emblems' is achieved? Which underlying social categories are objectified? And how can we, by considering these, account for the arbitrariness of the signs in modern manufacture?

Imagined Cuisines

Marketing may be analysed as a global system of knowledge. At the same time, marketing practice is localized, in the sense that the interpretations of the ways in which things are to be done are highly influenced by the local, cultural setting in which marketing practice takes place (see also Chapter 1). In what follows, I will take this particular interplay between the local and the global as a starting-point for the discussion. Following Wilk (1995), we may argue that, as a system of knowledge, marketing represents a *framework within which cultural diversity may be organized.* However, the exact ways in which diversities are expressed is subject to local interpretations. The present focus of interest is on the ways in which local interpretations of this system of knowledge serve to mediate particular patterns of difference.

As an example of a global structure mediating differences on a global scale, Wilk (1995) draws attention to international beauty contests, focusing especially on the preparations for enrolment in one such contest as it was organized by local beauty pageants in Belize in the Caribbean. While the Belizean pageants are fully localized in the sense that they encompass various dramas of power within Belizean politics, they are simultaneously observed with an intimate awareness of what Wilk refers to as the *global gaze*. To some extent, he argues, a *'global standard has become an ever-present . . . "significant other" by which the local is defined and judged'* (Wilk 1995:127). At each stage of the contest, Belizean beauty pageants organize and objectify certain kinds of difference while suppressing others. The awareness of this global gaze grows stronger as each pageant progresses towards the semifinals. As the contest proceeds towards the international level, a global standard of beauty tends to be compared to the Belizean, which is explicitly denounced, and Wilk thus maintains that beauty pageantry, like other global competitions, is hierarchical, moving upwards towards standards that are defined at the centre, which, in this case, is not Belize (Wilk 1995). On basis of this, Wilk concludes that the beauty pageants organize space into hierarchy, while time is organized into annual cycles of competition, linked by the careers of participants. According to Wilk, global contests such as beauty pageants do not eliminate the difference between the global and the local. Rather, they: *'provide a common channel and a point of focus for the debate and expression of differences,* [as they] *take the full universe of possible contrasts between nations, groups, locales, . . . political parties and economic classes, and systematically narrow our gaze to **particular kinds** of difference'* (Wilk 1995:130).

I contend that food marketing may be fruitfully approached as a common channel for the expression of differences, in a manner that resembles in many ways the beauty pageants described by Wilk.[3] What then, are the common idioms through which difference is being expressed in Norwegian food marketing? And in which ways is the universe of possible contrasts systematically narrowed down?

The presented cases indicate that one important way in which difference is communicated is by means of an *underlying dichotomy of foreignness and familiarity*, and that this dichotomy tends to be *conceptualized in idioms of nationality*. Frozen pizza products serve as a case in point. Frozen pizza is a fairly standardized product format, for which the possibilities of material variation are relatively limited. Yet, for the product manager, the main challenge was still to design the pizza product range in such a way that each product stood out as different from the others (Chapter 7). In his effort to achieve this, Kristoffer promoted one product as American, another as Italian, and a third as *'folkepizzaen i Norge'* (the Norwegian people's pizza). In other words, in the case of pizza, *the notion of national origin constituted a key element by means of which differentiation was expressed.* Achieving this particular type of differentiation, the product manager simultaneously aligned two different types of interest: First, he acted in accordance with a general marketing strategy which aims to avoid 'cannibalizing' by reaching a wider consumer segment. This rationale is based upon the notion of sameness between product and consumer, in the sense that, for example, American pizza is supposed to appeal to the taste of a particular consumer segment, while Italian pizza is supposed to appeal to another. Secondly, he appropriated a rich repertoire of national symbolism that could be elaborated in copy and visual design, and therefore made it possible to construct a differentiated product range in spite of a limited culinary format. In this way, the notion of national differences provided a conceptual scheme for differentiating a product range in a way that corresponds to differences between consumer segments.

An emphasis on national origin is salient in Norwegian food adverts, which frequently play upon notions of national, ethnic or regional origin (Lien 1995a). According to a survey of printed food adverts collected in 1992, foreign references appeared in as much as 20 per cent of all the adverts, making foreign reference one of the most frequent types of reference in Norwegian food advertising.[4] Many authors have argued that food provides a particularly suitable medium for representing 'the other', making ethnic cuisine an excellent paradigm, or metaphor, for ethnicity itself (see, for instance, van den Berghe 1984; Levenstein 1985; Appadurai 1988[5]). Clearly, references to foreign foods in Norwegian food adverts are locally constructed, referring to stereotyped idioms that are influenced not only by the countries they claim to represent, but also by the position and cultural preconceptions of the country in which they are applied. This implies that each national stereotype may be analysed as part of local imagery, or local images of the other. Foreign ethnic cuisines (as they are expressed in modern manufacture) are therefore basically imagined, and may be conceived as *imagined cuisines.*[6]

Localized interpretations of imagined cuisines apply to product development as well. Pepperoni and green pepper gave Pizza Romano a stronger taste – a feature that was associated with Mediterranean cuisine. Clearly, this does not imply that the final product was more similar to pizzas served in Italy than other frozen pizza products – my assumption is that they are all fairly different from their Italian counterparts. Yet the addition of pepperoni and green chilli served to differentiate the product in a way that *according to Norwegian interpretations* could easily pass as Italian. In this way, what was literally 'baked into the pizza product' was not only an image of its future consumers, but also assumptions about these consumers' images of Italian cuisine.

Claims of foreign origin are particularly relevant in relation to convenience foods. There is a significant tendency in Norwegian printed food adverts for combining reference to foreign origin with reference to convenience (Lien 1995a; see also Chapter 8). A similar tendency has been observed in articles on food preparation in women's magazines, which tend to present foreign dishes with easy 'do-it-yourself' instructions, a tendency described as the *'routinization of the exotic'* (Warde 1995). Bon Appétit provides an example of an appropriation of foreign culinary elements in a convenience food product range, featuring dishes such as Italian pasta (Chapter 8). According to the product manager, the use of pasta was partly due to cost–benefit considerations, as 'pasta dishes may taste good even without a lot of meat'. However, in the light of the discussion above, a supplementary explanation may be suggested.

Generally, convenience foods represent an alternative to home-made dishes. When traditional domestic culinary concepts appear as mass-manufactured convenience food, any difference detected in the mass-manufactured product is likely to be judged negatively as a sign of the imperfection of industrial pre-processing. This point is also expressed by Henrik, who certainly does *not* launch *'fårikål'* and *'kjøttkaker'* (Chapter 8) – both dishes that Norwegian consumers are likely to know how to prepare, and that are therefore likely to be critically examined and compared to the home-made versions. However, when it comes to more exotic products like 'Chinese chop suey' or 'Mexican enchiladas', consumers seem less likely to be critical in their judgement, simply because they will be less certain about what the product ought to taste like (if they do not like it, they are more likely to conclude that they don't like Chinese food than to complain about the manufacturer). Thus, a foreign cuisine that few consumers have firsthand knowledge of will easily lend itself to the technical requirements of mass manufacture. My suggestion is therefore that it is precisely the 'imagined-ness' of foreign cuisines that makes them particularly suitable to industrial production. This applies especially to convenience foods, for which scepticism with regard to product quality is perhaps most enhanced.

Considering the ways in which exotic culinary elements are appropriated in manufactured foods, we may conclude that in their efforts at differentiating the product range (while ensuring acceptance of novel culinary concepts), product managers contribute to *'colonialization' of the exotic*.

A colonialization of the exotic must, however, be balanced against a *notion of familiarity*. Even though the appropriation of food from The Congo or New Guinea would imply an extreme degree of freedom on part of the manufacturer to define the cuisine in a suitable (and potentially profitable) manner, this strategy is rarely pursued. The reason, I contend, is that both places fail to constitute the careful balance between foreignness and familiarity that is required. Most importantly, neither The Congo nor New Guinea may be said to represent a significant other nation, in the way that for instance 'America' or Italy do.[7] Although all these nations are 'foreign' in a strict sense of the term, only these last two nations are also familiar enough to elaborated in the construction of imagined cuisines.

Each time a locally defined image of the exotic is disseminated through a commercial food product on the Norwegian market, it will also contribute to a process of *familiarization* which will eventually alter Norwegian consumers' understanding of the exotic. Through processes of recodification, elements that were previously exotic will eventually become familiar to many consumers. As far as frozen pizza is concerned, it seems reasonable to assume that recent years' industrial exploitation of pizza in Norway has eroded the notion of an authentic Italian pizza and made the entire concept obsolete. To the extent that product managers succeed in a commercial colonialization of the exotic, they simultaneously contribute to the process of making previously exotic elements familiar. This, in turn, may force product managers to search for other, still unspoiled, imagined cuisines in order to present their products as exotic, thus contributing to a continuous accelerating proliferation of new culinary concepts offered to Norwegian consumers. These mechanisms, I contend, may account for the constant attempts in food marketing at appropriating and launching foreign novelties.[8]

The choice of exotic elements is both guided and restricted by other choices made before: a manufacturer's early introduction of a foreign culinary concept may pave the way for secondary entries, but at the same time, the very dissemination of products of 'foreign origin' will, as suggested above, gradually transform the foreign into something familiar. Each attempt to connect a product with its country of origin is therefore associated to previous attempts, for better or worse. Altogether, these mechanisms contribute to an arbitrariness that makes 'modern totemism' radically different from most traditional totemic systems described in anthropological literature.

Briefly summarized, the semiotic context in which products are interpreted is characterized by arbitrariness, dynamism and continuous recodification of meaning. This is partly due to mechanisms that rest upon imperatives of modern marketing according to which products must be differentiated and re-launched in order to 'survive', a process which – to the extent that it implies a colonialization of the exotic – implies a constant erosion of meaning.

The extent to which a manufacturer's definition of a certain product influences consumers' concepts of an exotic cuisine depends, however, on whether or not the manufacturer is able to present the product as 'authentic'. This ability, in turn, depends on the extent to which the product manager succeeds in choosing culinary elements that still retain a promise of something exotic or unique – i.e. elements whose meanings are not yet eroded by the mechanisms of familiarization. In the next section we will take a closer look at the ways in which authenticity is expressed in food marketing.

The Notion of Authenticity: A Modern Imperative and its Limits

I have suggested that a constant attempt at differentiation of brand products implies a colonialization of the exotic. This dynamic may erode the symbolic significance (meaning) of the images and concepts that product managers apply, and force them to search for novel signifiers. These processes may be described in terms of an enhanced awareness of the arbitrariness of the relation between cultural categories and their material representation, or a dis-continuity between a sign and its signifier. Such an awareness is clearly present among product managers, as evidenced by local

discourse on various possibilities for connections between products and advertising images. Consequently, to the extent that a
colonialization of the exotic implies frequent recodifications in the
food market, an awareness of such arbitrariness is likely to increase
among consumers as well.

Consumers' awareness of the arbitrariness of signs represents
an obvious constraint upon the manufacturers' claims for authenticity. At the same time, we may argue that the very fragility of
trustworthiness paves the way for even more fierce claims of
authenticity, simply because of an enhanced awareness of the
potential presence of the unauthentic! This seeming paradox
may partly explain the salience of claims for authenticity in
modern marketing, particularly with regard to claims of foreign
origin. Thus, the mechanisms that I have referred to as the
colonialization of the exotic may be part of the reason why the
notion of authenticity seems to be so powerful. At the same time,
frequent recodifications in the market-place serve to undermine
the trustworthiness of any claim, and thus represent an important
constraint upon the ways in which claims of authenticity may be
successfully achieved.

Claims of authenticity frequently appear in Norwegian advertising in general, and in food adverts in particular (Lien 1995a).
Sometimes, a quest for authenticity is associated with a nostalgic
image; in other cases it is connected to an exotic longing. In case
of the former, we are confronted with a kind of 'paradise lost',
which the producers – thanks to their access to traditional
recipes – have recreated. In case of the latter, authenticity plays
upon a longing for the exotic, which the product – thanks to its
ability to represent a foreign country symbolically – may fulfil (Lien
1995a).

An analysis of North American culture and consumption
confirms the prevalence of a notion of authenticity in American
advertising as well (Orvell 1989). In his account, Orvell argues
that the tension between imitation and authenticity has been a key
constituent in American culture since the Industrial Revolution.
Still, a major shift occurred around the turn of the twentieth
century, when a new appreciation of the authentic replaced the
culture of imitation that had been a key constituent of the previous
decade. Orvell describes this shift as a disenchantment derived
from a response to the vast consumer culture that was taking shape
in the early twentieth century: *'as the saturation of things reached*

the limit of containing space, the social and spiritual grace afforded by material objects was put to the question' (1989:69).

Disenchantment took many forms, and was expressed in art, in literature, in advertising and in mass production. One of the most famous examples is the marketing of Coca Cola under the slogan 'It's the Real Thing', which was the core of their campaigns in the 1960s and 1970s. The concept itself goes back to 1908, when the message was 'Get the Genuine' (Orvell 1989:144).

Orvell's account indicates that the notion of authenticity is neither a new phenomenon, nor confined to Norwegian marketing and consumption. A recent study from the Pacific further indicates that a preoccupation with the notion of authenticity is not confined only to the Western industrialized world. With reference to contemporary movies ('pirated scripts') in the Pacific, Thomas (1993) has pointed to the gap between routine consumption of imported or copied products on the one hand and what he refers to as *'the persisting power of a language of authenticity'* on the other (Thomas 1993:2). Thomas's account from the contemporary Pacific further attests to the fact that the notion of authenticity should not be approached simply as another example of North American influence, or of global homogenization. Rather, we should examine the contextual relevance, and the cultural dynamics inherent in claims of authenticity in each empirical context. Obviously, the recurrence of authenticity as a common theme does not preclude significant empirical variation of the ways authenticity is asserted and conceptualized. In the light of this, we need to examine more carefully the ways in which authenticity is made relevant in empirical cases from Viking Foods.

Authenticity in the Marketing Department

Authenticity does not refer to any detectable, objective quality of an object or a claim. As Daniel Miller notes: *'The authenticity of artefacts as culture derives, not from their relationship to some historical style or manufacturing process – in other words, there is no truth or falsity immanent in them – but rather from their active participation in a process of social self-creation in which they are directly constitutive of our understanding of ourselves and others'* (Miller 1987:215). Furthermore, it seems reasonable to assume that notions of authenticity are evoked whenever the trustworthiness of a certain claim may be questioned. Claims for authenticity thus indicate a certain awareness of the potential presence of the unauthentic. The question thus becomes: what kind(s) of trustworthiness are at stake when the notion of authenticity arises?

The three empirical cases indicate that authenticity is framed in different ways. In the poultry project, authenticity is negotiated with reference to turkey meat that comes in whole pieces, which consumers, according to Erling, experience as more authentic than meat that is more finely cut (see Chapter 6). The relevance of the concept has to do with an underlying scepticism among consumers regarding the quality of the raw material in manufactured foods. The assumed suspicion is that poultry raw material may have been treated during the process of mass manufacture in an unwanted, and possibly undetected, manner. The concept thus evokes *a dichotomy between raw material that is industrially processed, and that which is not.*

This point is also discussed by Fine and Leopold (1993), who maintain that scepticism towards the quality of mass-manufactured foods is due partly to '*the organic origins of food, the vulnerability of the human digestive system, and the dangerous passage over distance through time from one to the other*' (Fine and Leopold 1993:149). This intimacy between food and the body requires an absolute trust, which, according to the authors may be threatened by the awareness of deliberate intervention (Fine and Leopold 1993). Orvell makes a similar point about the relationship between authenticity and scale: '*One might imagine that the concept of authenticity begins in any society when the possibility of fraud arises, and that fraud is at least possible whenever transactions . . . routinely occur, especially when the society becomes so large that one usually deals with strangers, not neighbours* (Orvell 1989:xvii). Following Orvell, we might add that an awareness of the possibility of fraud is particularly salient in large scale mass-manufacture – which implies routine transactions with strangers. The salience of consumers' concern about the presence of harmful substances in food is also confirmed by other studies (Wandel 1994).[9] In the light of such scepticism among consumers, an emphasis upon nature and the natural qualities of food products is hardly surprising.

In the Bon Appétit case, authenticity is framed in a different way. In this case, the notion of authenticity relates to the female character's way of acting, or rather, a personal style that serves to substantiate an implicit claim of 'being herself'. This may be interpreted in the light of a general distaste among many Norwegians for ways of acting that are in opposition to what is considered to be 'natural' (Gullestad 1992). The notion of authenticity thus evokes a dichotomy between artfulness on the one hand and the virtue of 'naturalness' on the other.

In the case of frozen pizza, authenticity was most explicitly addressed in relation to culinary quality. In a 1990 target group analysis, an emphasis on authenticity was suggested as part of a strategy to reach the consumer segment located in the upper right of the sociograph, on the grounds that these consumers were cosmopolitan and had a good knowledge of cooking. However, according to the target group analysis two years later, the strategy had failed because of a latent conflict between 'manufactured food and authenticity' that was particularly salient in this particular consumer segment. Referring to these consumers' enhanced knowledge of cooking, the analysis concluded that 'machine-produced factory pizzas with soy-meat fall right through' (Chapter 7). What we encounter here is a latent dichotomy between that which is factory produced and that which is home-made.

This may be interpreted as another expression of an assumed suspicion among consumers about artificial manipulation of manufactured foods, similar to that encountered in the poultry project. This interpretation is confirmed through the emphasis in the text on terms like 'factory' and 'machine', i.e. negatively-loaded terms that serve to substantiate the rationale of such scepticism.

The alleged conflict between 'manufactured food and authenticity' in the case of frozen pizza may also be interpreted in terms of fundamental discontinuity between the sign (Italian) and its signifier (pizza). According to the target group analysis, the failure to reach the cosmopolitan consumer segment may simply be due to an inability of the frozen pizza product to evoke the image of authentic Italian cuisine. This, in turn, is explained by the fact that this consumer segment is particularly knowledgeable and interested in good cooking. Thus interpreted, the notion of authenticity relates to the trustworthiness of manufacturers' claims of the product's foreign origin. In this context, the concept evokes an underlying dichotomy between foods that 'authentically' represent an imagined cuisine and foods that fail to fulfil such claims.

I have indicated how the notion of authenticity appears meaningful within three different frames of reference. In each context, authenticity derives its meaning from an awareness of the opposite: an awareness that we may loosely refer to as scepticism. However, the causes of scepticism are radically different. One relates to the possibility of unwanted manipulation of raw material during industrial production. Another relates to an artfulness in social behaviour that is assumed not to reveal an inner self. A third cause of scepticism relates to 'false' claims of foreign origin. Within the first two contexts, authenticity is related to the concept of nature or being natural. In the third context, authenticity is related to a notion of 'true cultures', indicating that cultural distinction which may be expressed through distinct cuisines. In each context, however, the notion of authenticity relates to an expectation that things ought to be what they set out to be, or that things should not pretend to be what they are not.

In spite of the salience of the notion of authenticity in Norwegian food marketing, the possibilities for making such claims for authenticity are restricted. One such constraint relates to the inherent mechanisms in what I have referred to above as the colonialization of the exotic, which through large-scale dissemination of exotic elements contribute to making the foreign cuisines familiar, thus eroding their original meaning. Another constraint relates to the standardizing efforts that are inherent in the structural conditions of modern mass manufacture.

The expansion of modern mass manufacture may be partly attributed to one of its key features, namely economy of scale. Basically, this implies that profit is a function of large-scale mass production of uniform items. In order to maximize production, the company must not only produce and distribute large quantities of each product type, it must also ensure that each single item is a *perfect imitation* of the product prototype, and thus identical to every other item of the same type. In order to achieve this, modern mass manufacturing is organized according to sets of routines, specifically designed to ensure a standardized output. Often this is referred to as standardization or quality control. Any significant deviation from standardized output is generally interpreted as a failure on part of the manufacturer, and the final responsibility for such issues tends to be attributed to the product manager (see also Chapter 4).

The strategy of standardization in modern mass manufacture stands in stark opposition to the strategy of differentiation inherent in brand-building. Mass production of brand products may

therefore be described as an effort to achieve maximum differentiation *between* product series, while at the same time ensuring a
minimum of variation of each item *within* the series. Furthermore,
the routinization inherent in large-scale manufacture represents a
serious constraint upon the credibility that claims of authenticity
must seek to establish. Obviously, any large-scale manufacturer
that seeks to establish an authentic connection between a mass
manufactured product and concepts such as 'nature', 'home-
cooking' or 'foreign cuisine' is, on thin ice as far as credibility is
concerned. This paradox is also noted with reference to ethnic
cuisine. According to van den Berghe, any attempt to cater
commercially for the demand of what he calls 'ethnic tourism' in
food necessarily produces a *"staged authenticity" that adulterates
that which the tourist seeks'* (van den Berghe 1984:394).

In the light of the salience of imitation and copying inherent in
mass manufacture, the question we need to address at this point
relates to the *persisting power of the language of authenticity in the
mass marketing of consumer goods that continues to flourish in spite of
these factors.* Why is authenticity a salient issue when the credibility
of any such claim is so fragile? And where does this power of the
language of authenticity derive from? In order to illuminate these
issues, I suggest that we turn our attention to the broader cultural
context in which Norwegian food marketing takes place, the
context of Western modernity.

Western Modernity and the Disengaged Portrayal of 'True Selves'

In his attempt to construct a cultural theory of modernity, which
he delineates to cover the Western World and the history of ideas,
Charles Taylor introduces the concept *'modern inwardness'* as a
salient descriptive feature. 'Modern inwardness' refers to an
underlying opposition in our languages of self-understanding
between the 'inside' and the 'outside', in which thoughts and
feelings are thought of as somehow resting inside, awaiting the
development that will manifest them in the public world (Taylor
1992:93–4; for further discussion see Chapter 10).

In the following, I will argue that these aspects of Western
modernity are also applicable to an analysis of products in
the making, particularly as these products are metaphorically

conceptualized as having a 'personality'. To the extent that a product manager succeeds in his effort to portray a brand product as having a distinct and readily apparent 'personality', this personality ought, according to the modern way of conceptualizing a 'self', to reflect some 'deep core' of the product. However, if we consider the awareness among product managers of the arbitrariness of the relation between cultural categories and their material representation, the conceptualization of products as persons becomes somewhat problematic. On the one hand, product managers may literally pick and choose among a wide range of cultural idioms in order to construct a distinct 'product personality', and in this process both utilize and contribute to the arbitrariness characterizing the relationship between a signifier and its sign in modern marketing (see earlier in this chapter). On the other hand, in their efforts to establish brand products, they try to construct products with an image that is coherent and stable over time, a 'personality' that supposedly reflects some kind of authentic character of the product. As they conceptualize products as having a distinct 'personality', they simultaneously evoke a set of metaphors that is firmly embedded in the conceptual framework of Western modernity *according to which the 'true' personality resides on the inside.*

Not surprisingly, recent development of food marketing has been characterized by an increased involvement in (and influence upon) processes of product development (Hennion and Méadel 1989). This is also reflected in empirical cases, in which product managers try to ensure that the 'personality' of the product is also materialized at its very core. Such efforts literally to implant a symbolic image upon the material product prototype may, in fact, be interpreted as an attempt to reconcile both the awareness that all symbols are, in some sense arbitrary, and the simultaneous notion that any alleged 'personality' must reflect a true essence located on the inside. In light of this, the persistence of the language of authenticity may be understood as an attempt to recapture the 'true essence' of the product, an essence that is *both* arbitrary and (therefore) lost, *and* fiercely called upon and thus re-claimed.

The modern conceptualization of 'self' in terms of an inner–outer dichotomy also implies that authenticity is no longer a question of either/or, but rather a matter of degree. If we think of ourselves in terms of an 'inner' essence that is only partly manifested in public, any expression of the 'self' may, by definition, be *ranked according to the degree to which it reveals this authentic, inner self*. Similarly, as consumers, we may conceive products as 'more' or 'less' authentic representations of whatever they claim to portray, be it 'nature', 'Italy' or 'traditional Norwegian cooking'. Particularly with regard to claims of foreign origin, we may observe that a wide range of products are, in fact, 'Italian' – yet at the same time we may decide that some of them are more 'Italian' than others. Thus, the competition in the market-place is partly structured in terms of another contest, in which different products are ranked according to their ability to represent authentically what they are supposed to represent. Wilk (1995) briefly touches upon this point, when he cites a previous Miss Belize who, being asked to offer some advice to next year's Miss Belize with regard to her participation in the Miss Universe contest, maintains that: '. . . *she should be herself, never trying to imitate anyone else'* (Wilk 1995:1).

However, this 'authenticity contest' should not be interpreted too literally. As the former Miss Belize also seems to realize, the quest for authenticity ought to be matched by an awareness that being special is only valuable in so far as the specialness is comparable on a global scale. Thus, she advises her follower to go to the pageant *'feeling first that she is . . . just as special as every other contestant there'* (Wilk 1995:1). A closer look at these statements points up a striking reflexivity on the part of Miss Belize with regard to an alleged coherence between her notions of her 'self', her role as a participant in the contest, and the public expectations surrounding the contest. Most importantly, Miss Belize's advice reveals an awareness that *an authentic self is something that may consciously be made manifest in public*. Furthermore, she seems to be recognize that a successful manifestation of an authentic self also requires a certain state of mind, a 'feeling' which may be evoked by means of a conscious effort as well! Thus, Miss Belize speaks within the conceptual framework of modern inwardness. This disengaged and instrumental stance towards the self that is inherent in the advice provided by Miss Belize brings us on to another aspect of the inwardness of Western modernity; namely that of reflexive disengagement.

According to Taylor, the Cartesian notion of a disengaged subject articulates one of the most important developments of the modern era, and has brought about: '... *the growing ideal of a human agent who is able to remake himself by methodical and disciplined action. What this calls for is the ability to take an instrumental stance to one's*

given properties, desires, inclinations, tendencies, habits of thought, and
feeling so that they can be **worked on**, *. . . until one meets the desired*
specifications' (Taylor 1992:99).[10]

Considering product managers' attempts to differentiate their
products in the light of such reflexive disengagement, the idea
that a product's personality may be constructed makes a lot of
sense. Much like Miss Belize, who realizes that a successful
manifestation of the authentic 'self' may be consciously worked
upon, the product managers also know that any product's
'personality' is the result of their conscious effort to create an image
that is *both constructed and authentic* at the same time. The swiftness
by which this apparent contradiction may be reconciled by product
managers and Miss Belize alike may be interpreted as an indication
that we are dealing with ways of being in the world that are firmly
located within the condition described by Charles Taylor as
Western modernity.

These aspects of Western modernity also help us to understand
why certain cuisines that are locally perceived as exotic, such as
for instance New Guinea, and certain culinary formats from more
familiar places, such as 'Deutsche Knödeln' (see Chapter 8), are
not immediately appropriated in the Viking Food product range,
in spite of their exotic and authentic potential. Just like Miss Belize,
the product managers know that the 'authentic' is only valuable
in so far as it is made comparable within a common format. While
for Miss Belize this common format is represented by the global
gaze, the product manager's common format is defined by the
'gaze' of Norwegian consumers. Yet the idea that an image may
be both constructed and authentic is shared by both. Thus, when
Henrik quickly discards dishes such as 'Deutsche Knödeln' as too
strange, he acts in accordance with an immediate knowledge of a
common format that may be loosely referred to as 'the Norwegian
market'. At the same time, he demonstrates that the quest for
authenticity has its limits. It is precisely this awareness, and
the disengaged instrumentality with which he selects certain
properties and discards others, that enables him to construct
products that 'meet the desired specifications'.

Notes

1. One may argue that the image of product as weapon may aptly characterize the way products are negotiated in the marketing department. However, to the extent that products serve as 'weapons' they do so because they are *carefully designed* to 'hit' a particular consumer segment. Thus, we are talking about weapons that (in accordance with the metaphor) hit with an almost surgical precision that is the outcome of a complex network of technology and knowledge, rather than offensive violence.

2. This resemblance is also discussed by Brian Moeran, in his monograph on advertising in Japan (Moeran 1996).

3. This resemblance is particularly salient if we consider the international food exhibition called the ANUGA, in which food manufacturers were organized according to national origin, each presenting a carefully designed image of a national cuisine, staged in a way that clearly indicates an awareness of a global gaze (see Chapter 8).

4. The most frequent reference was Italian (6 per cent of all adverts), Chinese/oriental (4%), (North-) American (3%), French (3%) and Mexican (2%) and Russian (2%), followed by (in decreasing order) Danish, Greek, Swedish, Turkish, British, Taiwanese, Spanish, Creole, European, Indian, Peruvian, Chilean and Caribbean. The term Norwegian appeared in approximately 14% of all advertisements (Lien 1995a).

5. In his account of the American response to Italian food from the 1880s to the 1930s Levenstein (1985) demonstrates that the gradual transformation of American consumers' responses towards Italian food, from finding it unacceptable to regarding it as highly accepted, may be partly explained by the political situation of the United States, and especially the role of the US as Italy's ally during the First World War.

6. The term 'imagined cuisines' derives from the concept *'imagined communities'* (Anderson 1983). While Anderson applies this term primarily in relation to nations as they are imagined from within, the concept may easily be extended to imply images of a 'collective other' as well, and therefore also to material representations of the other, as in the notion of imagined cuisines.

7. Owing to a long history of interaction, first through vast migration during the nineteenth century, and then through massive influence during the post-war period, the United States (usually referred to as *'Amerika'*) represents a significant nation that most Norwegians will have some familiarity with, or at least have an opinion of. Italy represents a Latin Mediterranean culture in Norway, and derives its significance partly from a notion of differences in temperament and lifestyle between Northern Europe and Southern Europe.

8. This represents a supplementary explanation to what Colin Campbell (1987) approaches as one of the puzzles of modern consumerism, namely the rapid pace of change in fashion, and the accompanying *'apparently endless pursuit of wants'* (1987:37), features that he seeks to explain by referring to a broad historical–cultural shift to modern hedonism following the Romantic era.

9. According to a recent national survey, 39% of Norwegian consumers report that they are often concerned about food additives in the food they eat, while 43% report that they are often concerned about contaminants in food from environmental pollution (Wandel 1994).

10. These modern ideals of reflexivity and disengagement have also been described by others as aspects of modernity (e.g. Giddens 1991). The main differences between the two lie in the way Taylor limits his description to an account of Western modernity, and in his attempts to identify differentiating features that may characterize this condition, such as, for instance, what he calls 'modern inwardness'.

Chapter 10

Modernity in the Marketing Department

The main symptom of disorder is the acute discomfort we feel when we are unable to read the situation properly and to choose between alternative actions (Bauman 1991:1).

Consciousness is modern in as much as it reveals ever new layers of chaos . . . Modern consciousness . . . spurs into action by unmasking its ineffectiveness. It perpetuates the ordering bustle by disqualifying its achievements and laying bare its defeats (Bauman 1990:166).

Throughout the empirical description, *uncertainty* and *ambiguity* appear as central themes. These concepts relate both to various attempts to evaluate advertising agency performance and concomitant evaluations of creativity, and to various efforts at classification. The present chapter seeks to explore the social organization of the marketing endeavour in terms of what I will refer to as *strategies of separation* and *systems of mediation*.[1] I will argue that these two concepts serve to summarize much of what happens in the day-to-day activities of product managers in the marketing department, both at the level of social organization and in the institutionalization of knowledge. I apply these terms as a point of departure for a more thorough discussion of modernity in the marketing department. By and large, empirical findings correspond quite well with characteristics of modernity as described by Giddens (1991) and Bauman (1991) (see Chapter 1). However, such compliance does not necessarily help us any further in understanding the specific configurations of this particular instance of modernity. In the present analysis, I wish to discuss these 'modern' features in the light of comparative material from societies that are *not* considered to be modern. I wish to expand on the concept of modernity, by exploring its broader specificity and usefulness as a descriptive term. More precisely, I will ask: *What is it that makes 'modernity' modern?* In order to do this, I need a concept of the opposite of the modern, which, for lack of a better term, I will refer to as 'traditional'. In the following discussion, I draw upon a notion of the traditional derived from ethnographic descriptions of societies such as the Trobriand Islands (as described by Weiner 1988) and the Lele (described by Douglas 1975a). By explicitly juxtaposing empirical material from a modern setting to selected parts of traditional ethnographic accounts, I wish to inquire more specifically what modernity entails.

There is a general agreement that most anthropological analyses are ultimately comparative, as we have to translate in order to describe, and comparison is intrinsic to the process of translation (Holy 1987; Overing 1987; Berge 1992). In interpretative approaches, however, the comparative contrast often remains implicit in the analysis. This is most often the case when the explicit object of study is somehow distant or exotic, and the comparative contrast is the researcher's own cultural background (usually Western modernity). In the present analysis, these notions of 'us' and 'them' are turned around: the appropriate context of the object of study is Western modernity, while the comparative contrast that facilitates description is constituted mostly by selected ethnographic accounts of traditional societies.

Even though the present juxtaposition of rather different ethnographies has a comparative element, it should not be judged as a comparative analysis in a strict sense of the term. As a comparison, the following account is asymmetrical, in the sense that a comparative contrast is evoked only in order to highlight certain analytic issues necessary for a description of the marketing department. Thus, the ethnographic material from traditional contexts is applied in a fragmented and highly selective manner that does not give full credit to its complexity.

Ambiguity and Doubt

I think you'll find that the decision-making processes are really unsystematic, and far more contingent than you probably had thought (Marketing manager: comment before I started doing fieldwork).

In his book *Organizing Modernity*, John Law draws attention to three different aspects of the practice of making order in the modern world. Firstly, in spite of modern attempts at ordering, there is, he argues, no order. This is because orders are never complete, but remain *'precarious accomplishments that may be overturned'* (Law 1994:2). Secondly, there is no *single* order. To the extent that order is partially accomplished, there are plural processes taking place that cannot be reduced to a single underlying principle. Thirdly, although ordering is usually conceived as a social process (at least by social scientists), ordering is in fact materially heterogeneous. By this term he refers to the wide range of different entities that are implicated in, and perform, 'social' ordering, such as talk, bodies, texts, machines, and architecture (Law 1994:2). We might add manufactured products, consumer surveys and advertising as well.

As indicated by the empirical case studies (Chapters 6 to 8) and summarized in Chapter 9, marketing practice is characterized by contingency, ambivalence and doubt, rather than offensive action. Consequently, the situation of the product manager fits well with the state of reflexivity that has been referred to as a characteristic feature of modernity (Bauman 1990, 1991; Giddens 1991). What we have described is thus not only a state of uncertainty, but also a keen awareness of the inconclusiveness of each supposition. This corresponds very closely to what Bauman (1990:166) describes as modern consciousness, which *'is suffused with the awareness of inconclusiveness of order'.* [2]

For a large part, the closing of controversies implies the establishment of a classificatory kind of order, either in terms of a written document, a formulated decision or a material product prototype (see Chapter 6). Each new product idea is initially something undefined, which through meticulous negotiations gradually comes to be accepted as a product to be launched on the market, fully equipped with a name, a target group, and a set of symbolic and material instructions for use. During such negotiations, fragments of information are sorted according to a set of predefined concepts, models, and guides to action that are all inherent in the body of knowledge that is referred to as marketing theory. Marketing theory thus represents a firm anchor in a situation of uncertainty. Through the closing of controversies, the product manager and his or her associates succeed in *'giving their world a structure'* (Bauman 1991:1), and thus, as Bauman puts it: *'manipulate (the world's) probabilities; make some events more likely than some others; behave as if events were not random, or limit or eliminate the randomness of events'* (Bauman 1991:1).

Each new product launch is, in a sense, an encounter with something that is unknown. Through their preparatory efforts, the product managers and their associates are able to encounter that which is not yet known with what Latour refers to as the familiarity of previous experiences. The acts of classification enable the product manager to ensure the necessary adaptation between a set of potential allies (consumer and product) with whom/which a future alliance is crucial to the firm, and in one way or another also consequential for the future of the product manager.

During these negotiations, the arbitrariness of the classifications is constantly revealed. For, as Bauman notes, the struggle for order is an endless task, and the *least possible among the multitude of impossible tasks that modernity set itself* (Bauman 1991:4). This is precisely because ambivalence is, in itself, *'a side product of the labour of classification'*, and one that calls for yet more classifying effort (Bauman 1991:3).

Strategies of Separation: The Gap Between the Private and the Professional

To classify means to set apart, but what is it that is kept apart in the day-to-day practice of marketing? What are the strategies[3] of separation, and how do these, in turn, impinge upon the organization of tasks to be done and ways of doing them? Looking more closely at the empirical cases, we may identify strategies of separation at two different levels: (1) the conceptual level, as reflected through discourse and through the efforts to establish neat categories; and (2) the social level, as reflected in the social organization of daily activities and the division of labour. While these levels are clearly interrelated, I will treat them separately, in order to allow a more thorough analysis of each.

At the conceptual level, we may recall the continuous efforts at building brands, i.e. the conscious work of differentiation for commercial purposes. This may be achieved by a symbolic elaboration of selected aspects of product. Ideally, such product characteristics should reflect defined differences between categories of consumers. In this way, product differentiation also incorporates a notion of sameness between the product and the consumer (see Chapter 9). In other words, the elaboration of differences between products constitutes a central element of food marketing in Norway in the early 1990s, precisely through the emphasis on brand-building.

We may also note a conceptual distinction between 'us' and 'the market' (see Chapter 6), in which 'we' refers loosely to Viking Foods, while 'the market' refers to actual and potential purchases of a specific product by Norwegian consumers. In spite of the fact that Viking Foods holds a central position in Norway and is the dominant supplier of a wide range of food products to Norwegian consumers, the conceptualization of the market as something separate is rarely challenged. Generally, the strategies of separation seem to operate metaphorically, and are more a feature of conceptualizations than of day-to-day activities.

At the social level, we may note how strategies of separation are embedded in the preconditions of work itself. Firstly, this appears through the underlying separation of private and professional spheres. This distinction serves as one of the main organizing principles of life and work in modern societies, and thus operates both at a structural level (as the underlying precondition for the entire marketing endeavour), and at a personal level (as the key organizer of the daily life of the product managers themselves).

To the extent that mechanisms separating the professional from the private spheres are apparent in the marketing department, they seem to serve primarily to protect the 'boundedness' of the professional sphere from intrusion from the private sphere (keeping privacy from filtering into the marketing department), rather than the other way around. This impression may be a result of my empirical focus on the professional, rather than on the private sphere.[4] Statements such as 'Since I had children, I've tried not to work overtime' may indicate that the private sphere is also, in some sense a protected realm. Still, the main impression from fieldwork during office hours is that of mechanisms protecting the professional sphere from intrusion. Partly, these mechanisms may be assumed to operate within each individual person, as part of the acquired ability to distinguish between acceptable and unacceptable behaviour at work. Partly they operate at the structural level, embedded in social (and partly formalized) contracts between employer and employee.

These separations between the private and professional spheres are not unique to the Viking Foods marketing department. Rather, as studies of working life repeatedly demonstrate (or take for granted), such a distinction pervades the organization of life and work in modern societies (see Chapter 4). What makes this distinction especially intriguing in the present context is the fact that the subject-matter, i.e. marketing food products, is intrinsically related to the consumption of food in the domestic sphere. In the light of this, one might assume that there are specific conditions under which the private sphere may be of particular relevance to the professional as a potential source of knowledge. As we have seen, this is rarely the case. In spite of the vast range of experience each product manager has as a consumer, this knowledge is rarely explicitly referred to in marketing decisions. I do not suggest that the competence acquired as consumer is entirely irrelevant, nor that the value of general experience within the domestic sphere is denied altogether. Still, I suggest that in the day-to-day practice of marketing, *competence derived from the domestic sphere largely remains invisible or unarticulated*. In the very few instances in which such reference occurs, it is either in a joking manner, or through a humorous play on words that metaphorically transforms the domestic sphere into a branch of the professional. An example of this is when Erik jokingly refers to his home kitchen as the 'test institute in Edvard Griegs vei 54' (see Chapter 8). In this case, the use of the private kitchen is legitimized by metaphorically 'transforming' it into a laboratory, which, in itself *'has become a theoretical notion in our understanding of science'* (Knorr Cetina 1995:144). Through such play on words, the home kitchen is temporarily incorporated into the professional sphere.

Rather than disproving the suggestion above, these cases of exception serve to indicate that *the boundedness of the professional sphere is, simultaneously a boundedness of knowledge*. More precisely, I suggest that the social rhetoric of the marketing department serves effectively to separate the competence that each product manager may possess as a consumer from the competence derived within the marketing profession. This is achieved through filtering processes, in which implicit criteria render certain claims of knowledge legitimate and others not. Consequently, when Erik gets the chance to watch six randomly selected consumers through a screen in the laboratory of a market research institute and to study the written summary report afterwards (Chapter 6), this represents a source of knowledge that is by definition far more legitimate than a comparable response elicited from Erik's friends and neighbours.

These strategies of separation have important implications for the social organization of marketing practice. Most importantly, they pave the way for a wide range of *intermediary translators*, such as advertising and marketing research agencies. In the following, I will examine the relationships to such intermediary translators.

Structures of Mediation: Imagining Consumers

When product managers from Viking Foods' marketing department participated at a two-day consumer segmentation seminar arranged by a market research institute, the activities included a personal survey of each product manager by means of which participants were informed of their individual score and location on the *Norwegian Monitor* sociograph (see Chapter 5). Afterwards, several participants told me that they found this exercise extremely useful, because it revealed *'how different many of them were from the average Norwegian consumer'*. Many found themselves in the upper right corner of the sociograph, and one product manager even discovered that she was located so far to the upper right that they couldn't fit her into the figure, and had to indicate her position somewhere up on the wall.

Market research institutes may be described as intermediary translators that mediate *from* the consumer *to* the manufacturer. Often, their surveys are referred to as part of the system of 'decision-making-support' (*'beslutningsttøttesystemer'*). Advertising agencies represent another category of intermediary translators that primarily serve to mediate *from* the manufacturer *to* the consumer (see also Figure 7.1). However, as the sociograph exercise may indicate, the product managers' need for intermediary mediators is not entirely self-evident. It is founded upon a recognition of distance, or a recognized inability really to understand the consumers that the market research institute itself provides the evidence to sustain. According to marketing managers, the exercise is also a tool for self-reflection. Still, as this particular device for self-reflection is a statistical tool that serves to emphasize differentiation, the effect of the exercise will inevitably be a realization of the limitations of one's own knowledge. Thus, while serving as an intermediary translator between the manufacturer and the consumer, the market research institute may *simultaneously* take part in what we have described as processes of separation between the two. This is important, because intermediary translators are not merely functional assistants in the effort of aligning the interests of food producers with those of consumers, they are also producers of a distinct kind of knowledge which is highly commoditized. This commoditization presupposes a separation of spheres that the intermediary translators themselves provide the 'evidence' to sustain.

Appadurai notes that *'as commodities travel greater distances (institutional, spatial, temporal), knowledge about them tends to become partial, contradictory, and differentiated'* (Appadurai 1986:56). While this is true of all types of commodity exchange, there is one feature that, according to Appadurai, characterizes capitalist societies; namely the fact that *'knowledge **about** commodities is itself increasingly commoditized'* (Appadurai 1986:54). Appadurai's basic argument may easily be extended to include knowledge about consumers, thus attributing to the intermediary translators a double edge: that of offering their knowledge of the product to the consumer (through advertising), while at the same time offering their knowledge of the consumer to the producer (through market research).

Most transactional exchanges between different groups of individuals occur without the aid of the professional advertiser or market research agency. Even in industrialized, Western societies, products are being mass-produced and mass-distributed with minimal involvement of advertising agencies and market research institutes. In the light of this, it is reasonable to ask what it is that the manufacturer actually seeks to acquire when purchasing the services of intermediary translators. What are the key elements of this commodity, and how is its value negotiated?

In order to analyse this, we have to make a separation once again between the commodities offered by advertising agencies and those offered by market research agencies. On the one hand, there are the advertising agencies, whose distinguishing characteristic is that of offering *creativity*, i.e. coming up with names, logos, design and text for advertising campaigns. On the other hand, there are the market research institutes, whose primary and most indispensable service is that of offering *information about consumers* and whose main sales argument is their ability to describe in great detail the specific characteristics of differentiated target groups, an ability that is largely an effect of the application of modern statistics.[5] Let us take a closer look at each of these commodities, as they appear through transactions between Viking Foods and advertising agencies.

Trusting Advertising Agencies: A Tournament of Value

As we were discussing advertising during lunch time, a staff director once told me that he often questioned the value of advertising. He continued: *'Advertising is like the arms race. Everybody does it, so no one dares take the risk of staying out.'* This comment echoes a saying that is frequently quoted, in which a manufacturer complains that he knows that half his advertising budget is a waste of money: the problem is that he doesn't know which half.[6] In the following, I will not discuss the value of advertising in terms of sales results or profit return. Rather, I wish to illuminate the ways in which professionals in the marketing department justify, negotiate and challenge the value of their advertising costs.

In his description of strategies of presentation in Japanese advertising, Brian Moeran draws attention to what he calls a *competitive presentation,* in which an advertiser invites two or more agencies to submit advertising material in an open competition for an advertising account (Moeran 1993; 1996).

During my fieldwork period, several situations of competition took place that resemble Moeran's description of a competitive presentation. For instance, during the poultry project, in an effort to find a proper name, Erik's scepticism towards the suggestions from Publicity led him to contact a second advertising agency, called Promotion. As it turned out, their suggestions were no more convincing than the earlier ones, and Erik ended up choosing a third name that had come up during an internal brainstorm meeting (see Chapter 6). A similar incident took place while preparing a pizza commercial, when Kristoffer's dissatisfaction with the film idea presented at 'Film Makers' brought about a meeting with a second film director (see Chapter 7). In both these cases, the introduction of a competitor came as a result of dissatisfaction with the first suggestion. These events are not identical to what Moeran defines as competitive presentations. In both cases, however, the client initiates the presentations (or, in the case of Film Makers: the advertising agency, after an initiative from the advertiser), even if the invitations were sent out one by one. We may therefore refer to the events as a competitive presentation occurring in a diachronic manner.[7]

The distinction between a diachronic and a synchronic presentation is closely related to budgeting. In the poultry project case, each advertising agency that came up with a name was paid a specific amount of money for its advice. Consequently, for Erik, introducing a second (or third) competitor was a costly endeavour, which was postponed until the results of the first presentation had turned out to be unsatisfactory. Moeran's analysis of competitive presentations refers to a situation in which no such provisional payment is being made, and the situation for the competing agencies is that of 'winner takes all'. Consequently, in such cases, the prospective client who invites the competitive presentation is not charged by the agencies, and there is no extra cost involved in inviting several agencies simultaneously.

The most dramatic example of a competitive presentation in Moeran's sense of the term took place when a new marketing director decided to invite eight different advertising agencies (including Publicity and Promotion) to participate in a competitive presentation, on the basis of which the entire mode of partnership and the prospective partners would be re-evaluated. Since the firm had relied almost exclusively on a single advertising agency (Publicity) for several years, this relationship was seriously challenged by this decision. According to informants, there were several reasons for this re-evaluation. A certain dissatisfaction with the previous advertising agency was sometimes referred to, along with the recent hiring of the new marketing director, who took an active role in staging the event. Another background for the re-evaluation was a recent fusion that prompted the need to select a primary advertising partner. Finally, the enhanced emphasis on brand-building implied a greater priority of so-called strategic issues. The marketing director put it this way:

> We are looking for one main agency which may serve as ... a strategic 'sparring-partner'.[8] They must be particularly well qualified in brand-building. How to establish brand products. That's our focus, all the time. But we also need one or two supporting agencies that may contribute with creative solutions, within the framework which is plotted out by our strategic partner.

In order to undertake a re-evaluation, each agency was invited to present a model of cooperation, and details about their organizational structure, ownership, economic results, creative teams, and competence in various fields, including in-store marketing, international networks, brand-building and film production.

These invitations led to a sequence of eight separate meetings, each lasting approximately two hours, in which each of the advertising agencies presented themselves to a group of Viking Food marketing managers and marketing directors. On the basis of this first sequence of presentations, four agencies were invited to a second round of meetings, of which a presentation of earlier work was also requested. The second letter of invitation also included a brief description of Viking Foods' brand-building strategy, and asked the agencies to comment specifically upon the tenability of this strategy, and possibly suggest an alternative strategy.

During the second sequence, consisting of four separate meetings, the Viking Foods vice-president and the managing director were also present. The meetings took place in an elegantly furnished meeting-room next to the office of the managing director. A dark polished oval table with two sharply pointed edges fitted harmoniously with the oval shape of the room itself. One of the walls was covered by a giant woven textile decoration, substituting for the more common graphic reprints usually used for decorations in other meeting-rooms.

The entire process of competitive presentations lasted from early January until March, and resulted in a selection of three agencies, one as a strategic partner, and the remaining two as supporting partners in the creative work. For one agency, this implied a less dominant position *vis-à-vis* Viking Foods, and also a less lucrative account. For a second agency, the competitive presentation implied a considerable enhancement of the present account in terms of far more involvement on strategic issues. For the third, it implied a continuation of a previous account.

It seems reasonable to assume that the competitive presentation served to destabilize the relationship between product manager and advertising agency. Thus, when Erik sent his first brief on the poultry project to Publicity in late March, he was well aware that he might also consult the services of other agencies, while Tom (the account manager) knew that his agency no longer held the secure position of an exclusive supplier of such services. However, considering the heavy involvement of Publicity even *after* the competitive presentation, the consequences of this event for day-to-day activities should not be over-rated.

The competitive presentation taking place at Viking Foods is quite similar to the one described by Moeran (1993, 1996), in which a major European car manufacturer (PKW) invited four Japanese agencies to compete for its advertising account in Japan. Following the events from one agency's position, Moeran describes in great detail the frantic preparations for the dramatic performance, the intense excitement while waiting for the results, and the disappointment when the account is lost. Still, even though the results implied a dismissal of the agency, the agency's contacts with the car manufacturer PKW did not come to an end, as they were already involved in numerous practical activities – *'activities that could hardly be brought to halt just because a contract had been terminated'* (Moeran 1993:85). Furthermore, shortly after this event, rumours circulated that PKW's rival was going to call for a competitive presentation a few months later. Consequently, in spite of the seeming brutality of the 'winner takes all' principle, there are always other potential clients, and other competitive presentations in which an agency may get a second chance.

Competitive presentations represent an instance of what Appadurai (1986) refers to as *'tournaments of value'*.[9] According to Appadurai, a tournament of value may be defined as:

> *complex periodic events that are removed in some culturally well-defined way from the routines of economic life. Participation in them is likely to be both a privilege of those in power, and an instrument of status contests between them. . . . what is at issue in such tournaments is not just status, rank, fame, or reputation of actors, but the disposition of the central tokens of value in the society in question* (Appadurai 1986:21).

Appadurai derives his concept from descriptions of the Kula ring (Weiner 1988), and applies it to describe contemporary Western phenomena, such as art auctions. Yet the definition of a tournament of value fits equally well with the competitive presentation at Viking Foods. Appadurai insists that even though tournaments of value occur in special times and places, their forms and outcomes are always consequential for the more mundane realities of power and knowledge in ordinary life. As in the Kula Ring, competitive presentation in the advertising trade is both a ritual set apart from ordinary life, and a dramatic event with implications far beyond the event itself. Although a dismissal does not necessarily put an end to an account, at least not immediately, it still has consequences for the reputation of the agency, and also for the relationships of those involved.

As in the Kula ring, the exchanges taking place at Viking Foods are more than mere monetary transactions; they also involve a *'reciprocal construction of value'*. According to Appadurai, the kula system is a dynamic process in which *'shells and men are reciprocally agents of each other's value definition'* (Appadurai 1986:20; see also Weiner 1988). Similarly, we may approach the competitive presentation of advertising agencies at Viking Foods as a situation in which the basic token of exchange is the prospect of an advertising account. While the final outcome of the competitive presentation depends on the client's evaluation of the relative merits of the agencies in question, the acquisition of the account will enhance the future opportunities for the winning agency, thus strengthening their relative position (symbolically and financially) *vis-à-vis* the other agencies in question. In this way, the competitive presentation involves a reciprocal construction of value, in which a transactional exchange is not only a result of an evaluation of relative merits, but also an agent in defining social rank.

Still, one question remains, namely: How do they know? Which criteria are used by marketing experts at Viking Foods to distinguish the 'good' from the 'bad'? Which qualities do they look for?

As I posed these questions to various informants, emotional and subjective aspects were always emphasized. A marketing manager put it this way:

> *It's all very subjective, it's a matter of how you feel, how the personal chemistry fits ('hvordan kjemien passer'). Of course, there are also other things that we look at, such as their present client situation, their international networks, like how good are their day-to-day systems for following up on what's going on in the rest of the world, and how clever they are at brand-building. That's important to us. Another important question is how well they seem to handle the strategic part . . . But their strategic solutions are mostly the same. I'd say that what we select **people** more than we select **agencies**.*

This statement echoes the answer of a marketing director when asked by which criteria the agencies are distinguished from each other:

> [smiling] *It's very difficult. We spend a lot more time on this now, more than what is normally done in the field of food manufacturing . . . It boils*

down to a lot of 'synsing'.[10] *The agency brings the creative team that they*
will put us up with. What we consider is:
1. *Whether the chemistry fits ('om kjemien stemmer').*
2. *What they have done the last two years. That is, a professional evaluation.*
3. *Their answers to our questions regarding brand-building.*
4. *The agency's economy, formal ownership, etc. That is, solidity. In addition,*
   it is a key requirement that the company is of a certain size – we are not
   going to give them two assignments a year, you know, but many . . .
   Another requirement, of course is that we are dealing with people who
   are clever and professional ('dyktige'), people who are willing and able to
   discuss strategic solutions.

Then I ask: So you are not afraid of involving advertising agencies
in strategic decisions on a higher level? *'No, I'm not. I don't want*
them on the board of directors. But I wish to involve advertising agencies
when we prepare a strategic plan, defining where we want to be five
years from now, and deciding how many resources we shall allocate to
the various activities – then I want them to be part of these discussions.'

Another marketing manager mentions the integrity of the
agency as an important criterion for selection. When asked which
criteria he considered to be important, he replied: *'Good question.*
Buying advertising services is a bit like buying consultancy services,
you buy the people, it's a question of confidence ('tillit') in the people
you meet.'

Inviting him to be a bit more concrete, I ask: What ought they
to tell you in order for you to have confidence in them?

They should have the courage to say what they think, and not just echo our
own viewpoints ('ikke snakke oss etter munnen'). If we buy consultancy, I
want somebody to say: 'Hey, Anders, this is just rubbish . . .'. I think the
advertising agencies easily get into a position of yes-saying. They are often
not critical or offensive enough.'

These statements suggest that in the process of selecting a new
advertising partner, subjective feelings and personal preferences
play a central role. The reliance on such preferences, often referred
to as 'gut-feeling' (*'magefølelse'*) or *'synsing'*, is especially relevant
with respect to the marketing directors' judgement of the quality
of the relationship between agency and client. This is indicated
by frequent metaphorical references to the 'chemistry' between
the people involved, and through a consistent emphasis that 'it's
a question of confidence in people, rather than in the agency as
such'. This is quite in accord with a recent study of Norwegian

advertising professionals, in which most agencies identified themselves as *'strategic partners in an intimate agency–client relationship'* (Helgesen 1994:51). The stress on the relational dimension is also emphasized in other studies, alongside an emphasis on creativity (Wackman *et al.* 1986; Verbeke 1988).

In addition, the *professional integrity* of the agency and the persons involved are explicitly appreciated. This is also reflected in agencies' modes of presentation. A printed hand-out distributed at a competitive presentation by one of the four finalists, entitled *'A presentation of the agency and the people'*, summarizes the role of the agency as follows: *'[The agency should be] a serious, real discussion partner, that is even paid for disagreeing, if it is for the benefit of your company and your customers. Search for a "no-agency", not a servile partner!'*

Furthermore, a strong sense of *identification* with the client and its products is frequently emphasized by agency staff, and by account managers especially, who may sometimes refer to the strategy of Viking Foods as 'our strategy', and the products as 'my products'.

The reliance on subjective feelings in the final evaluation of advertising partners is not very surprising. In their attempt to evaluate advertising agencies and their pieces of work, the marketing managers and directors move beyond the sphere in which most things can be classified; they enter a sphere in which things can no longer be known in a 'semi-scientific' manner, and thus they have few options in the final evaluation other than to rely on what they feel. The question that begs to be explored is therefore not so much *why* they rely on subjective judgements, but rather *why uncertainty is thematized so frequently* – or even, why it is an issue at all. We will return to this question shortly. First, let us explore in some more detail another salient aspect of the transactions between agency and client: the notion of creativity.

Purchasing Creativity: Between Commodity and Friendly Favour

> *Of course, every person is creative. But some are more creative than others* (Copywriter, advertising agency).

The product managers' reliance on subjective preferences ('*syn-sing*') is particularly relevant with respect to the concept of *creativity*. In the marketing department, the term 'creativity' is sometimes referred to as the key commodity of their transactions with advertising agencies, as indicated in the phrase *'creativity is what we buy'*. Creativity may thus be analysed as the ultimate quality defining the actual value of any piece of advertising that is purchased.

However, a closer examination of the negotiations that take place indicates that it is not that simple. For instance, during the competitive presentation, creativity is hardly mentioned as a distinguishing criterion at all. This subordination of creativity as a distinguishing criterion was further confirmed during an agency presentation. After a lengthy description of organizational structure, consumer segmentation systems and financial solidity, the managing director of the advertising agency mentioned advertising awards. Referring to his agency's high number of awards, he claimed that his agency was among the leading advertising agencies in terms of what '– *if creativity may be measured – is the most important measurement of good advertising in Norway'*, whereupon the managing director of Viking Foods abruptly exclaimed: *'You can get as many awards as you wish, as far as I'm concerned. It does not interest me!'*

This statement reflects a general worry often expressed by product managers, regarding an alleged tendency for the advertising agency's creative team to get *too* involved in the creative aspects of the advert, at the expense of the need to sell. The latent conflict of interest between an emphasis on aesthetics vs. one on effectiveness may also be seen as an expression of differences in the objectives and strategies of advertisers and agencies (Helgesen 1994). On the basis of a recent survey among major Norwegian advertisers, Helgesen maintains that, from the perspective of advertising agencies, creative excellence still *'functions as a valid and largely unrivalled criterion of professional advertising agency performance'* (Helgesen 1994:51). A systematic enforcement of creative excellence, manifested for instance through advertising awards, takes place even though the *effectiveness* of the creative element in advertising in terms of sales returns is seriously questioned (Helgesen 1991). Thus, from the advertiser's point of view, the value of creativity is somewhat ambivalent. Rhetorically, creativity is *'what we buy'*, but the feasibility of this particular 'investment' remains highly uncertain. In addition, as creativity is difficult to evaluate and measure, for the product manager the content of the transaction remains somewhat obscure.

To the extent that product managers need to make judgements pertaining to creativity as a quality of an advert, it implies that they must tread the sharp edge between marketing and aesthetics, i.e. between a *publicly recognized kind of knowledge*, which may be classified, falsified and even measured against clear criteria, and expressions that result from the subjective imagery of someone else. When a market research institute concludes that modern materialists may be reached by the use of American symbols (Chapter 7), this particular connection is assumed to refer to a cultural pattern to which the market research consultant has some kind of privileged access. When a film director, on the other hand, suggests the combination of a red Corvette, a beautiful woman, a pizza and a burp within a thirty-second commercial (Chapter 7), the connections are assumed to be based primarily on the film director's subjective imagery, and the concept is subject to far more critical consideration, and is more likely to be turned down. While both suggestions are 'creative' in the sense that they connect elements in unfamiliar ways, the difference in the degree to which they are seen as the outcome of subjective imagery makes a great difference for the product manager. In the former example, all s/ he has to do is to pass on a creative element that is assumed to be part of a general cultural pattern. In the latter example, however, the product manager represents one of the first audiences with the power to decide whether a result of subjective imagery is likely to be tolerated by the general public. Yet, s/he has few clues as to how to make this decision except for his or her own subjective reaction, and the *'synsing'* of a few colleagues, clues that are generally not accepted as valid criteria for judgement.

However, these difficulties are partly alleviated through the institutionalization of an account manager, who serves as a mediator between the creative team and the advertiser (Chapter 3). Before an idea is presented to a client, it has been subject to internal judgement by a group of professionals within the advertising agency, consisting of both creative director and account manager. Ideally, the former will serve to guarantee the aesthetic quality, while the latter will make sure that the client's interests are taken into account. In this way, the *latent conflict between aesthetics and commerce is transformed and embedded into a social structure* that, to some extent, relieves the product manager of the problem of evaluating – with any sense of certainty – the relative merits of the various aesthetic expressions. This may partly explain why the evaluation of advertising agencies is, to such a great extent, described in terms of an evaluation of the social relationships involved.

It also provides a necessary context for understanding the final outcome of the competitive presentation. In spite of the alleged intention to select an agency that is particularly well qualified, the competitive presentation brought about few changes: out of the four agencies that were invited to do a second presentation, three succeeded in establishing an account: one as a strategic partner, the other two as creative partners. As it turned out, these three agencies were all previous advertising partners of enterprises that had merged with Viking Foods. Thus, the final decision implied maintenance and some redefinition of the content of previous accounts rather than the establishment of new ones. In the final evaluation, well-established social bonds appeared to be decisive. Shortly after the decision had been made, I asked a marketing manager whether there had been much discussion, whereupon he replied: *'No, there was not much dissent ("det var lite dissens"). The four final agencies were mostly equally good, so actually, we ended up with a pragmatic choice in which we decided to carry on [the relationship] with those [agencies] that we had been using before [the merger]'* (Marketing manager).

Summarizing the nature of the judgement involved in the competitive presentation, we may conclude that after a preliminary elimination based on quantifiable criteria, the final evaluation is based upon both subjective judgements (*'synsing'*) and pragmatic social considerations. This is in accord with the conclusion reached by Moeran regarding the competitive presentation in Japan, in which he argues that the outcome is essentially a social matter, depending for a large part on the successful cultivation of relations with the client 'target man' through what is known in Japanese as *'newaza'*, or in Moeran's English translation: human chemistry (Moeran 1993:83).

This finding is particularly relevant in the light of a persistent tendency in social science discourse to reify the difference between traditional and modern societies by reference to systems of exchange, mostly in terms of a dichotomy between, for example, gift exchange and commodity (market) exchange (Bloch and Parry 1989:7–8). While gift exchange is based on an exchange of *inalienable* objects between *interdependent* transactors, commodity exchange is assumed to represent an absolute contrast, based on an exchange of *alienable* objects between *independent* transactors (Gregory 1982). According to its rhetorical framing, the competitive presentation represents a 'market type of event'. According to informants, it will enable the marketing experts to select the agency that represents the 'best buy' when all relevant aspects are considered, thus emphasizing the legitimacy of a market principle. Yet, a closer analysis indicates that this is not the way it works. In fact, it is the dependency that turns out to be decisive. Furthermore, the object of exchange (the service provided) was hardly alienable, but closely connected to, and even evaluated in terms of, the social relationships involved. The competitive presentation thus serves to illustrate that, in spite of an *emic* justification in terms of a market principle, in the final evaluation the interdependency of the transactors and the inalienability of the commodity are very much involved. This observation is particularly interesting in the light of the fact that the competitive presentation occurs in the marketing department of a modern, profit-oriented, industrial enterprise. Thus it occurs at an empirical location at which we might expect to find all the typical characteristics of a capitalist commodity principle of exchange, characteristics that nevertheless tend to slip away when we focus more closely on the actual transaction.

Let us consider once more the similarities between the competitive presentation and the Trobriander Kula system. According to Weiner (1988), the Kula ring is much more intricate and deeply endowed with social meaning than the system of exchange of armshells and necklaces first described by Malinowski in 1922. This is especially salient with regard to the path along which particular shells are passed from one partner to another. When judging the value of an item of exchange, such as a necklace, the distinguishing criteria include not only aesthetic values related to its material qualities as judged by weight, dimension, colour, age and tactile qualities (S. Campbell 1983), but also the history of its circulation around the islands, and especially, its association with particular men. Weiner writes: '*Just as a man gains renown through the circulation of his name with particular shells, so too, as the shells continue to move from one partner to another, they likewise gain value from their association with particular men*' (Weiner 1988:144).

Just as the value of the kula necklace depends upon its previous path and the reputation(s) of its previous owner(s),[11] so too does the evaluation of the advertising agencies include a consideration of their previous work and their association with (previous and) contemporary clients. Furthermore, as in the Kula exchange, the evaluations rest upon a sense of knowledge of the persons involved. As such, we may argue that both systems of transactions are both constitutive of and constituted by social relationships. Upon closer examination of the actual transactions involved in a 'market economy' like Viking Foods and a 'gift-economy' such as the Trobriands, this aspect of the alleged difference tends to collapse.

Purity and Pollution in Modern Exchange

Considering the social embeddedness of the competitive present-ation, and especially of the final judgement, we may ask: Why was it ever staged in the first place? Even if the new marketing director felt there was a need to re-negotiate the value of the present agencies' services against some others, why did he choose the format of market exchange rather than simply a low-key sequence of meetings at which matters could be discussed more informally?

In order to understand this, I suggest we consider the division between the private and the professional in the light of general principles of market exchange. Bloch and Parry suggest that the assumed dichotomy between gift exchange and commodity exchange may be due to a peculiar power that Westerners attribute to money: *'For us, money signifies a sphere of "economic" relationships which are inherently impersonal, transitory, amoral and calculating'* (Bloch and Parry 1989:9).

This impersonality of money, they argue, seems to be a pecu-liarity of Western culture. It tends to reinforce a romantic idealization of the world of gift exchange, which is constructed as an antithesis to the economic sphere of market exchange (Bloch and Parry 1989).[12] The tendency to distinguish sharply between the economic sphere of monetary exchange and a social sphere from which money is excluded, runs parallel to, and is partly connected to, the general division in modern soc-ieties between the private sphere and the public sphere, or, as it appears in the present context: between the private and the professional.

For most product managers, purchasing advertising services implies cooperation and frequent encounters with a few professionals in the advertising agencies. Especially in relation to the agency account manager, and also to some extent to the creative staff, the relationships established are characterized by continuity, offering possibilities for developing a closer relationship than the professional task strictly requires. However, if such relationships get too friendly and personal they may in fact be conceived to represent a challenge to the implementation of an underlying principle of 'pure' market transaction. This echoes the Weberian emphasis on formal or instrumental rationality in modern, bureaucratic organization, which, according to a current interpreter: *'established an objective decision-making mechanism based on impersonal rules and specialist knowledge, which **excluded all subjective, moral or similarly irrational considerations**'* (Reed 1992:40, my emphasis).

In this case, the market principle serves symbolically as a 'decision-making device', apparently rearranging partnerships to advertising agencies in a way that ensures 'the best buy'. This interpretation is in accordance with Weber's description of the principal conditions for obtaining formal rationality in productive enterprises.[13] In the light of these principles, the establishment of a too close relationship to persons in the advertising agency would imply a threat to the principle of absolute freedom to renegotiate or terminate the account.

On the one hand, a long-lasting relationship to a single group of advertising professionals represents a definite advantage, in terms of a mutual knowledge of products, persons and enterprise. On the other hand, such a relationship may represent a challenge to the ideal of a free market principle when selecting an advertising partner. Caught in this dilemma between the need for social continuity on the one hand and the threat of dependence on the other, the competitive presentation offers a temporary solution. Even if the outcome does not significantly alter the state of affairs, it serves as a ritual 'purification' of the relationships involved. In order to serve in this way, the event must be staged formally and within a format that complies with the general principle of market exchange.

Through the competitive presentation, the initiators demonstrate to their superiors that the choice of agencies is the result of a close examination of the best agencies available. Simultaneously, they demonstrate to the agencies that their ongoing relationship cannot be taken for granted, thus providing an impetus for optimal performance in present and future assignments. In this way, the competitive presentation may, through temporarily destabilizing the relationship, actually serve to legitimize the continuation of a relationship that is in fact both personal and long-lasting. As such, it may be seen as a purifying ritual that celebrates the overarching ideology of free market exchange.

To summarize, even within a profit-oriented enterprise in a modern Western society, the principles of exchange may be socially embedded, and in this manner are remarkably similar to those adhered to in societies that are generally characterized by a far more traditional and gift-oriented mode of exchange, such as for instance the Trobriand society. To the extent that the alleged dichotomy between gift and commodity modes of exchange is actually reflected in the empirical material, it is a distinction that is most apparent at the level of rhetorical discourse, but that tends to disappear once we turn our attention to actual implementations and evaluations of the exchange.

Thus the difference between the advertising transactions in the marketing department and the Trobriand tournament of value relates first and foremost to the moral interpretation of the exchange and the way it is rhetorically justified. While the Trobriands seem to have no need to 'alienate' the necklace from its previous owner, the professionals in the marketing department must go a long way to demonstrate that a re-negotiation of the contract is, in fact, independent of any relationships that may have become established along the way. Thus, in modern marketing, competitive presentations may serve symbolically to separate the professional sphere (in this case, free market enterprise) from the privacy of personal bonds.

Concluding Remarks: Modernity in the Marketing Department

In spite of the social nature of exchange both in the marketing department and in relation to the Kula-system of exchange, one significant difference remains, which relates to reflexivity and doubt. In the light of the social embeddedness of the transaction, and the product managers' reliance on subjective judgement, their reflexive stance may not seem so surprising to us. Yet, when compared to Weiner's account of the Kula-ring, which *also* involves highly subjective and socially embedded evaluations, the ambiguity and doubt so often expressed by product managers stands apart as something radically different. We are confronted with a kind of radical doubt and reflexivity that has been described by Giddens (1991) as a characteristic feature of high modernity (Chapter 1).

Throughout Weiner's description of the Kula, reflexivity and doubt seem to play a minor role. This is not because participants of the Kula system of exchange do not face up to difficult decisions. Difficulties arise especially when high-ranking *'kitomu'* shells are to be entered into kula circulation, a move that may be extremely profitable for the owner, but that also implies an element of risk. According to Weiner, the most crucial step in the circulation of a *kitomu* shell is how its particular path is established (because the path publicly proclaims the value of the shell, and eventually, the talent and fame of its owner). Thus, facing up to this decision, a *kitomu* owner: '. . . *thought carefully about each man who . . . signified that he wanted his kitomu shell. How big is his name? Is he trustworthy, or does he sometimes take the shells directed for his partners and give them to other men for other paths? How reliable are his partners around the other islands? How big are their names?'* (Weiner 1988:150). In other words, when a crucial, strategic move was considered, the questions posed by the player related primarily to the trustworthiness and reputation of potential partners, and not so much to the inherent value of armshells and necklaces.

Generally, Weiner describes the Kula as a system of exchange that is carried out with strategic cunning on the part of the participants. In her description, she evokes the metaphors of game and play, describing the Kula system as a game, the activity as 'Kula playing' and the participants as players. Through extensive training, Kula players may become experts at the game, but, as her informants say *'the kula takes a lot of work'* – work that implies taking care of your (Kula) friends (Weiner 1988:148). Thus the Kula system appears as a complicated game, a kind of lifelong chess: the rules are known, the criteria for evaluating armshells are well established, and the only thing that one cannot fully control is the future moves of other player(s). Based on Weiner's account, we may thus conclude that it is primarily social skills (and lifelong training) that distinguish an expert from a novice in the Kula game.

In short, following Weiner, Kula playing is something that one may learn.

In the marketing department, feelings of doubt seem more pervasive. They relate not only to the trustworthiness of partners (although including that as well), but also to the quality of products, the quality of a piece of advertising, and even the criteria by which products and advertising may be judged. Moreover, the doubtful and reflexive stance even seems to persist after the judgement has been made. They may, for instance, doubt the quality of a piece of advertising, they may release it in spite of such doubt, and, if the promotion happens to be followed by an increase in demand, they may *still* doubt the quality of the advertising, claiming that they do not know exactly *what it is about this particular piece of advertising* that made it succeed. In other words, no matter what they do, the product managers seem to have to accept that there are always things they do not know, and perhaps cannot know, but still *ought to know*. Searching for an ultimate explanation that is always slightly beyond reach, the product managers thus have to confront the inevitable gap between that which is known and that which ought to be known. This gap is continuously reinforced by a simultaneous requirement for documentation of a semi-scientific kind.

According to Bauman, ambivalence is a by-product of the labour of classification, and as such, it is associated with modernity (Bauman 1991:3). In accordance with Bauman's thesis, we might pursue an argument according to which feelings of doubt in the marketing department are basically a result of their classifying efforts, and as such an expression of a typically modern condition. However, even if the argument makes sense at the descriptive level, it is not satisfactory in the light of comparative material.

Classification is hardly a modern phenomenon. Ever since Durkheim and Mauss first published their essay on primitive classification in 1903 (Durkheim and Mauss 1963), the connections between systems of classification and the social order has been a salient theme in anthropology. Since then, numerous ethnographies have demonstrated that classifying is a common endeavour, not least among cultural groups who have been referred to as 'traditional' (see for instance Douglas 1975b; Howell 1984). Furthermore, Douglas demonstrates that in traditional societies, the classifying effort may (also) give rise to ambiguity, especially when things do not fit with the order of classification. Among her numerous empirical examples, we may for instance consider the case of the pangolin among the Lele, an animal *'with the body and tail of a fish, covered in scales [but with] four little legs [that] climbs in the trees'* (Douglas 1975a:33). Because of what appear to the Lele as its anomalous characteristics,[14] the pangolin is both avoided and associated with the spirits. Douglas extends her argument to all elements that are culturally avoided – for instance to food taboos and pollution (Douglas 1966). According to Douglas, such anomalies (taboos) are by-products of classificatory efforts, and as such an inevitable aspect of the classification itself.

Douglas's argument resembles the proposition set forth by Bauman in the sense that both speak about ambivalence as a necessary by-product of classification. The difference appears, however, in their respective accounts of *ways of dealing with* ambivalence or ambiguity. Douglas's argument about the Lele implies that ambiguity is generally handled through ritual physical or ritual avoidance or control. Bauman, in his discussion of modern ambivalence, draws attention to feelings of discomfort regarding the ambiguous, and to efforts to *eliminate* the ambiguous element, either physically or by means classifying efforts, (i.e. by means of a mental operation) (Bauman 1991). While ritual avoidance of anomalies may imply inclusion at a higher conceptual level (Douglas 1966), the classifying efforts described by Bauman hardly allows any inclusion of anomalies as such. Where Douglas speaks of fear, and a reverence for the natural order, Bauman speaks of management, engineering and the efforts at creating order. Thus, while Douglas describes a way of handling ambiguity that primarily operates through rituals of avoidance, Bauman describes a way of handling ambivalence that implies both classifying efforts, and in some cases also a deliberate physical elimination of the cause of discomfort (an effort which may also include violence, as in the case of the Jews during the Second World War). While Douglas's thesis is based on a wide varieties of studies, including those of traditional societies,[15] Bauman bases his theses entirely on modern societies and a notion of modernity as a cultural-historical phase.

How can these two approaches to classification and ambi-vaguity help us to understand the doubt of the product managers? First of all, we may simply note that the classifying efforts of the product managers are not particularly modern (see Douglas 1975a). Yet, in terms of ways of *dealing with ambivalence*, the efforts of informants differ considerably from avoidance rituals described in traditional societies such as the Lele.[16] Rather than symbolically transforming the anomalies (the unclassifiable) into taboos, the product managers tend to approach the 'unknown' with persistence and relentless classifying efforts. Through efforts, which often imply the gathering of information, ambiguity is sought to be replaced by order. Yet in their efforts at eliminating the gap between the 'known' and the 'ought to be known', the product managers are constantly in doubt. This feeling of doubt is not fully explained by reference to the social embeddedness (cf. the Kula), nor is it simply (as Bauman might argue) a by-product of classification itself (cf. the Lele). How then, can this particular phenomenon be understood?

In his description of modernity, Giddens suggests that *institutional reflexivity* may explain the peculiarly dynamic character of social life in high modernity (Giddens 1991). According to Giddens, the reflexivity of modernity actually serves to undermine the certainty of knowledge, even in a core domain such as science. He writes:

> *No matter how cherished, and apparently well established, a given scientific tenet might be, it is open to revision – or might have to be discarded altogether – in the light of new ideas or findings. The integral relation between modernity and radical doubt is an issue which, once exposed to view, is not only disturbing to philosophers but is **existentially troubling** for ordinary individuals* (Giddens 1991:21).

Highlighting the close linkage between modernity and radical doubt, Giddens offers a very accurate description of a specific feature of the modern condition, a feature that may partly account for the dynamic character of modernity. Following Giddens, the feelings of doubt among product managers may be interpreted in terms of their realization that any assumption about the market or about consumers is *always open to revision*. In this way, radical doubt in the marketing department may be understood as a necessary consequence of a relativistic stance in relation to knowledge.

Still, the explanation offered by Giddens is not entirely satisfactory. Assuming that their doubtfulness is nourished by relativism, why do they act as if the knowledge is still to be found? In order to account for the persistence with which product managers search for their 'truth', I suggest that we turn our attention once more to Taylor's description of one of the typical features of Western modernity, namely the 'modern inwardness', or the underlying opposition between 'inside' and 'outside' in our languages of self-understanding (Taylor 1992). According to Taylor, the notion of an inner self is a typical feature of modernity as it has developed in the cultural context of the Western world. While Taylor focuses primarily on inwardness within discourses of self-understanding, his concept of inwardness may be extended to other realms as well. Following this line of reasoning, we may argue that when product managers keep searching for an ultimate kind of truth (of products, of consumers), *they are envisioning a world in which the true character of any element is hidden just below the surface.* We may also speak of this in terms of a constant quest for *authenticity*, in the sense that it attributes to any element an aspect of absolute essence.

This is particularly salient in the evaluation of advertising agencies, when the agency's integrity was emphasized as a key feature. Thus, when the courage to disagree (with the client) is appreciated, it is because the product managers assume that, behind a surface of servility and yes-saying, the advertising agency may conceal a more authentic kind of 'truth'. Similarly, in every piece of advertising there is an aesthetic element that is appreciated, but yet hard to judge. Consequently, the product manager must rely on the judgement of others (most notably the account manager), aware that the true quality of a piece of advertising is not always apparent 'on the surface'. Thus, when product managers keep struggling to bridge the gap between the 'known' and the 'ought to be known' *in spite of* a relativistic stance, they are acting within a conceptual framework in which a quest for authenticity also plays a part. The origin of their feelings of doubt may thus be understood as a *constant tension* between an understanding of truth as something that resides on the inside, just below an immediate surface, and the awareness that any truth is provisional. Applying the terminology of Giddens and Taylor, this tension may be described as a tension in Western societies between institutional reflexivity and modern inwardness. This, I suggest, is the essence of the feelings of doubt so frequently encountered in the marketing department.

To conclude, feelings of doubt in the marketing department are not simply by-products of classification, as Bauman seems to suggest. Rather we may approach this feature as a typically *modern* way of dealing with ambiguity. Drawing on comparative material, I suggest that the characteristic feature of modernity is not ambivalence in itself, but rather the specific way in which ambivalence is dealt with. In the present case, ambivalence occurs in the twilight zone between that which may be 'scientifically' known and the realm of tacit, intuitive knowledge, or between rational logic and intuitive creativity. Avoidance of instances of ambivalence is achieved through different procedures of separation and mediation, some of which may be referred to as rituals of purification:

1. by an institutionalized division of labour by which 'creativity' is handled by a defined group of professionals in advertising (an instance of separation);
2. by subjecting tacit, intuitive knowledge to formal logical procedures (and instances of mediation); and
3. by subjecting long-lasting relationships of cooperation to a re-evaluation within the idiom of market exchange, for example by means of competitive presentation (a ritualized instance of separation). To the extent that ambivalence still remains, it is handled by a meta-discourse that serves the function of *setting apart*, either by means of jokes and humour (cf. the 'test-institute' at the home address), or through apologetic remarks (*'synsing'*), both instances of separation.

Finally, I suggest that these specific ways of dealing with ambivalence in the marketing department rest upon a more fundamental division in modern societies between the private and the professional. This division may be identified both at an institutional level, at the level of personal identity and role identification, and at the level of knowledge and discourse. However, the inwardness of Western modernity and the search for authenticity that such inwardness implies account for certain dilemmas in relation to these divisions between private and professional. On the one hand, things are kept apart through ritual purification of the professional sphere; on the other hand, decisions are made with reference to a truth that is effectively 'located' in the realm of personal, subjective and 'inner' knowledge. This dilemma, arising out of the peculiar combination of modern inwardness, the quest for order and the simultaneous division between the private and the professional, contributes to the feelings of uncertainty so common in the marketing department.

Notes

1. These concepts are partly inspired by readings of Zygmunt Bauman and his understanding of the modern quest for order. According to Bauman, much of social organization can be interpreted as '*sedimentation of a systematic effort to reduce the frequency with which hermeneutical problems are encountered*' (1990:146). Two methods of separation are referred to: the functional and the territorial. With regard to the activities in the marketing department, separation appears to be both functional (as expressed through a division of labour between e.g. advertising agency and client), and territorial (as expressed through a parallel separation in space between different functions). In addition, I find it fruitful to point to strategies of separation occurring at the level of professional knowledge, as expressed through mechanisms by which certain types of experience are made legitimate while others are not.

2. I should add that this does not necessarily exclude a considerable potential power of the battlefield metaphor in the mind of the product manager. In fact, one may argue that strong feelings of uncertainty and doubt may actually call for courage on the part of the actor in order for him/her to act at all. Consequently, from the perspective of the product manager, the image of a courageous warrior may be at least partially correct. Still, I contend that such feelings of courage may be interpreted primarily as part of a feeling of overall uncertainty and risk. Thus, as an overall description, reflexivity and doubt seem more pervasive.

3. The use of the term 'strategies' in the present context is not restricted to the intentional pursuit of particular ends by individual actors. Rather, I use the term in a broader sense, denoting all those mechanisms by which distinct spheres are set apart, as they are reflected in discourse and practice.

4. During fieldwork, I did not follow people to their homes after office hours. This circumscription is obviously limiting, in that I was not able to observe the protection of the private sphere from intrusion. At the same time, it is also a result of the sphere division: any attempt on my part to transgress these invisible boundaries between spheres would imply an undue violation of the social contract that had been established.

5. This distinction is not as clear-cut as it may appear from looking at Figure 6.1. While market research institutes *primarily* offer information about consumers, and advertising agencies *primarily* offer a fully designed advertising campaign, there are frequent overlaps. Some advertising agencies offer exclusive access to complete consumer segmentation systems, while market research agencies may offer suggestions as to what an advertising campaign should or should not look like.

6. According to Helgesen (1991), this saying may be traced back to an American owner of a warehouse chain called John Wanamaker.

7. There are also examples of competitive presentations that are directly comparable to Moeran's case. Some of these are minor events, such as when a product manager asks two or more market research institutes for an estimate and a proposal for qualitative group discussions, or an in-home test for a specific product. Sometimes, these invitations may also be extended to an advertising agency that offers market research services as well. In these cases, the most important criterion for distinguishing between the competitors is that of cost.

8. The English term is used.

9. For Appadurai, the application of the concept of a "tournament of value" is an attempt to create a general category *'for comparing the kula system to the art world in the modern West'* (Appadurai 1986:21). I find the concept very suitable for transactions in marketing as well, and especially as a conceptual bridgehead in the analysis of competitive presentations of advertising agencies. With regard to the applicability of Appadurai's term to the latter, I am indebted to Moeran (1993), who first introduced this linkage in his article about Japanese advertising.

10. The Norwegian term *'synsing'* is a phrase commonly used when referring to subjective judgement. It is often used in an apologetic or critical manner, in order to describe the lack of

precise, scientific or professionally valid criteria for judgement. The term is derived from the Norwegian verb '*å synes*', whose meaning may be translated into a wide variety of English terms including: 'to think, to mean, to imagine, to consider, and to feel'.

11. This observation is, of course, not restricted to the Kula exchange. Rather, the idea that the life force ('*hau*') or characteristics of a person may be transmitted to his or her possessions (and consequently to gifts) is a significant ethnographic observation which has informed a wide range of analyses of gifts in anthropology (Mauss 1954; Weiner 1992).

12. The idea that gifts may also involve self-interest is not new (see for instance Mauss 1954).

13. According to Weber, the principal conditions necessary for obtaining a maximum of formal rationality of capital accounting in productive enterprises include market freedom, autonomy in the selection of managers, freedom in the selection of workers, substantive freedom of contract, a mechanically rational technology, a formally rational administration and '*the most complete possible separation of the enterprise and its conditions of success and failure, from the household or private budgetary unit*' (Weber 1947:275). While some of these conditions are challenged and modified in practice, they still seem to serve as underlying principles for market enterprises in general. Recent reinterpretations of Max Weber have challenged the general understanding of Weber's perspective on bureaucracy as an 'iron cage' based strictly on the principle of formal rationality. For a critical reading, see for instance du Gay (1994).

14. While she distinguishes between the terms anomaly and ambiguity, Douglas maintains that there is little advantage in making this distinction in practical application (Douglas 1966:37). In the discussion that follows, I will not distinguish sharply with these terms.

15. In the light of her analysis of the Abominations of Leviticus, Douglas reformulated certain statements regarding the original analysis of the Lele in her article 'Self-Evidence'. Based on her argument that classification is a necessary human activity, accompanied by a universal human tendency to pass adverse judgements on that which refuses to fit into the tidy compartments of the mind, she suggests that the treatment of

anomalies in terms of boundaries and mediations is a proper
subject of comparative analysis (Douglas 1975b). (For critical
discussion of some implications of her earlier analysis of
classification, see Douglas 1996.)

16. Rituals of avoidance are subject to some variation, even in so-
called traditional societies. Avoidance may be substituted by
physical control, or it may be achieved through the inducement
of fear, or by what Douglas refers to as reduction (Douglas
1966:38). The latter occurs for instance when a monstrous birth
among the Nuer is 'labelled' a baby hippopotamus, and gently
returned to the river where it belongs. While this example
could certainly be seen as what Bauman describes as a physical
act of elimination, I suggest on the basis of the description
provided by Douglas that it is not quite the same. Returning a
monstrous birth to the river may rather be interpreted as
an attempt at restoring order, rather than an attempt at
elimination. Provided that this understanding is shared among
the Nuer, this way of dealing with ambiguity may even be
more 'successful' than the relentless efforts at classification
and elimination of ambiguity described by Bauman.

Bibliography

Anderson, Benedict (1983), *Imagined Communities*. London: Verso.

Appadurai, Arjun (1986), *The Social Life of Things*. Cambridge: Cambridge University Press.

Appadurai, Arjun (1988), 'How to Make a National Cuisine: Cookbooks in Contemporary India', *Comparative Studies in Society and History*, 30(1), pp.3–24.

Appadurai, Arjun (1990), 'Disjuncture and Difference in the Global Cultural Economy'. In: M. Featherstone (ed.), *Global Culture*. London: Sage.

Balasubramanyam, V. N. and Nguyen, D. T. (1991), 'Structure and Performance of the U.K. Food and Drink Industries', *Journal of Agricultural Economics*, 42(1), pp.56–65.

Barth, Fredrik (1966), *Models of Social Organization*, Occasional Paper no. 23. London: Royal Anthropological Institute of Great Britain & Ireland.

Bauman, Zygmunt (1990), 'Modernity and Ambivalence'. In: M. Featherstone (ed.), *Global Culture*. London: Sage Publications.

Bauman, Zygmunt (1991). *Modernity and Ambivalence*. Cambridge: Polity Press.

Beck, Brenda (1978), 'The Metaphor as Mediator Between Semantic and Analogic Modes of Thought', *Current Anthropology*, 19(1), pp.83–8.

Berge, Gunnvor (1992), 'Sammenligning i ulike retninger av antropologien' [Comparison in Different Anthropological Traditions], *Norsk Antropologisk Tidsskrift*, 3(1), pp.6–21.

Berger, Peter and Luckmann, Thomas (1967), *The Social Construction of Reality*. Garden City NY: Anchor.

Bijker, Wiebe E., Hughes, Thomas P. and Pinch, Trevor J. (eds) (1987), *The Social Construction of Technological Systems*. Cambridge, MA: The MIT Press.

Bloch, Maurice and Parry, Jonathan (1989), 'Introduction: Money and the Morality of Exchange'. In: J. Parry and M. Bloch (eds), *Money and the Morality of Exchange*. Cambridge: Cambridge University Press.

Bourdieu, Pierre (1984), *Distinction: A Social Critique of the Judgment of Taste*. London: Routledge & Kegan Paul.

Callon, Michel (1986), 'Some Elements of a Sociology of Translation: Domestication of the Scallops and the Fishermen of St Brieuc Bay'.

In: J. Law (ed.), *Power, Actions and Belief; A New Sociology of Knowledge?*, Sociological Review Monograph. London: Routledge & Kegan Paul.

Campbell, Colin (1987), *The Romantic Ethic and the Spirit of Modern Consumerism*. Oxford: Basil Blackwell.

Campbell, Shirley F. (1983), 'Attaining Rank: A Classification of Kula Shell Valuables'. In: J. W. Leach and E. Leach (eds), *The Kula; New Perspectives on Massim Exchange*. Cambridge: Cambridge University Press.

Cockburn, Cynthia (1988), *Machinery of Dominance*. Boston: Northeastern University Press.

Collins, H. M. and Yearly, Stephen (1992), 'Epistemological Chicken'. In: A. Pickering (ed.), *Science as Practice and Culture*, pp.369–89. Chicago: University of Chicago Press.

Czarniawska-Joerges, Barbara (1992), *Exploring Complex Organizations*. London: Sage.

Dahl, Hans Fredrik (1986). 'Those Equal Folk'. In: S. R. Graubard (ed.), *Norden – The Passion for Equality*. Oslo: Scandinavian University Press.

Dalseg, Trygve (1983), Fra Adressecontoir til reklamebyrå; En dokumentasjon av reklamens historie frem til 1940 [A History of Norwegian Advertising until 1940] Oslo: Instituttet for Markedsføring.

Dilley, Roy (1992), 'Contesting Markets'. In: R. Dilley (ed.), *Contesting Markets, Analyses of Ideology, Discourse and Practice*. Edinburgh: Edinburgh University Press.

Douglas, Mary (1966), *Purity and Danger*. London: Routledge & Kegan Paul.

Douglas, Mary (1975a), 'Animals in Lele Religious Symbolism'. In: M. Douglas, *Implicit Meanings*. London: Routledge & Kegan Paul.

Douglas, Mary (1975b), 'Self-Evidence'. In: M. Douglas, *Implicit Meanings*. London: Routledge & Kegan Paul.

Douglas, Mary (1996), 'Anomalous Animals and Animal Metaphors'. In: M. Douglas, *Thought Styles*. London: Sage.

Douglas, Mary and Isherwood, Baron (1980), *The World of Goods: Towards an Anthropology of Consumption*. Harmondsworth: Penguin Books.

Douglas, Mary and Nicod, Michael (1974), 'Taking the Bisquit: The Structure of British Meals', *New Society*, 19 December, pp.744–7.

Du Gay, Paul (1994), 'Making up Managers: Bureaucracy, Enterprise and the Liberal Art of Separation', *British Journal of Sociology*, 45(4), pp.655–74.

Dulsrud, Arne (1994), 'Mat, Marked og Makt, Betingelser for forbrukerinnflytelse' [The Food Market, Conditions for Consumer Power], Report no. 9. Lysaker, Norway: National Institute for Consumer Research.

Durkheim, Emile (1961 [1912]), *The Elementary Forms of the Religious Life* (trans. Joseph W. Swain). New York: Collier Books.

Durkheim, Emile and Mauss, Marcel (1963 [1903]), *Primitive Classification* (trans. Rodney Needham). London: Cohen & West.

Evans-Pritchard, Edward E. (1962), 'Social Anthropology: Past and Present'. In: E. E. Evans-Pritchard, *Social Anthropology and Other Essays*. Glencoe, Ill.: The Free Press.

Fabian, J. (1983), *Time and the Other. How Anthropology Makes its Object*. New York: Columbia University Press.

Feldman, Jacqueline, Lagneau, Gérard and Matalon, Benjamin (1991), *Moyenne, milieu, centre, Histoires et usages*, Introduction, pp. 9–28. Paris: Éditions de l'Ecole des Hautes Études en Sciences Sociales.

Fernandez, James (1974), 'Persuasions and Performances; Of the Beast in Every Body and the Metaphors of Everyman'. In: C. Geertz (ed.), *Myth, Symbol and Culture*. New York: Norton.

Fine, Ben and Leopold, Ellen (1993), *The World of Consumption*. London: Routledge.

Firat, Fuat, A. (1994), 'Gender and Consumption: Transcending the Feminine'. In: J. A. Costa (ed.), *Gender Issues and Consumer Behavior*. London: Sage.

Fischler, Claude (1988), 'Food, Self and Identity', *Social Science Information*, 27(2), pp.275–92.

Friedman, Jonathan (1991), 'Consuming Desires: Strategies of Selfhood and Appropriation', *Cultural Anthropology*, 6(2), pp.154–63.

Geertz, Clifford (1966), 'Religion as a Cultural System'. In: M. Banton (ed.), *Anthropological Approaches to the Study of Religion*. London: Tavistock Publications.

Geertz, Clifford (1973), 'Thick Description: Toward an Interpretive Theory of Culture'. In: C. Geertz, *The Interpretation of Cultures*. New York: Basic Books.

Gewertz, Deborah and Errington, Frederic (1996), 'On PepsiCo and Piety in a Papua New Guinea "Modernity"', *American Ethnologist*, 23(3), pp.476–93.

Giddens, Anthony (1991), *Modernity and Self-Identity*. Cambridge: Polity Press.

Graubard, Stephen A. (ed.) (1986), *Norden – The Passion for Equality*. Oslo: Norwegian University Press.

Greenley, Gordon E. and Bayus, Barry L. (1994), 'A Comparative Study of Product Launch and Elimination Decisions in UK and US Companies', *European Journal of Marketing*, 28(2), pp.5–29.

Gregory, C. A. (1982), *Gifts and Commodities*. London: Academic Press.

Gullestad, Marianne (1989), 'Small Facts and Large Issues. The Anthropology of Contemporary Scandinavian Society', *Annual Review of Anthropology*, 18, pp.71–93.

Gullestad, Marianne (1992), *The Art of Social Relations*. Oslo: Scandinavian University Press.

Hallsworth, Alan G. (1992), 'Retail Internationalization: Contingency and Context', *European Journal of Marketing*, 26(8/9), pp.25–34.

Hamilton, Gary G. and Lai, Chi-kong (1989), 'Consumerism Without Capitalism: Consumption and Brand Names in Late Imperial China'. In: H. J. Rutz and B. S. Orlove (eds), *The Social Economy of Consumption*, Society for Economic Anthropology, Monographs in Economic Anthropology, No. 6. Lanham: University Press of America.

Hannerz, Ulf (1990), 'Cosmopolitans and Locals in World Culture'. In: M. Featherstone (ed.), *Global Culture*. London: Sage.

Hastrup, Kirsten (1987), 'Fieldwork Among Friends'. In: A. Jackson (ed.), *Anthropology at Home*, ASA Monographs 25. London: Tavistock Publications.

Helgesen, Thorolf (1983), 'Reklamebyråene i fortid, nåtid og fremtid' [Advertising Agencies in the Past, the Present and the Future]. In: RRF 50 år, IFM 25 år. Oslo: Registrerte Reklamebyråers Forening [Norwegian Advertising Agencies Association].

Helgesen, Thorolf (1991), 'Bedre planlegging, styring og kontroll av reklametiltakene' [Better planning, surveillance and control of advertising efforts], *Praktisk økonomi og ledelse*, 3, pp.13–17.

Helgesen, Thorolf (1992), 'The Rationality of Advertising Decisions', *Journal of Advertising Research*, 32(6), pp.22–30.

Helgesen, Thorolf (1994), 'Advertising Awards and Advertising Agency Performance Criteria', *Journal of Advertising Research*, 34(4), pp.43–53.

Hellevik, Ottar (1991), *Forskningsmetode i soisologi og statsvitenskap* [Research Methods in Sociology and Political Science]. Oslo: Scandinavian University Press.

Hennion, A. and Méadel, C. (1989), 'The Artisans of Desire: The Mediation of Advertising between Product and Consumer'. *Sociological Theory*, 7(2), pp.191–209.

Holy, Ladislav (1987), 'Introduction; Description, Generalization and Comparison: Two Paradigms'. In: L. Holy (ed.), *Comparative Anthropology*. Oxford: Basil Blackwell.

Howell, Signe (1984), *Society and Cosmos; Chewong of Peninsular Malaysia*. Chicago: University of Chicago Press.

Hower, Ralph M. (1949 [1939]), *The History of an Advertising Agency: N. W. Ayer & Son at Work 1869–1849*. Cambridge, MA: Harvard University Press.

Hughes, Thomas P. (1987), 'The Seamless Web: Technology, Science, Etcetera Etcetera.' *Social Studies of Science*, 16, pp.281–92.

Hviding, Edvard (1994), 'Indigenous Essentialism? "Simplifying" Customary Land Ownership in New Georgia, Solomon Islands'. In: P. van der Grijp and T. van Meijl (eds), 'Politics, Tradition and Change in the Pacific.' *Bijdraagen tot de Taal-, Land en Volkenkunde*, 131(4), pp.1–11.

Jacobsen, Eivind and Dulsrud, Arne (1994), Kjedenes makt til forbrukernes beste? Konsentrasjon og integrasjon i dagligvarehandelen med matvarer i Norge [Retailer Power to the Benefit of the Consumer? Concentration and Integration in Food Retailing in Norway], Report no. 4. Lysaker, Norway: National Institute for Consumer Research.

Jasanoff, Sheila, Markle, Gerald E., Peterson, James C. and Pinch, Trevor (eds) (1995), *Handbook of Science and Technology Studies*. London: Sage Publications.

Jensen, Thor Øivind (1994), The Political History of Norwegian Nutrition Policy. In: J. Burnett and D. J. Oddy (eds), *The Origins and Development of Food Policies in Europe*. London: Leicester University Press.

Kanter, Rosabeth Moss (1977), *Men and Women of the Corporation*. New York: Basic Books.

Kjærnes, Unni (1994), Mat, forbrukerpolitikk og internasjonalisering [Food, Consumer Policy and International Integration], Report no. 11. Lysaker, Norway: National Institute for Consumer Research.

Kjærnes, Unni (1995a), 'Milk: Nutritional Science and Agricultural Development in Norway 1890–1990'. In: A. Den Hartog *et al.*, *Food Technology, Science and Marketing: The European Diet in the 20th Century*, pp.103–16. East Lothian: Tuckwell Press.

Kjærnes, Unni (1995b), 'Fra husmødre til aktivister. Om kvinner og matpolitikk' [From Housewives to Activists. On Women and Food Policy]. *Sosiologi idag*, 25(3), pp.49–66.

Knorr Cetina, Karin (1995), 'Laboratory Studies: The Cultural Approach to the Study of Science'. In: S. Jasanoff, G. E. Markle, J. C. Petersen and T. Pinch (eds), *Handbook of Science and Technology Studies*. London: Sage.

Kotler, Philip and Armstrong, Gary (1987), *Marketing: An Introduction*. Englewood Cliffs: Prentice-Hall.

Kvande, Elin and Rasmussen, Bente (1990), *Nye kvinneliv, Kvinner i menns organisasjoner* [New Lives of Women. Women in Men's Organizations]. Oslo: Ad Notam.

Lakoff, George and Johnson, Mark (1980), *Metaphors We Live By*. The University of Chicago Press, Chicago.

Latour, Bruno (1987), *Science in Action*. Cambridge, MA: Harvard University Press.

Latour, Bruno (1988), 'The Prince for Machines as Well as for Machinations'. In: B. Elliott (ed.), *Technology and Social Process*. Edinburgh: Edinburgh University Press.

Latour, Bruno (1993), *We Have Never Been Modern*. Harvester: New York.

Latour, Bruno and Woolgar, P. (1986 [1979]), *Laboratory Life*. Princeton: Princeton University Press.

Law, John (1994), *Organizing Modernity*. Oxford: Blackwell.

Leiss, Willian, Kline, Stephen and Jhally, Sut (1990), *Social Communication in Advertising*. Scarborough: Routledge.

Leopold, Marion (1985), 'The Transnational Food Companies and Their Global Strategies', *International Social Science Journal*, 37(3), pp.315–30.

Levenstein, Harvey (1985), 'The American Response to Italian Food, 1880–1930', *Food and Foodways*, 1(1), pp.1–24.

Lévi-Strauss, Claude (1963), 'The Bear and the Barber', *Journal of the Royal Anthropological Institute of Great Britain and Ireland*, 93, pp.1–11.

Lévi-Strauss, Claude (1966 [1962]), *The Savage Mind*. Chicago: Chicago University Press.

Lien, Marianne (1989 [1987]), *Fra 'Bokna Fesk' til 'Pizza': Sosiokulturelle perspektiver på mat og endring av spisevaner i Båtsfjord, Finnmark* [From 'Bokna Fesk' to 'Pizza'. Sociocultural Perspectives on Food and Changes of Food Habits in Båtsfjord, Finnmark], Occasional Paper in Social Anthropology, 18. Oslo: Institute and Museum of Anthropology, University of Oslo.

Lien, Marianne (1990), *The Norwegian Nutrition and Food Supply Policy; Accomplishments and Limitations of a Structural Approach*, Working Report no. 4. Lysaker, Norway: National Institute for Consumer Research.

Lien, Marianne (1992), 'Grasping Food Cultural Change through Public Discourse', Working Paper no. 2. Lysaker: National Institute for Consumer Research.

Lien, Marianne (1993), 'From Deprived to Frustrated; Consumer Segmentation in Food and Nutrition'. In: U. Kjærnes *et al.* (eds), *Regulating Markets, Regulating People: On Food and Nutrition Policy*. Oslo: Novus Press.

Lien, Marianne (1994), 'Offer, strateg eller iscenesetter; Bilder av forbrukeren i forbruksforskning' ['Victim, Strategist or Choreographer, Images of the Consumer in Consumer Research'], *Sosiologisk Tidsskrift*, 2(1), pp.41–62.

Lien, Marianne (1995a), 'Fuel for the Body – Nourishment for Dreams: Contradictory Roles of Food in Contemporary Norwegian Food Advertising', *Journal of Consumer Policy*, 18(2), pp.1–30.

Lien, Marianne (1995b) Food Products in the Making; An Ethnography of Marketing Practice. PhD dissertation submitted at the Institute and Museum of Anthropology. Oslo: University of Oslo.

Linn, Carl Eric (1985), *Metaproduktet og Markedet* [The Metaproduct and the Market]. Oslo: Bedriftøkonomens Forlag.

Luckmann, Benita (1978), 'The Small Life-Worlds of Modern Man'. In: T. Luckmann (ed.), *Phenomenology and Sociology*. Harmondsworth: Penguin.

Machiavelli, Niccolò (1961 [1514]), *The Prince*. London: Penguin Classics. (Translated from Italian to English for the first time in 1649.)

Mackay, Hughie and Gillespie, Gareth (1992), 'Extending the Social Shaping of Technology Approach: Ideology and Appropriation', *Social Studies of Science*, 22, pp.685–716.

Mauss, Marcel (1954 [1922]), *The Gift*. London: Cohen & West.

Meyer, J. W. (1983), 'Institutionalization and the Rationality of Formal Organizational Structure'. In: J. W. Meyer and R. W. Scott, *Organizational Environments: Ritual and Rationality*, pp.260–82. London: Sage Publications.

Meyer, J. W. and Rowan, B. (1977), 'Institutionalized Organizations; Formal Structure as Myth and Ceremony', *American Journal of Sociology*, 83(2), pp.340–63.

Miller, Daniel (1987), *Material Culture and Mass Consumption*. Oxford: Blackwell.

Miller, Daniel (1992), 'The Young and the Restless in Trinidad'. In: R. Silverstone and E. Hirsch (eds), *Consuming Technologies*, pp.163–82. London: Routledge.

Miller, Daniel (1994), *Modernity: An Ethnographic Approach*. Oxford: Berg Publishers.

Miller, Daniel (1995a), 'Consumption Studies as the Transformation of Anthropology'. In: D. Miller (ed.), *Acknowledging Consumption*, pp.264–95. London: Routledge.

Miller, Daniel (1995b), 'Artefacts and the Meaning of Things'. In: T. Ingold (ed.), *Companion Encyclopedia of Anthropology*, pp.396–419. London: Routledge.

Mintzberg, H. (1980), *The Nature of Managerial Work*. Englewood Cliffs: Prentice Hall.

Moeran, Brian (1993), 'A Tournament of Value: Strategies of Presentation in Japanese Advertising', *Ethnos*, 58(1–2), pp.73–93.

Moeran, Brian (1996), *A Japanese Advertising Agency. An Anthropology of Media and Markets*, ConsumAsiaN Book Series. Richmond, Surrey: Curzon.

Myers, Kathy (1983), 'Understanding Advertisers'. In: H. Davis and P. Walton (eds), *Language, Image and Media*. Oxford: Basil Blackwell.

Nielsen, Harriet B. and Rudberg, Monica (1994), *Psychological Gender and Modernity*. Oslo: Scandinavian University Press.

Nielsen, Norway (1993), Unpublished statistical material. (Reproduced with permission from Jacobsen and Dulsrud 1994.)

Norwegian Advertising Statistics (1994), Unpublished statistical material. Oslo: A/S Norsk Reklamestatistikk.

Norwegian Official Statistics (1992), *Tidsbruk og tidsorganisering 1970–90* [Time Expenditure and Organization of Time 1970–1990]. Oslo: National Bureau of Statistics ('Statistisk Sentralbyrå').

Okely, Judith (1992), 'Anthropology and Autobiography: Participatory Experience and Embodied Knowledge'. In: J. Okely and H. Callaway (eds), *Anthropology and Autobiography*, ASA Monographs 29. London: Routledge.

Okely, Judith (1996), *Own or Other Culture*. London: Routledge.

Ortony, A. (ed.) (1979), *Metaphor and Thought*. Cambridge: Cambridge University Press.

Orvell, Miles (1989), *The Real Thing; Imitation and Authenticity in American Culture 1880–1940*. Chapel Hill: University of North Carolina Press.

Overing, Joanna (1987), 'Translation as a Creative Process: The Power of the Name'. In: L. Holy (ed.), *Comparative Anthropology*. Oxford: Basil Blackwell.

Paul, Robert (1990), 'What Does Anybody Want? Desire, Purpose and the Acting Subject in the Study of Culture', *Cultural Anthropology*, 5(4), pp.431–51.

Pelto, Gretel H. and Pelto, Pertti (1983), 'Diet and Delocalization: Dietary Changes since 1750', *Journal of Interdisciplinary History*, 14(2), pp.507–28.

Pinch, Trevor J. and Bijker, Wiebe E. (1987), 'The Social Construction of Facts and Artifacts: Or How the Sociology of Science and the Sociology of Technology Might Benefit Each Other'. In: Wiebe E. Bijker, Thomas P. Hughes and Trevor J. Pinch (eds), *The Social Construction of Technological Systems*. Cambridge, MA: MIT Press.

Prus, Robert C. (1989), *Pursuing Customers: An Ethnography of Marketing Activities*, Sage Library of Social Research, 171. Newbury Park: Sage.

Reed, M. (1992), *The Sociology of Organizations*. Hemel Hempstead: Harvester Wheatsheaf.

Sahlins, Marshall (1976), *Culture and Practical Reason*. Chicago: University of Chicago Press.

Said, Edward W. (1979), *Orientalism*. New York: Vintage Books.

Salmond, Anne (1982), 'Theoretical Landscapes, On Cross-cultural Conceptions of Knowledge'. In: D. Parkin (ed.), *Semantic Anthropology*, ASA Monographs, No. 22. Washington DC: ASA.

Scholte, B. (1984), 'Comment on: The Thick and the Thin: On the Interpretive Theoretical Program of Clifford Geertz. By P. Shankman', *Current Anthropology*, 25(3), pp.540–2.

Silverman, D. (1970), *The Theory of Organizations*. London: Heinemann.

Sørensen, Bjørg Aase (1982), 'Ansvarsrasjonalitet; Om mål-middel tenkning blant kvinner' ['A Rationality of Responsibility. On Instrumental Rationality Among Women']. In: H. Holter (ed.), *Kvinner i fellesskap*. Oslo: Universitetsforlaget.

Sørensen, Knut H. and Andersen, Håkon W. (1988), 'Teknologi – fra konsekvensskapende til samfunnsskapt' [Technology – from 'Consequence-creator' to 'Society-created']. *Sosiologi i dag*, 3, 81–99.

Sorj, Bernardo and Wilkinson, John (1985), 'Modern Food Technology: Industrializing Nature', *International Social Science Journal*, 3, pp.301–14.

Steen, Arild H. (1989), En næring i nytelse? Utviklingstrekk i nærings- og nytelsesmiddelindustrien [Development Trends in Food and Drink Industries], FAFO-report no. 094. Oslo: FAFO.

Steen, Arild H. (1991a), Nye vilkår; Nye handelsbetingelser for norsk nærings- og nytelsesmiddelindustri [New Trade Conditions for Norwegian Food and Drink Industries], FAFO-report no. 125. Oslo: FAFO.

Steen, Arild H. (1991b), Ingen over – ingen ved siden? Konkurransem- uligheter for norsk nærings- og nytelsesmiddelindustri. [Possibilities for Competition in Norwegian Food and Drink Industries], FAFO- report no. 126. Oslo: FAFO.

Taylor, Charles (1992), 'Inwardness and the Culture of Modernity'. In: A. Honneth (ed.), *Philosophical Interventions in the Unfinished Project of Enlightenment.* Cambridge, MA: MIT Press.

Thomas, Nicholas (1993), 'Pirated Scripts: Appropriations of History and Culture in the Pacific'. Paper presented at the ASA Decennial Conference, Oxford 1993: *'The Uses of Knowledge: Global and Local Relations'* (unpublished manuscript, cited with permission).

Turner, Bryan S. (1987), 'A Note on Nostalgia', *Theory, Culture and Society,* 4(1), pp.147–56.

Van den Berghe, Pierre L. (1984), 'Ethnic Cuisine: Culture in Nature', *Ethnic and Racial Studies,* 7(3), pp.387–97.

Verbeke, Willem (1988), 'Developing an Advertising Agency – Client Relationship in the Netherlands', *Journal of Advertising Research,* 28(6), pp.19–27.

Wackman, Daniel B., Salmon, Charles T. and Salmon, Caryn (1986), 'Developing an Advertising Agency–Client Relationship', *Journal of Advertising Research,* 26(6), pp. 21–7.

Wandel, Margareta (1994), 'Consumer Concern and Behaviour Regarding Food and Health in Norway', *Journal of Consumer Studies and Home Economics,* 18(3), pp.203–15.

Warde, Alan (1995), 'Vocabularies of Taste; Changes in Discourse about Food Preparation'. In: E. Feichtinger and B. M. Köhler (eds), *Current Research into Eating Practices: Contributions of the Social Sciences,* AGEV Publication Series, Vol. 10, pp.101–4. Frankfurt: Umschau Zeit- schriftenverlag.

Weber, Max (1947), *The Theory of Social and Economic Organization.* New York: The Free Press.

Weiner, Annette B. (1988), *The Trobrianders of Papua New Guinea.* New York: Holt, Rinehart and Winston.

Weiner, Annette B. (1992), *Inalienable Possessions: The Paradox of Keeping While Giving.* Berkeley, CA: University of California Press.

Wilk, Richard (1995), 'Learning to be Local in Belize. Global Systems of Common Difference'. In: D. Miller (ed.), *Worlds Apart: Modernity through the Prism of the Local,* pp.110–32. London: Routledge.

Williams, Raymond (1983), *Keywords*. London: Fontana Press.
Williamson, Judith (1978), *Decoding Advertisements*. London: Marion
    Boyars.

Index

advertising: agencies 152–3, 155; building stable alliances 18; characteristics of Norway 52–3; competitive presentation by agencies 267–71; conflict over burp in commercial 188–93, 195–7; creativity as a favour and as commodity 273–8; diachronic and synchronic presentation 268; expenditure 53; growth and development of agencies 48–51; imagined cuisines 244–7, 248; knowledge gap 282; metaphor 21–2; offer creativity 266–7; pizza commercial 181–93; professional integrity 273; relationship with marketing people 279–80; role of 4; scepticism of value 267; search for person 213–221; television studio and equipment 184; tournaments of value 270–3; visual design 50

agriculture: protection of market 41–3

alliances: building 15–18

ambiguity and ambivalence 3–26, 260–2, 282; relativity 284–5

ANUGA world market for nutrition 202–4

Appadurai, Arjun 11, 266; tournaments of value 270–1

Armstrong, Gary 102; market research 113; product positioning 227

authenticity: awareness of discontinuity between sign and signifier 247–8; culture of imitation 247–9; in marketing 249–53; modern inwardness and the disengaged self 253–6, 285

Ayer (N.W.) & Son 50

Barth, Fredrik 162–3, 164

Bauman, Zygmunt 5, 149–50; ambivalence and classification 282–4; defining modernity 8, 259; randomness and order 261–2

Beck, Brenda 118

Berger, Peter 15

Bijker, Wiebe E. 18

Bloch, Maurice 278

Bon Appétit project 227–9; authenticity 250–1; commercial using famous but ordinary person 213–21, 228; developing the dishes 208–10; formulating strategy 205–8; Henrik considers convenience foods at international fair 202–4;